HUMAN TRAFFICKING

SASHA JESPERSON, RUNE HENRIKSEN,
ANNE-MARIE BARRY and MICHAEL JONES

Human Trafficking

An Organised Crime?

HURST & COMPANY, LONDON

First published in the United Kingdom in 2019 by
C. Hurst & Co. (Publishers) Ltd.,
41 Great Russell Street, London, WC1B 3PL
© Sasha Jesperson, Rune Henriksen, Anne-Marie Barry and
Michael Jones, 2019
All rights reserved.
Printed in India.

Distributed in the United States, Canada and Latin America by Oxford
University Press, 198 Madison Avenue, New York, NY 10016, United States
of America.

The right of Sasha Jesperson, Rune Henriksen, Anne-Marie Barry and
Michael Jones to be identified as the authors of this publication is asserted
by them in accordance with the Copyright, Designs and Patents Act, 1988.

A Cataloguing-in-Publication data record for this book is available from the
British Library.

ISBN: 9781787381285

www.hurstpublishers.com

CONTENTS

ACKNOWLEDGEMENTS

This book is based on research funded by the UK government to enhance our understanding of human trafficking and the role of organised crime. It involved extensive fieldwork in source, transit, and destination countries, where many people willingly contributed their time and knowledge to build the evidence picture on which this book draws. The people we met were generous with their time but also told us many stories—some amusing, some quite terrifying—that made working on this project stimulating beyond the research itself.

Because of the geographical spread of the research, it relied on a small team working closely together to conduct fieldwork, share findings, and draw conclusions. In addition to the chapter authors acknowledged below, the research also benefited from the knowledge and expertise of Karen Anstiss, Abimbola Ayodele, Kokunhre Eghafona, Giulia Nicoloso, Stephanie Schwandner-Sievers, Daniel Silverstone, Diem-Tu Tran, and Seefar—particularly Nathaniel Logan and Paul Clewett, among others.

NOTES ON CONTRIBUTORS

Anne-Marie Barry is a research associate with the Centre for the Study of Modern Slavery at St Mary's University, where she has managed this research project on human trafficking and organised crime. Before coming to St Mary's, Anne-Marie worked in the NGO sector where her research focus was on forced labour and exploitation within major industries. She has worked with companies across multiple sectors in their response to the UK Modern Slavery Act and to address issues of modern slavery within their operations and supply chains.

Dr Rune Henriksen is the Deputy Director of Rhipto (the Norwegian Centre for Global Analyses), where he focuses on the dynamics of illicit trade and intersections with security threats, including violent extremism. He completed his PhD in International Relations at the London School of Economics. He has published in the *Journal of Strategic Studies* and in *Terrorism and Political Violence*.

Dr Sasha Jesperson is the co-founder and Director of ITERU, a boutique consultancy that addresses the challenges that arise with the movement of people and goods across territories and borders. Sasha provides technical expertise on migration, human trafficking, and organised crime to governments and international institutions. Prior to this, she was the Director of the Centre for the Study of Modern

Slavery at St Mary's University. She holds a PhD from the London School of Economics and has an academic background in migration and organised crime.

Michael Jones is a Research Fellow in the National Security and Resilience Team at the Royal United Services Institute, where he focuses on conflict and counter-terrorism. He has conducted research into violent extremism and militancy, with particular reference to East Africa. Before starting at RUSI, Michael was lead researcher in the Africa programme for the Institute of Islamic Strategic Affairs, focusing on the intersections between crime, insurgencies, and transnational terrorism in Sub-Saharan Africa. He holds an MSc in Conflict Studies from the London School of Economics.

LIST OF FIGURES

SELECTED ACRONYMS

COR	Commission of Refugees (Sudan)
ECOWAS	Economic Community of West African States
NCA	National Crime Agency (UK)
NCCT	National Committee for Combating Human Trafficking (Sudan)
NGN	Nigerian Naira
NISS	National Intelligence and Security Service (Sudan)
NRM	National Referral Mechanism
OCG	Organised Crime Group
RSF	Rapid Support Force (Sudan)
UNODC	UN Office on Drugs and Crime

1

THE HUMAN TRAFFICKING INDUSTRY

AN ORGANISED CRIME?

Sasha Jesperson

Mention 'human trafficking', and many people will immediately think of gangsters forcing people, often women and girls, to leave their homes and engage in dangerous activities against their will under the threat of violence in order to make money. Numerous films have been made portraying young women being forced into the sex industry, held in captivity, beaten and drugged by their captors.[1]

Human trafficking is not limited to the sex trade—exploitation can occur in many different industries and targets many different people, not just women and girls.[2] Yet regardless of the type of exploitation, the impact trafficking has on its victims has received considerable attention. Many NGOs have been formed to identify and support trafficking victims, providing accommodation, medical treatment, trauma counselling, legal support, and other services.

Much has been written about the experiences of victims of human trafficking and modern slavery, with numerous books, articles, and documentaries recounting their experiences. In drafting the UK Modern Slavery Act, the Home Office summed up the experience of trafficking victims as 'working long hours for little or no money or food, forced into a life of crime or pushed into the sex industry. Their entire life and liberty is in the hands of another, with no say and no way out.'[3]

While human trafficking and modern slavery are intrinsic problems because of the impact they have on victims, a greater threat emerges from the involvement of organised crime. The profit motives and violence associated with organised crime make human trafficking more dangerous for victims and difficult to detect and address, as the networks behind trafficking are always two steps ahead of law enforcement.

But compared with other forms of criminality, the involvement of organised crime in human trafficking is poorly understood. There are many unanswered questions about the relationship between organised crime and human trafficking: What form does organised criminal involvement take? How cohesive are criminal networks across the supply chain? What elements of human trafficking are criminal networks involved in? How much violence is involved?

In 2012, an alliance of UK NGOs identified how little we know about this aspect of human trafficking, pointing out that 'although such studies may be seen as difficult to conduct, they are not impossible, and the knowledge acquired would greatly inform effective intervention'.[4] However, since then, there has not been a considerable growth in research.

Yet there is an increasing recognition that human trafficking and modern slavery are an organised crime problem. The UK's first independent anti-slavery commissioner, Kevin Hyland, frequently referred to the organised crime elements that underpin slavery, drawing on his experiences as head of the Metropolitan Police Human Slavery and Kidnap Unit.[5] The UK Modern Slavery Act, which came into force in 2015, includes provisions to target slave drivers and those facilitating exploitation. In response, the National Crime Agency (NCA) created a Modern Slavery and Human Trafficking Unit to address the criminality that underpins human trafficking and in 2017 established a Joint Slavery and Trafficking and Analysis Centre to share and analyse intelligence.

In response to this renewed attention, this book investigates the role of organised crime in the facilitation of human trafficking, seeking to answer the questions posed above. The book analyses trafficking from four source countries—Albania, Eritrea, Nigeria, and Vietnam. According to the US Trafficking in Persons Report, none of these countries meet the minimum standards for the elimination of trafficking. Albania, Nigeria, and Vietnam are making significant efforts to meet these standards, whereas Eritrea is not.[6] For the UK, these countries frequently have the most referrals to the National Referral Mechanism (NRM), which identifies victims of trafficking.[7]

The authors have conducted in-depth field research in source, transit, and destination countries for trafficking from these four countries to understand the role of organised crime.[8] Although the research has highlighted the business models and tactics of criminal groups, it also challenged some of the commonly held assumptions on human trafficking. Rather than being completely coercive, a blurred line between human trafficking and people smuggling emerged in all four case studies. This has implications for a policy response that focuses purely on criminality, as the way criminal groups are organised and operate is affected by this fluidity between categories. These two issues are explored in more detail in Chapters 6 and 7.

To set the scene, this introduction engages with what we know about the role of organised crime in human trafficking, drawing on research on organised crime more broadly, considering what that means for a response to human trafficking, which differs from other forms of organised crime because of the human commodity.

Human Trafficking and Organised Crime

Following the adoption of the UN Convention against Transnational Organised Crime, the head of what was then the UN Drug Control and Crime Prevention Programme (now UN Office on Drugs and Crime; UNODC) argued that human trafficking was the fastest growing form of organised crime.[9] Pino Arlacchi pointed to 'reports that drug traffickers are switching to human cargo to obtain greater profit with less risk'. That was in 2001, and one of the protocols to the UN convention focused specifically on human trafficking—seeking to prevent and punish traffickers and protect trafficking victims. UNODC was subsequently tasked with assisting state parties in drafting legislation, developing strategies, and providing resources to implement the protocol.

Although the protocol came into force as international law in 2003, the UK Anti-Trafficking Monitoring Group released a report in 2012 that pointed out that

> little is known about the profile of people who essentially fuel this criminal industry, what level they occupy within the criminal chain, their characteristics and personal circumstances, their reasons for becoming involved in trafficking activities, their perceptions of their activities and their opinion of those they traffic.[10]

UNODC itself highlighted how

> the global landscape of organised crime, whether it is in smuggling of migrants or trafficking in persons, drugs, weapons, etc. has changed. The overall common ground in this respect is that not only is there an enormous diversity in the landscape of organised criminal involvement in both phenomena but that overall there is an enormous diversity as to the different actors active in these markets. The actors involved may be organised criminal groups, individual traffickers or smugglers, or even friends and family of migrants or trafficking victims.[11]

Echoing UNODC's emphasis on the diversity of actors and the diverse ways in which organised crime engages with human trafficking, the Institute for International Research on Criminal Policy developed a typology of how criminal structures are organised that includes hierarchical structures that resemble traditional mafia-type organisations, networks of loosely connected individuals, as well as unorganised criminal involvement.

Despite the lack of understanding of what form organised crime takes in relation to human trafficking, it is increasingly being recognised as an organised crime problem. This is primarily because it is such a lucrative industry. In 2014, the International Labour Organization estimated that the profits made from forced labour amounted to USD 150.2 billion per year.[12] This breaks down to USD 99 billion from commercial sexual exploitation, USD 34 billion in construction, manufacturing, mining, and utilities, and USD 9 billion in agriculture, including forestry and fishing.[13] Not all of this profit is harnessed by criminal groups, however, as it also includes savings within the industry by using cheaper forms of labour. The figure also includes USD 8 billion that is saved annually by private households that employ domestic workers in exploitative conditions. Gary Craig et al. also argue that 'it is difficult to conclude other than that we all do [profit], however unknowingly, in the goods we buy which come from unknown destinations'.[14] Despite this dispersal of profits, trafficking remains a lucrative activity for criminal groups. A UNODC estimate from 2012, for instance, claimed that traffickers make USD 32 billion annually.[15]

A major motive for organised criminal groups to engage in human trafficking is the low threshold costs, the low risk of getting caught, and the ability to conduct this business model anywhere in the world.[16] A core difference between historical slavery and modern slavery is that those considered trafficking victims today 'invariably want to move, and generally have excellent reasons for wishing to do so'.[17] Julia O'Connell Davidson cites research on debt-financed migration and debt bondage, where migrants know the risks but nonetheless consider the potential benefits worthwhile.

In some cases, however, the role of criminal groups is redundant. In the UK at least, forced or exploitative labour occurs at a greater rate than sexual exploitation, and this is primarily a result of increasing deregulation of the UK economy, opening the door to low wages, long hours, insecure contracts, poor working conditions, and limited organising by trades unions.[18] These factors mean that organised crime networks are not necessary to circumvent labour regulations—employers or agencies can exploit workers directly. These circumstances have in turn created a role for 'middlemen' who exploit individuals from their own country of origin, finding them jobs but charging them for travel and accommodation. When their language skills are inadequate, they may be duped into opening a bank account that they do not control. The Gangmasters Licensing Authority (GLA) explained that

> sometimes ... workers are being exploited, but they are being exploited by somebody who works for the same company that they do. ... In that situation you find that it's either, for example, Lithuanian workers

exploited by a Lithuanian who works for the same company, or, for example, a Slovak Roma exploited by a Czech Roma who are in the same company.[19]

The ease with which anyone can become involved in the exploitation or trafficking of people reduces the need for organised crime networks. However, crossing borders still requires more technical expertise, and the profit motive ensures that criminal groups want to be involved.

Learning from Countering Other Crimes

Much of what is known or thought about organised criminal involvement in human trafficking comes from research on other forms of criminality, with human trafficking being viewed as one aspect of a rapid growth in all forms of organised crime. Louise Shelley acknowledges that 'trafficking has become an important component of the expanding illicit global economy. Globalisation has facilitated the rise of all forms of transnational crime and the internationalisation of corruption.'[20]

Drug trafficking has received the most attention, both in research and policy responses. Accordingly, it is from drug trafficking that the response to human trafficking has drawn most of its lessons. Although there are frequent discussions of building a toolbox to address organised crime, particularly among development agencies, the main strategies to address organised crime continue to rely on law enforcement techniques, particularly arrest and seizure.

For drug trafficking, this approach involves crop eradication and decapitation or 'king pin' strategies in source countries, arresting traffickers and seizing commodities in transit, and arresting users and distributors in destination countries, while also attempting to disrupt networks along the transit route. For human trafficking, this translates to arresting traffickers in source countries and disrupting criminal networks, which may include tracking financial flows and asset seizure. In transit countries, law enforcement also attempts to arrest traffickers and disrupt the networks, while in destination countries the focus is also on arresting facilitators of exploitation, and potentially arresting users, depending on the type of exploitation and the legislation in place.

Even in response to drugs, however, law enforcement approaches have not been effective. Successful law enforcement strategies rarely stop organised crime and merely push it elsewhere. This 'balloon effect' has been well documented. For example, the West African route for cocaine was attractive for many reasons—its proximity to South America, weak governance, and limited capacity to patrol borders and territorial waters. The popularity of this route was also attributed to effective strategies to deal with the flows from South America into North America.[21] More recent reports point out that this shift has come 'full circle' as the route through the Caribbean into North America and Europe has regained its popularity with drugs gangs after significant resources were invested in building the capacity of law enforcement in West Africa.[22]

Rather than shifting into new regions, or moving their commodities along different routes, criminal groups have also diversified into other commodities. This is not new. Early narco-traffickers in South America were initially engaged in the trade of numerous illicit goods. The specialisation in cocaine arose because the profits overshadowed other commodities. A number of more recent cases have highlighted the involvement of key organised criminals in several lucrative trades. For example, Feisal Ali Mohamed was arrested by Interpol in Dar es Salaam, Tanzania, for dealing and possessing elephant ivory. However, he is also reportedly linked to the Akasha family, well-known drug traffickers in the region. This case is more indicative of collaboration between criminals, through the sharing of corrupt officials, legal support, and knowledge of the marketplace. In other instances, there has been more direct crossover, such as the smuggling of Afghan minors with backpacks full of heroin.

The business-like nature of organised crime has long been recognised. For instance, the bootlegging trade in the United States involved a complex business structure to create the product and bring it to market. In 1963, Thorsten Sellin was writing about organised crime as a business enterprise.[23] As business has evolved, becoming more agile and dynamic, so too have organised crime groups. In most cases, they have had to become even more agile and dynamic to stay ahead of law enforcement, to the point where some commentators have asked 'what business can learn from organised crime'.[24] As part of this continual shift, organised crime groups are now also shifting into new commodities and new tactics, away from traditional high-risk activities to new areas that may even have been legal.

There is some value in applying the same strategies as drug trafficking to human trafficking. Phil Williams contends that

> one of the most pernicious and demeaning aspects of trafficking in women and children is that it reduces people to the status of commodities. Understanding this, however, is also an important insight since it suggests that what we are seeing is the operation of a commodity market that is subject to the same kinds of laws, impulses and trends as any other illicit market, whether drugs, nuclear materials, illicit arms, fauna and flora or art and antiquities.[25]

A Centre for Social Justice report also identified several cases that involved similar structures to drug trafficking networks—'power pyramids' with 'divisions of foot soldiers who will play their role in whichever division they are employed to operate within to recruit, transit or run the daily management of controlling victims'.[26] Shelley also points out how traffickers interact with other criminal networks: 'they obtain false documents for their victims from criminal specialists, hire thugs from outside their network to intimidate women and traffic labourers, and move their proceeds through established money-laundering channels'.[27]

But there are challenges in addressing human trafficking through law enforcement strategies. Because human trafficking involves a human commodity, strategies to respond place victims at risk. Some of the investigative techniques applied to drug trafficking, such as controlled deliveries, where police track the delivery of a shipment and then move in for arrests, or covert tactics and surveillance, put individuals at risk of exploitation. For these tactics to be effective, the crime has to have taken place, giving law enforcement the evidence it needs to prosecute a case. This creates a tension between the need to safeguard victims, the development of criminal intelligence, and the collection of evidence. As a result, there is a heavy reliance on testimony, which is particularly difficult because of the trauma experienced by victims, but also potential threats against family members or other control mechanisms, including *juju* in the Nigerian context.[28]

The methods criminal groups use for human trafficking also differ from other illicit activities such as drug trafficking. While there are some overlaps in the need for false documentation, corruptible border officials, the use of violence, and conduits to launder money, other areas differ significantly. Recruiting victims is very different from harvesting drugs. There is a need for large numbers of victims, and there is a tendency for traffickers to target their own ethnic group to capitalise on the trust that exists.[29] In addition, other strategies are used, such as advertising for false jobs, or marriages. Transport and entry relies on bribes to border officials or the receipt of visas through clandestine means, but human cargo needs to be fed, housed, and delivered in a reasonable condition.[30] Finally, compared with inanimate commodities, the victim needs to be controlled upon arrival—they need to have legitimate residence and be prevented from escaping, usually through a combination of violence, the confiscation of documents, psychological intimidation, and threats to family.[31]

These factors require a more nuanced understanding of how organised crime is involved in human trafficking in order to identify more strategic entry points for intervention.

The Diversity of Organised Crime

Organised crime is not a monolithic entity. Definitions vary, usually focusing on the groups or actors involved; the activities or markets these groups engage in; or the motives for criminal activity.[32] Vanda Felbab-Brown has identified a further way to distinguish between criminal economies—differentiating between labour-intensive, transactional illicit economies and non-labour intensive, predatory crimes. She argues that 'transactional crimes violate laws and procedures and supply black markets for prohibited or semi-prohibited products for which there is a demand', and they rely on extensive labour—from farmers to traffickers to distributors.[33] In contrast, predatory crimes have a clear victim, and include rape, robbery, extortion; they involve predation, victimisation, and abuse.[34]

Predatory Crimes

Human trafficking doesn't easily fit within these categories. On the one hand, it is predatory, in that it relies on people as a commodity and profit is derived from their exploitation and abuse. In this regard, sex trafficking is viewed as the most violent and depraved form of trafficking. The common perception of sex trafficking is of young women and girls, drugged and beaten, locked in rooms and forced to engage in sexual acts from which their exploiters profit.

Labour exploitation can be just as violent, however. As modern slavery has moved up the UK policy agenda, more and more cases have surfaced of vulnerable individuals held in slave-like conditions. In 2011, as part of Operation Netwing, seven people were arrested following a raid on Greenacres Caravan Park in Bedfordshire. Those arrested had targeted homeless and isolated men with false promises of work, food, and accommodation. Work began at 5 a.m. and continued into the night, laying driveways, doing groundwork, or cleaning and domestic work at the traveller site. Workers were beaten, psychologically abused, forced to live in squalid conditions, and were not paid.[35] The Passage, a homelessness charity in London, has recorded many more cases of homeless men being targeted and held in slave-like conditions.[36]

The profitability of exploitation is not the only driver for predatory crime. In conflict situations, human trafficking is used as a tactic of war with glaring parallels to the use of rape as a weapon of war. In 2008, the UN Security Council passed Resolution 1820, which recognised that 'women and girls are particularly targeted by the use of sexual violence, including as a tactic of war to humiliate, dominate, instil fear in, disperse and/or forcibly relocate civilian members of a community or ethnic group'.[37]

Traditionally, the link between human trafficking and conflict groups has been the most explicit in the forced recruitment of children—whether as soldiers, porters, cooks, lookouts, or sexual slaves. Conflicts in the 1990s and 2000s were notorious for the use of child soldiers, particularly Sierra Leone, Liberia, and also the Lord's Resistance Army in Uganda, which was publicised by the Invisible Children campaign.

However, an additional trend has been the use of women and girls as sex slaves. This is not new—during the Second World War, Japanese forces established 'comfort stations' in occupied territories with women and girls abducted or falsely recruited to be factory workers or nurses and forced to work as prostitutes. The stated aim was to comfort soldiers, prevent rape, and avoid espionage. However, comfort stations were violent and coercive.

More recently, however, conflict groups have been targeting particular groups to degrade a segment of the population and contribute to genocide. Islamic State targeted Yazidi women and girls, which the UN Human Rights Council considers to have been part of a genocidal strategy:

> Captured Yazidi women and girls are deemed property of ISIS and are openly termed *sabaya* or slaves. ISIS made eighty percent of the women and girls available to its fighters for individual purchase, the apportioning being drawn directly from religious interpretation. ISIS sells Yazidi women and girls in slave markets, or souk *sabaya*, or as individual purchases to fighters who come to the holding centres. In some instances, an ISIS fighter might buy a group of Yazidi females in order to take them into rural areas without slave markets where he could sell them individually at a higher price. The remaining twenty percent are held as collective property of ISIS and were distributed in groups to military bases throughout Iraq and Syria.[38]

Slave markets were organised by the Committee for the Buying and Selling of Slaves; information about how to participate in IS-run slave auctions was circulated to IS combatants, and IS troops who controlled slaves received a USD 50 stipend per week.[39]

Labour-intensive Crimes

In contrast, there are also examples that suggest human trafficking is a labour-intensive crime. As British police forces have prioritised slavery and increased raids on sites suspected of slave-like practices, they have met resistance. In early 2018, a raid on a daffodil farm in Cornwall resulted in the arrest of three farmers. In response, over 100 workers travelled to the police station to protest. Workers had been paid eight pence a bunch and worked up to nine hours a day, but said that they had agreed to work in these conditions. Of the 200 workers interviewed by police, however, fourteen did ask for assistance in leaving the farm.[40]

This is not an isolated case. Numerous police forces conducting raids on suspected sites of slavery have encountered push back from the purported victims who state that police are taking their livelihoods away. Even in Operation Netwing, discussed earlier, nine men also found at Greenacres Caravan Park refused to help the police inquiry.[41] Police suggest this may be because of the structure of the workforce, where 'alphas' would oversee the work of others and receive better conditions, generally becoming more loyal to the employer.[42]

Some victims even view sex work as a valid source of income. Belgian Federal Police picked up a Nigerian prostitute in Brussels and were transporting her to an NGO for assistance. Because she was young and beautiful, she was earning 3,000 euros per week and was able to send a large proportion home to support her mother and four siblings. She demanded to be let out of the police car, so she could continue to earn.[43]

This line between predatory and labour-intensive crime is very thin and can easily become blurred when there is profit to be made. Williams points to 'situations in which women are trafficked in the full knowledge that they will be engaged in prostitution at their destination'.[44] But he argues that this does not eliminate coercion, as

> women who are trafficked knowingly for prostitution often have the expectation that they will make enough money to live well and send funds back to their families. Instead they find themselves in a form of indentured labour that all too often is more akin to slavery than to traditional forms of prostitution in which the women themselves at least reap significant financial gains.[45]

Similarly, Misha Glenny has pointed to the difference between Czech girls who began prostituting themselves on the highway linking Dresden and Prague in the early 1990s and the creation of brothels in Prague and Northern Bohemia by Bulgarian organised crime groups filled with Bulgarian girls who had been promised jobs as shop assistants and waitresses but were beaten and raped into submission.[46] While this example indicates a clear distinction, the case studies discussed in this book reveal a messier picture, particularly when exploitation is intertwined with migration.

Human Trafficking versus People Smuggling

There is a blurred and constantly moving line between categories of human trafficking and people smuggling. In legal terms, the two categories are substantially different. Both practices are defined by protocols that supplement the UN Convention against Transnational Organised Crime. People smuggling is 'the procurement, in order to obtain, directly or indirectly, a financial or other material benefit, of the illegal entry of a person into a state party of which the person is not a national'.[47] In this sense, people smuggling is a crime against the state to which a person is being taken. Criminal networks that facilitate smuggling are seen to be providing a service to individuals that want to be moved.

In contrast, human trafficking is a crime against the individual being trafficked. It refers to

> the recruitment, transportation, transfer, harbouring or receipt of persons, by means of the threat or use of force or other forms of coercion, of abduction, of fraud, of deception, of the abuse of power or of a position of vulnerability or of the giving or receiving of payments or benefits to achieve the consent of a person having control over another person, for the purpose of exploitation. Exploitation shall include, at a minimum, the exploitation of the prostitution of others or other forms of sexual exploitation, forced labour or services, slavery or practices similar to slavery, servitude or the removal of organs.[48]

Aside from the target of criminality suggested by the type of activity, the primary distinction is the role of consent. People smuggling is a service chosen by individuals to move them across borders—whether because they are fleeing conflict or persecution or simply seeking better opportunities. In contrast, human trafficking is done without the consent of those being trafficked, either through the use of force or other forms of coercion as outlined in the Palermo Protocol above. Further, the Palermo Protocol states that any consent given is irrelevant if any coercive mechanisms are used, such as deceit, fraud, abuse of power, and so on. For individuals under eighteen years of age, none of these factors need to be employed for it to be considered trafficking. Their age defines the practice as human trafficking regardless, as they are deemed unable to give informed consent.

In reality, however, the distinction between people smuggling and human trafficking is not clearly defined, as even those who choose to move are vulnerable to a form of exploitation that meets the definition of human trafficking, particularly when they have clearly been deceived. As border controls are tightened globally in response to growing migration flows, more and more people are forced into irregular migration, which relies on smugglers to circumvent borders and provide transport through unfamiliar countries. Many irregular migrants need to work along the way to pay for their journey, making them vulnerable to forced and exploitative labour, which would put them into the human trafficking category. Tuesday Reitano disputes this, stating that in many African countries what is labelled human trafficking is 'simply a quest for a better life': 'often what the international community labels as human trafficking are in fact locally acceptable labour practices that offer the only meaningful employment available'.[49]

Because it is so difficult to draw a clear line between human trafficking and people smuggling, it is difficult to define the role of criminal networks, how they operate, and where the crime takes place.

Structure of the Book

The book is structured around three sections—the role of organised crime, how organised criminality in relation to human trafficking is understood, and the agency of trafficking victims. As the book seeks to interrogate current understandings and responses to human trafficking, this chapter has sought to provide an overview of the current landscape and the problems associated with it.

The second section begins the analysis through four country case studies: Nigeria, Albania, Vietnam, and Eritrea. Each chapter draws on extensive fieldwork in source, transit, and destination countries to uncover the dynamics of criminality and victimhood.

Nigeria

Nigeria is a key source country for human trafficking for sexual exploitation. Benin City, to the east of Lagos, is a hub for the recruitment of women who are trafficked to Europe. Trafficking in Nigeria is closely connected to *juju* rituals, which means there is less need for coercion as victims feel compelled to comply with the demands of their traffickers for fear of *juju* curses. Nigeria is widely understood as a classic case where coercive sex trafficking is facilitated by organised crime. In the early 2000s, trafficking was much more organised, with criminal networks moving women and girls through Lagos Airport into Europe, identifying and exploiting immigration loopholes, which required more sophisticated methods.[50] However, with the opening of the overland route via Libya, networks facilitating movement have become increasingly cell-based, and the barrier to becoming a trafficker or smuggler has become much lower.

In the case of Nigeria, shifts in the regional context have influenced how criminal facilitation is organised—focusing on the opening of the overland route, the criminalisation of smuggling in northern Niger, and the increasing involvement of armed groups in Libya.

The Nigeria chapter also emphasises the blurred line between trafficking and smuggling, as many victims believe they are travelling for legitimate employment or further education, while others willingly (often with family or community pressure) travel to engage in the sex trade, as they can earn more money than in Nigeria. In both cases, victims are exploited—forced to repay large sums to cover their transportation, and they only receive a small amount of their earnings. Madams that facilitate this exploitation were all previously prostitutes who had been trafficked from Nigeria, and the goal of many women and girls is to eventually become madams themselves.

The overland route from Nigeria has become the primary journey for both migrants and trafficking victims. The dynamics within the Economic Community of West African States (ECOWAS) are similar. The Libyan crisis initially 'opened the road', but fighting between different militias has made this part of the route increasingly dangerous and exploitative. Accordingly, Libya has been separated from Nigeria into its own chapter.

Albania

Albania is commonly thought of as a source country for women and girls trafficked into sexual exploitation. In contrast to Nigeria, trafficking is seen to be much more coercive, with victims often kidnapped and sold on to trafficking rings. While this was the case in the 1990s, there has been a shift by Albanian gangs to using other nationalities for sexual exploitation, as well as the deprioritising of trafficking in favour of drugs and arms, which are much higher-value commodities.

It is believed that the Albanian mafia controls human trafficking from Albania. However, the movement of people has historically been less organised and more ad hoc. In some cases, small-scale human trafficking operations have been used to generate revenue to move into the trafficking of drugs.

The trafficking routes from Albania have also shifted. Previously, women and girls were moved by boat into Italy. With Albanians now able to access Schengen visas, movement is usually by air into Europe and then overland to the UK. Most people moving currently, however, are not trafficked but smuggled. While the groups facilitating this movement are highly organised and business-like, this activity is not connected to coercive trafficking or exploitation.

Vietnam

Vietnam presents a different case. While trafficking for sexual exploitation is a problem, trafficking for labour exploitation, particularly of minors, is a much greater issue, and it is far less understood. Trafficking for labour exploitation is closely intertwined with people smuggling for economic opportunities. In the UK, many Vietnamese migrants are employed on cannabis farms, the illegality of which often prevents victims from seeking assistance from law enforcement. Victims are also controlled through debt bondage, the confiscation of documents, threats of deportation, and threats to family members still in Vietnam.

From Vietnam, victims are transported to Europe by commercial airlines or overland via Russia where they are held for days or weeks before being moved on to the UK. Although not coercive, those smuggled end up in exploitative conditions in the UK, mostly because of their irregular status. The networks that facilitate their movement are highly organised.

Eritrea

While the first three cases are all recognised as human trafficking, but in reality cross into people smuggling to varying extents, the book also includes a fourth case study—Eritrea. Movement from Eritrea begins as people smuggling, as individuals fleeing political violence seek out assistance to cross the border into Sudan and on to Libya or Egypt. In some cases, Eritreans are able to travel all the way to Europe with the assistance of smugglers. As irregular migrants in transit, however, Eritreans are vulnerable to exploitation, and there is an increasing risk that their journey will shift from people smuggling to human trafficking.

For those with the means to pay for their journey, there is a high risk of being kidnapped for ransom. Interception by authorities can also lead to extortion and human rights violations. Those who need to work to fund their journey may be held in debt bondage or forced into exploitative labour in gold mines or agriculture. With limited access to recourse, these migrants remain at the mercy of their smugglers and can be held for long periods. By adding this case study, the book will unpack the connections between trafficking and smuggling.

The third section of the book draws out two themes that undermine the current perception of human trafficking. The first theme is the prioritisation of human trafficking, which embeds a well-established dichotomy of helpless victim/barbaric exploiter. The case study chapters highlight how the categories of victimhood are fluid and change along the journey, making the dichotomy unhelpful when developing appropriate responses. The second theme engages with the nature of criminality. In all cases, victims have more agency than is commonly recognised, and to varying extents they have become complicit in a criminal pyramid scheme. From victims, to their families and communities and on to the criminal facilitators themselves, human trafficking and people smuggling are lucrative businesses, and everyone in the pyramid wants to benefit. This makes the trade less violent than it has been previously, but the challenge is that no one is willing to reveal the identity of the perpetrators because it risks undermining their economic interests.

2

NIGERIA
COMMUNITY COMPLICITY FOR WEALTH

Rune Henriksen and Sasha Jesperson

I am afraid of going back because I haven't paid the money back yet. If I am in Nigeria, the man can do anything to me. I have no money. The police only believe those who have money. The police is not protecting you in Nigeria.

—May Ikeora [1]

It works in a way that a girl that arrives in Sabha will never be able to pay us back in a reasonable time, and this will justify the fact they we will pass her to other operators who will offer to pay her price, but in fact they will do the same thing that we do. Some of them will do it in Sabha, or in Bani Walid, or in Tripoli, and most of the girls will end up in Italy where the profit for the operators is so high ...

— Sabha [2]

Introduction

Nigeria has become notorious for human trafficking, with numerous reports of women and girls transported to Italy and farther afield to work as prostitutes. While sex trafficking continues in high numbers, the situation is more complex. Children are being used by both Nigerian security forces and Boko Haram. Sexual exploitation of women and girls displaced by violence in the north-east is common, and they are vulnerable to trafficking. Domestic servitude and forced or exploitative labour in plantations, brick factories, and fishing is rife, both in Nigeria and across West Africa. However, it is trafficking to Europe that has received the most attention.

Trafficking of Nigerians to Europe primarily revolves around two forms of organised trafficking: domestic servitude and sex work, with historical links forming the genesis of both these flows.[3] The main origin for sex trafficking is Edo State in Nigeria, and the prevailing destination has been Italy, with 10,000 to 12,000 Nigerian prostitutes in 2003.[4]

Just as the Muslim north of Nigeria has historically had links to the Middle East, the predominantly Catholic south developed a similar relationship with Italy, as the hub of Catholicism. The entrepreneurialism of Nigerians quickly turned this into an economic relationship as well, shifting from agriculture to fashion to prostitution.

Destinations have since expanded, moving to France, Belgium, the Netherlands, the UK, Scandinavia, and even Russia. Origins have also expanded to neighbouring states, although Edo remains the primary origin hub.

This chapter will engage with how domestic servitude and labour exploitation are organised before turning to sex trafficking, which is the most lucrative, and thus the most attractive, to organised crime networks. As will be shown, sex trafficking is not a straightforward crime to categorise. A basic distinction begins with the difference between sex work and forced sex work. In addition, complications arise around how sex work is initiated, and in some cases how it continues even with serious and longstanding exploitation, or how sex trafficked victims transition into traffickers themselves.

Sex trafficking of Nigerian women originates in its most basic sense as economic opportunity. For onlookers around the world, the trafficking of women and girls is abhorrent, not least because the product is not objects, but human beings. Yet, for the community from which the girls and women originate, it is about business and about opportunities for social advancement, even with the foreknowledge of the hardships the girls can expect to endure.

Domestic Servitude

Domestic servitude is a specific kind of forced labour that takes place in a private home and is very different in its dynamics from sex trafficking. Traditionally, it has been a common practice in Nigeria for wealthy families to bring less advantaged children into their home in exchange for accommodation, food, and basic education. Domestic servitude is a commercial form of an old tradition. It is customary to give up your daughter to someone richer, as a kind of support system in the culture. The children are generally not held in slave-like conditions.[5] Domestic servitude thus exemplifies the complexity in the degree of legality, voluntarism, and exploitation related to human trafficking.

In many instances, domestic servitude has become a matter of good intentions going bad—where traditions have evolved into exploitation. According to a report by the Nigeria Federal Ministry of Women's Affairs: 'The practice of extended family fostering and apprenticeship provides the framework for most cases of abuse of children as domestic workers.'[6] Because of demand, there is also a reverse flow of young people being trafficked into Nigeria and held in domestic servitude.[7]

The practice has also attracted international attention as it has extended abroad. Wealthy Nigerian expats see themselves as doing charity work by reaching back to the poor villages and taking in someone else's girl.[8] The underlying assumption is that the trafficked victim travels abroad to receive a better education, for example to the UK. Because the practice is widespread across Nigeria, it is less centred in Edo State than sexual exploitation.[9]

Depending on how it is viewed, domestic servitude can be seen as much more organised or much more ad hoc compared with other forms of human trafficking. In Nigeria, there are agencies that recruit and provide domestic workers for families. However, the revenue domestic servitude generates is not high enough to make it lucrative to organised crime networks. Accordingly, the actual organisation of a domestic servitude agreement between the victim's family and the host family is usually done by word of mouth. It is a form of negotiation stipulating what the payment to the originating family is to be (e.g. whether school fees are paid). If the arrangements include going to school, stays typically last months rather than years. Instead, the arrangements can be serialised, involving different children replacing each other, which avoids the child becoming strongly attached to the host family.

Nonetheless, these arrangements are often facilitated by a middleman, who will negotiate on behalf of the families and control the distribution of workers. These middlemen can earn as much as NGN 5,000 per month (USD 14), or NGN 55,000 per year (USD 150) providing domestic workers to families, which are usually girls between the age of ten and eighteen. The child is typically replaced by another at Christmas and very often works throughout the day, does not go to school, and does not earn any money. In some cases, the families are paid for the girls' work, though she is not paid herself. There are even some cases where the domestic servitude arrangement may be entirely bilateral between the girl's family and the hosting family, without any other people or networks involved.

The Nigerian government has been slow to acknowledge that this practice is a problem, particularly when compared with its more active engagement with sexual exploitation. Engagement by the Nigerian government on domestic servitude only really took place when it became a global problem. The focus has until recently come primarily from NGOs.[10]

Even internationally, it is difficult to identify victims of domestic servitude. There have been several cases in the UK where families have been prosecuted for domestic servitude. In June 2017, for example, a Nigerian couple were sentenced to a six- and nine-month period of imprisonment and ordered to pay GBP 10,000 compensation for exploitation. In February 2007, the couple had brought a twenty-nine-year-old woman from Nigeria to look after their children. Despite being contracted to work from 7 a.m. to 5 p.m., Monday to Saturday, for GBP 500 a month, when she eventually escaped in June 2009 she had only received GBP 350 for the entire period. The victim's father was employed in a similar role by one of the couple's parents in Nigeria.[11] Similarly, in August 2017, a High Court ruling found that Teresa and Joel Abu held Nigerian Rashida Ajayi in domestic servitude for ten years between 2005 and 2015 while only paying her GBP 300 a year with little or no personal freedom.[12]

The Middle East is also increasingly becoming a destination for victims of domestic servitude, with 40 to 50 per cent of Nigerian victims travelling to the Gulf.[13] In parallel, trafficking for sexual exploitation in the Middle East has also increased.[14] In one case, three Nigerian girls in Dubai were attempting to run away from the apartment where they were kept; however, when the police attempted to intervene, the girls threw themselves off a high building rather than allow themselves to be caught.[15]

Because domestic servitude occurs at a lower rate than other forms of human trafficking it is harder to trace. When families recruit directly, they may apply for legitimate visas, or they may use fake passports. But once in the home, the conditions are invisible.

Labour Exploitation

Other forms of labour exploitation in Nigeria primarily target boys and men. A number of female victims of sexual exploitation are offered opportunities to pay their way through Libya by cleaning, cooking, or child minding. But they all end up being sexually exploited, as they cannot make enough money to move by doing non-sexual labour.[16] For men and boys, on the other hand, exploitative labour conditions are often the only available economic option. Exploitative labour primarily arises from the economic situation in Nigeria, where men and boys migrate for opportunities in typically unregulated industries, including plantations, brick factories, and fishing. Tuesday Reitano debates whether this should be considered human trafficking at all, as in many African countries this is 'simply a quest for a better life'.[17]

Labour migration occurs across West Africa, with Guinea Bissau a hotspot for exploitation due to lack of rule of law. Victims are also transported into East Africa. Travel is often facilitated by false documents, with the Oluwole cartel notorious for factories in Lagos that produce false documents and vehicle plates that facilitate movement.[18] According to the International Organization for Migration (IOM), Bauchi and Kano States in Nigeria are the major source of men and boys subject to labour exploitation, both domestically and internationally.[19] In comparison with other forms of exploitation, labour exploitation is less deceptive, as those who become involved are eager for economic opportunities.

Sex Trafficking

Origins

Although sex trafficking from Nigeria has gained increased attention, in part due to the Mediterranean migrant crisis, movement from Nigeria to Europe for sexual exploitation actually stretches back to the 1980s. There are numerous explanations for why and how it started. In one version, the oil boom in Nigeria generated a market for high-profile consumer goods. The wives of top military figures wanted designer shoes and handbags, so Nigerian textile traders travelled to Italy in search of products. Another version holds that Nigerian Catholics started making pilgrimages to Rome, imitating Nigerian Muslims who had gone on Haj to Mecca for generations. A third version says Nigerians were in Italy working in tomato picking, but as the tomato industry became heavily controlled by the Italian mafia, they were forced into other industries.

After arriving in Italy, Nigerians sought out other business opportunities. For example, the textile traders saw how the Albanians were organising the red-light districts in the suburbs of Turin, giving them the idea that they could bring Nigerian girls and sell them to the madams that were already established there.[20] Turin has been a key node and arrival destination for human trafficking from Nigeria since the mid-2000s.[21] Nigerian women who became involved in buying fashion and taking it back to Nigeria to sell for profit discovered that they could also engage in sex work and make large profits in a short period of time, money that could then be used to buy more fashion pieces. The fashion industry provides a good secondary income, but it may also serve as a cover and can be a money laundering front for sex work.[22]

While it is difficult to ascertain the veracity of these stories, they all rest on the same premise: Nigerians already in Italy identified a business opportunity and used their networks to take advantage of it. A parallel across all these stories is the transition of Nigerian women to madams that accrue greater profit from the sex trade—as the first generation of women retired from their own sex work, they became madams and started recruiting girls from Nigeria, using their personal networks. The first generation of Nigerian women involved in sex work in Italy predominantly came from Edo State, particularly Benin City.

During the 1990s, most of the young street prostitutes in Italy came from Nigeria and Albania, albeit with no connection between the different nationalities' networks.[23] After Italy, Belgium and the Netherlands were the next largest destinations for Nigerian prostitutes at that time. In all these countries, there was a market segment of thirteen to seventeen year olds from Nigeria who earned two to three times more than their adult counterparts per day. They had higher debts to start with, but they were able to pay them down quicker.[24] This may explain why there are Nigerian madams of a very young age in Europe. In 2005, madams tended to be between twenty-five and thirty-five in Italy, but as young as nineteen in the Netherlands. Often, the Dutch madams had married in pro forma marriages and then started their own network of child prostitutes.[25]

Today, more than half of those identified as sexually exploited still come from Benin City and Edo State. The recruitment through personal networks has reinforced the dominance of Edo State as a source. When Italy deported 800 sex workers back to Nigeria in 1999–2001, 86 per cent were from Edo State and 7 per cent from neighbouring Delta State.[26] In 2008, most Nigerian victims either came from Benin City or its outskirts. But today the source demography is more spread out into rural areas, although it is still centred in Edo State. There is also increasing knowledge about what is happening with the girls who travel to Europe. Nonetheless, the social pressure remains towards going rather than not going, and parents become very angry when a trip is interrupted.[27]

Prostitution also takes place domestically in Nigeria, as poor girls in particular cannot afford to travel far. But once they have been doing sex work in Nigeria, they are more exposed to trafficking. The girls believe they are going to be working in the same conditions in Europe. The recruiters' pitch is simple: 'You are doing the same work, just making much more money.'[28] Inside Nigeria, prostitutes are used to keeping about 90 per cent of their earnings and naturally will be inclined to imagine that working conditions are similar and with similar margins in Europe, albeit with much higher prices.

In more recent years, the trafficking from Edo State has continued but spread to European countries beyond Italy, particularly the Netherlands, Belgium, Scandinavia, the UK, and Germany. In Belgium,

Ghanaian women originally dominated the prostitution scene, as far as African origin was concerned, and they trafficked and exploited Nigerian women alongside others. Later, Nigerian women sought to control this trade themselves, so they took over from the Ghanaians.

The role of madams in managing the exploitation of Nigerian women and profiting from the trade has created a dual system of trafficking—the madams control prostitution in Europe and are mostly responsible for recruitment, while another network that operates as a syndicate or loosely affiliated group rather than a structured hierarchy manages the transportation of girls to Europe.[29] Both groups rely on the other for the industry to function but have different functions and skills.

Recruitment

Women working as prostitutes in Europe rarely last more than four or five years in the industry. After that, they are either worn out, ill, addicted to drugs, or have serious sexual diseases, although after this time, some have paid off their debts and have become madams themselves. Whatever the cause of the attrition, there is a need for new girls from Nigeria, and usually there is a madam in both the destination and the origin countries. The origin country madam contacts a recruiter in Edo State, sometimes referred to as an 'Italo Sponsor'.[30] Recruiters use word of mouth to market the journeys they sell and often travel to rural areas where the people are less educated. This type of recruitment appears to be ad hoc, rather than systematic.[31] Recruiters typically tell the girls a series of half truths about what awaits them, and even if they realise they are going into prostitution, they do not know the extent or duration of the hardship they will face on the journey or at the destination.[32]

Girls leave and return by the thousands, and some of those who return, or have been sent back from Libya, turn back and try going to Europe once again. Some of the rural areas where the girls come from are very deprived, both of political representation and infrastructure. Benin City used to be endemically affected by trafficking, but this has now moved out into the more rural areas (see Map 1). The recruitment process is constant. Each month, a handful of recruiters come to rural villages and persuade girls, who may even be their girlfriends, to be trafficked to Europe. The recruiters are often boys who have attempted to travel and who have returned. These boys know the routes and conditions of travel and also have contacts along the route. Recruitment is widespread in the villages and towns and may even take place in the streets, in church, or in family homes.

Madams have also been known to assist with recruitment. They occasionally return to Nigeria and swan around with expensive handbags and clothes to show the girls what they can have if they travel to Europe. Most recruiters, however, are men.[33] The recruiters and the transporters are often a relative of the madam and receive plenty of referrals from relatives.[34]

Many families in Edo State have a relative who has gone to Europe, which they associate with opportunity and social status.[35] The decision to send a girl away is always made collectively by the family, as they are described as the girls that can restore the dignity of the family,[36] thus placing pressure on the girls to travel. In one example, a second wife coerced her daughter to travel because the first wife's daughter had sent back enough money to build a house, and the second wife needed to do the same. This pressure extends to the community as a whole: 'if the industry stopped, Edo State would be bankrupt'.[37] The community interest in sending girls to Europe means that many organisations seeking to prevent trafficking, or supporting returnees, are threatened. Because of this, however, most girls are able to raise the funds and pay upfront.

In some cases, girls arrange with the mini bus drivers, often referred to as 'trolleys' or 'trolley boys', to pay for their transportation when they get to their destination. These girls are particularly at risk of exploitation and are made to take *juju* oaths to bind them to the agreement to ensure that they do not run away. The trolley boys think that they are recruiting in a very innocent way as they see themselves only as facilitators because it is what the girls want: 'I just want to help, I know it is what your parents want ...'[38] The recruiters also use agents to pressure parents into accepting the departure of their daughter as a good deal. This may work in instances where the parents are too ignorant or poor to be able to resist the apparent attractiveness of the pitch.[39] When the recruiters are at work in the local rural communities, they typically deal with a community leader who is a

27

'gatekeeper'. The recruiters give gifts to the gatekeeper while posing as helpers themselves. In one case, a girl who was a good singer in church was recruited by her pastor, who said she could make it as a singer in Europe. The pastor took her to his own sister, who was a madam. The girl worked for four years until she suffered from an illness and was no longer able to make money.[40]

The families who send girls to Europe are sworn to secrecy, and they pledge their commitment to the deal. They are presented with a letter that functions as a contract, which states the amount owed by the girl.[41] This is presented as the full cost of the journey. Since the girls have never travelled abroad, they have no idea that a realistic price would be no more than EUR 3,000. The girls are usually inspired by the successes of previous victims-turned-madams, who have impressive new houses in the community, and they decide that they want the same success. While the girls may know that the house owner has been away for a few years in Europe, they have no detailed knowledge of what has happened there. The family want to help the girl, who may be coming of age without having married, for example, or remains unemployed.[42]

Control Mechanisms

Once recruited, there are two mechanisms that ensure the girls continue to work as prostitutes after reaching their destination—traditional beliefs and social prestige. A significant part of the recruiting of girls is the power of sorcery, witchcraft, and magic. The belief in the power of juju is held with absolute conviction by many Nigerians, and not just the uneducated.[43] The beliefs come into play when the recruiters take the girls to swear to deities at a shrine. The deities in question can vary according to location, but in Edo State the deities Ogun, Isango, and Ayelala, particularly Ayelala, are typically used. Ogun is a deity for travel and beauty, so it has a key role.[44] Ayelala is so popular that this deity is a genuine challenger to the formal justice system. This means that the juju priests bind the girl to their agreement using a well-known, feared, and respected spiritual guarantor.[45] This use of the spiritual world is not necessarily associated with loss of agency, since mobilising the spiritual deities can also help the girl travel, which is what she wants.[46]

After the initial recruitment, paperwork is sometimes signed by a lawyer. The girls then go to a traditional local priest—often referred to as a *juju* priest—who initiates a ritual at a holy shrine. They believe they remain spiritually at the shrine, even when they are physically in Europe.[47] As part of this rite, the girls may have to give pubic hair, menstrual fluid, underwear, or nails. The girls swear an oath that binds them to the deity. They are told that they are spiritually bound to the contract and will be plagued by nightmares if they do not work and pay back their debt in full.

In addition, there is an underlying threat against their family if the girls do not fulfil their obligation under the contract and the oath. This was discovered by one girl who went to the police in Ceuta, Spain, and whose family's house was burnt down in reprisal.[48] In some cases, the girls return to the holy person to have their oath revoked after they return. In other cases, councillors try to help, but it is extremely hard to break the belief in the spiritual bond.[49]

Social prestige is the other powerful push factor in the local communities in Edo State, where returning successfully from Europe means dramatic upward social mobility. Prostitution is seen as one of the few means of social mobility, with the revenue from prostitution estimated to be 65 per cent of revenue in Edo State.[50] As long as the girls return wealthy, there is no stigma attached to their involvement in sex work.

The information at origin, such as it is, is heavily biased towards the positive aspects, since the social dynamics reinforce the success stories, forming a lingering 'narrative of success' around those girls who come back wealthy. This narrative of success means that girls are very keen to go, and there is a scramble to get there first. Some of the girls even steal from their family, or sell the family home, to fund the journey. After the economic boom in the 1980s in Benin City, houses often had signs saying 'this house is not for sale' as a countermeasure against an increasing trend where parents had found that their house had been sold by daughters funding their travel to Europe.

In 1999, the Nigerian First Lady started an initiative against human trafficking, an issue close to her heart. The First Lady convinced the Oba of Benin City—the traditional ruler—to commit to work against trafficking by showing him video footage of trafficking victims' stories.

He was shocked and condemned the practice, as well as the role of the *juju* priests who take the oaths from the girls. However, the First Lady and the Oba encountered a great deal of grass roots resistance from women in Benin City. Many women marched naked to the Oba's palace, protesting the initiative and arguing that the First Lady and the Oba were stealing their livelihood.

At that time, most Nigerian families sought to have a child abroad.[51] As an example, local workers from NGO International Reproductive Rights Action Group, one of the first NGOs actively working against trafficking in Edo State, received threats for their engagement and were told 'you're poisoning our food'.[52] Even as late as 2008, there was still resistance towards interfering with trafficking in Benin City, and today sources say that 'everyone' is on the take in Edo State from the trafficking.[53]

Nonetheless, the local chiefs have gradually come around to supporting countermeasures.[54] In the past, the national agency for counter-trafficking work—the National Agency for the Prohibition of Trafficking in Persons (NAPTIP)—has initiated 'reverse ceremonies', which were aimed at investigating and finding the 'native doctors' who have performed the oath-taking ceremonies and getting them to reverse the curse placed on the victim.[55] Today, the support from the Oba is unequivocal. Indeed, on 9 March 2018, the Oba of Benin, Oba Ewuare II Ogidigan, met with all the local *juju* priests in Benin City and had them revoke all the oaths they had administered on victims of human trafficking.[56]

There is also pressure from below to allow the girls to go abroad. Almost every family has a family member abroad. It is a status symbol and a source of pride. In Benin City, numerous businesses are run on products received from abroad, as the girls send container loads of cheap consumer goods home so the family can sell them in order to buy land or a house. This has been happening since the 1980s and is a way of life, although the market is becoming saturated with cheap products. The girls who are in Italy illegally, for example, ship products together with the Nigerians who are there legally.[57]

Reinforcing the pull factors is the role of money as king in Nigeria. Those who have money will be respected, even if they have no education. Social status is very important. Many trafficking victims are stranded because of this. They cannot return as ashamed losers, especially if they have friends who made it.

Some of the girls who are recruited know what they are going to be doing in Europe. Some of them are returnees, and they know and go deliberately anyway. For most, however, the knowledge is piecemeal, and they have no idea how exposed they are to exploitation, which primarily takes place once they have arrived in Libya. With the current perception of wealth acquisition in Nigeria, sources of wealth are hardly investigated or questioned, and the end is believed to justify the means; hence trafficking becomes highly contingent on these social views and processes.[58] The successful girls contribute to the economy of the family and the state. They are given power, status, and a voice in the local community and are seen as successful businesswomen who are to be emulated. They become well-connected powerbrokers.[59]

Those who return home empty-handed are stigmatised in several ways. One stigma comes from having been involved in sex work, which is frowned upon unless you are successful, in which case the woman is not a former sex worker, but a businesswoman. It does not really matter what the girl is going through. If she complains, the family may say that so-and-so is also in Europe and they are not complaining. Stigma also arises from having squandered the savings of the family who were paying the journey as a future investment. Such multiple stigmas make the women who return as losers not divulge any details about what they have endured, because it reinforces their position as victims rather than winners. Similarly, the successfully returning madams have no incentive to share the dark side of their experience and will not be made to do so, since the local population shows deference to them due to their success.

At destination, those who succeed in the sex trade become madams, having typically worked for three to four years to pay their debt. All the madams were once sex workers themselves.[60] As they become madams, effectively facilitating trafficking, they are able to secure their family wealth for the next three to four generations. Benin City, for example, has the highest share of house ownership by women.[61]

When the girl arrives in Italy, they will be handled by a madam who typically cooperates with her 'black boy' male counterpart in controlling ten to fifteen girls. She will buy clothes and condoms for the girl, and for some girls this used to be the point when they would realise they were going into prostitution,[62] although in more recent years most have worked in prostitution during their journey, certainly in Libya. The other women who are already working are made responsible for training the new arrival, since they tend to live together and the controller is usually an aspiring madam.[63] The girls may suffer violence, but typically that is not necessary since they are controlled by the power of their pact. This is in contrast to Eastern European prostitutes who are more prone to suffering violence as a control mechanism, although in the mid-2000s there was a trend whereby Albanian and other Eastern European networks would copy the Nigerian style, where the women are given some degree of ownership over the sex work, which makes control easier and makes law enforcement harder.[64]

Smuggling and Trafficking Routes: Airside and Overland

Since 2010, trafficking from Nigeria has undergone an evolution from comparatively fewer numbers travelling by air—and requiring much more criminal sophistication and assistance in acquiring fraudulent documents in doing so—to mass movement overland through Libya, where a large number cross the Mediterranean. These two main models of trafficking are airside and overland.

Airside

Relying on lax controls at Murtala Muhammed International Airport in Lagos, airside trafficking was the most dominant form of trafficking in the 1990s and 2000s. However, as international attention has increased, and the airport has become more professional, the numbers involved in airside trafficking have fallen a great deal.[65] It is much more difficult to successfully get trafficking victims on board aircraft today. It requires more sophistication, with back stories ranging from victims being portrayed as refugees from Liberia, to fake newlyweds on honeymoon. Such flights would typically arrive at Schiphol Airport in the Netherlands, where the victims would claim asylum. With a simple phone call, they would be picked up from asylum centres by traffickers and then moved around Europe by a smuggling network of madams.[66]

To function effectively, the airside model also requires corrupt officials. Traffickers often recruit immigration officers to facilitate airside trafficking. But NAPTIP is now operational on the airside as well, and there have been a series of arrests of corrupt immigration officers and other law enforcement officers. As a result, the airside route has increasingly been replaced by the overland route, not only because the latter makes more business sense but also because the growing use of biometric data makes it harder to fake the identities and documents that are necessary to fly.[67] In addition, airport personnel have received a great deal more training. One example of airside fraudulent identities are fake honeymooning couples, several of whom have been arrested by NAPTIP based on profiling. When interviewed separately, it becomes clear that the girl is being trafficked abroad and the marriage is fake.[68] Airside trafficking has not completely stopped, but there has been a shift towards trafficking to the Middle East, where arrivals checks are less rigorous. Flights typically go via Nairobi and Addis Ababa and arrive in Oman. Trafficking victims then receive a legitimate two-year work visa and go into domestic servitude.

The price to forge a genuine visa with false personal data in Nigeria is about NGN 30,000 (USD 85). It is possible to buy Nigerian passports for a fee, for example through subcontractors involved in issuing them. In some cases, genuine documents are used, but with fake stamps. Although this happens, it does not take place on a large scale. Another approach is to fraudulently acquire genuine papers, even British passports.

When the individual tries to enter the UK, they are helped to acquire supporting documents by organised crime groups. Such documents include false tax returns or employment records stating that they work for a non-existent CEO. In part, people use false documents because they believe it is difficult to obtain a real visa.[69]

Overland

The overland route has existed as long as people have wanted to travel from West Africa to Europe (see Map 4). For many, travel to Libya was sufficient and even the desired destination, and after working for a period they would return home. The rule of law vacuum in

Libya since 2011, arising from ongoing fighting between factions, has created an easy route to the Mediterranean and an opening for traffickers.[70]

The routes broadly stay the same. It is all but impossible, and for the purpose of maintaining an overview, it is also unnecessary, to identify day-by-day changes to routes. Generally, it is fairly difficult to get into Morocco and farther to Ceuta into cross over to Spain. There is virtually no interest in stopping migrants from the Algerian side. Thus a lot of the migration and its concurrent smuggling and trafficking of people coalesce around and through Niger and into Algeria and Libya, where weapons and drugs are also smuggled, and smuggling routes mirror the trafficking routes to a great extent.[71]

In terms of the papers needed for the journey, it is possible to travel visa-free within the ECOWAS zone (i.e. for northbound journeys up through Mali and through Niger), although not without identity papers,[72] all the way up to the border with Libya. Until recently, there has not necessarily been any clear-cut criminal feature (other than the fraudulent expectations that are pitched at the origin) to the journey undertaken until the migrants reach Libya, where they illegally cross the border.

The northern part of Niger and Libya itself constitutes the proverbial bottleneck that separates three vast free movement areas: ECOWAS to the south, and the high seas and EU to the north. On the high seas, there is no law against smuggling, only against piracy. For this reason, there is effectively free movement of people and products on the high seas.[73]

The overland trafficking route currently has the highest volume of people trying to get to Europe. The main mode of transport is minibuses controlled by 'trolley boys' who hand the women over to colleagues who take them through the next sections of the journey. The trolley boys do not organise any kind of clandestine transportation but are using public transport and simply facilitate the journey. However, there will be someone waiting at the end of the leg to take the girls and introduce the next set of trolley boys who will be in charge for the following part of the journey. There is a qualitative difference between what happens before Libya, when the girls want and need help to find their way, and inside Libya, where the girls are in a lawless situation and entirely unprotected unless in the hands of traffickers who force them into prostitution for an undetermined period.

The smugglers and traffickers do not see themselves as criminals but rather as someone providing a sought-after service. They call themselves 'sponsors' or 'facilitators', and they negotiate any practical obstacle to the journey.[74] Overland trafficking to Europe is both cheaper, although less convenient, and more accessible than flights and can involve far more people. There are also no problems with immigration control, which means a much lower risk.[75] For the smugglers, it is a McDonald's-type business model, with high volume, low risk, and low expenses. The airside route is more boutique, more expensive, and higher risk.

During the overland journey, the girls can be sold on to another trafficker, or they may beg to be released. But due to social pressure, a huge investment in the journey and manipulation from *juju* rituals, the girls start working as madams themselves when they are freed, rather than return home. And this may have been their motivation all along. The girls may make excuses for not making it to Europe, whether to the trolley boys, the madams, or their family, blaming a shortage of boats or the security situation. They tell their family they are waiting to cross the Mediterranean Sea and are not disclosing that they are working, often permanently, in Libya rather than in Europe as had been expected. The family may start applying pressure if they understand that their girl has not yet crossed the sea.[76]

The journey overland is usually very slow and long, but there is also an express option that can be completed in as little as a week. Yet as this route is prohibitively expensive, it is not used by many migrants. The express journey is either paid for by the migrants themselves, or in some cases (e.g. if the girl is very attractive to a madam) the girl's journey is paid for by a madam. Most of the women being trafficked travel for a period of anywhere from three months to two years.[77] Some migrants believe they are embarking on an express route but are duped and it in fact takes two years, and they do not travel beyond Libya.[78]

The opening of the overland route has lowered the barrier to entry to becoming a trafficker. It does not take much to be a trafficker these days, as the only prerequisites are access to girls and transportation.[79] The more sophisticated airside route required greater

35

skill, organisation, and a network of corrupt officials. Many argue that this was managed by university cults or confraternities, which have become the foundation of organised crime in Nigeria. The Black Axe cult, which hails from the University of Benin, as well as the Air Lords (or Supreme Eiye), which originally hail from the University of Ibadan, have been associated with human trafficking.[80] These cults have networks across Europe that would greet girls at Schiphol, for example, before transporting them to the madams.

The networks facilitating the overland route are horizontally linked, flexible in their grouping, highly specialised, and discreet.[81] Such networks are difficult to defeat because of their structure. In contrast to hierarchies that can be collapsed, these networks easily regenerate if a cell is removed. Dutch officials claim that arresting human traffickers has not had an appreciable effect on the number of Nigerian prostitutes in the country.[82] The criminal element of the recruiters' activity in Nigeria is difficult to define, but it lies in the fraudulent exploitation, for example in the vast overcharging of the cost for the journey, which traps the girl in financial bondage. There is a large element of deception in this, which also applies in the case of domestic servitude. There is no oversight or transparency between the claimed contents of the transaction (when the girls or their family pay upfront) and what the facilitators offer en route.[83] Accordingly, transportation has become a marketplace, with multiple trolley boys operating on the same sections.

How the Money Travels

The movement of money is where the two networks—the madams and the transporters—most clearly intersect. The way money is transported varies, but there is an interplay between different money transporting modes and their attendant degrees of indebtedness for the girls.

In many cases, the girls need to pay upfront for their journey. In some cases, girls have secretly sold their family home to raise the cash. But often families, or communities, are eager for the girl to travel and will find the cash, expecting to profit in return. In other cases, the madam may cover the costs of travel herself if she is requesting another girl, from the madam's position in Italy. The madam will then pay in instalments, and the girl who is travelling may be stuck in Libya, because the madam does not have the money to pay for the last leg.[84] Regardless, once the required funds have been raised, they need to be distributed to all the key players participating in transporting the girl to Europe. Once she reaches her destination, she will also need to send money home to repay the debt.

The hawala system is widely used, both because of its practicality and immediacy and the difficulties involved in policing it. Money is paid out along stages of the route, sent from the woman's home or the madam depending on the arrangement, and collected by the person who is controlling her at a given stage.[85] In some cases, the traffickers also use the conventional banking system, despite the comparative ease with which national and international authorities can investigate money flows.[86] Primarily, this is because smuggling and trafficking are not seen as criminal.

Sometimes a dedicated money man is responsible for payments along the route. A money man is paid by the girl's family, and he charges 2 to 5 per cent commission for his service. He can work for five to six traffickers at any given time. The benefit is the woman does not need to carry any cash, so she is less vulnerable to being mugged and being unable to pay for the remainder of her journey. The money man pays the traffickers so that the victim can be transported on the next leg of the journey, and he facilitates transport (he has contact details for trolley boys at the various stages), security where relevant, and bribes.[87]

In some cases, the traffickers pay the trolley boys a given amount that includes the necessary bribes. It is then up to the trolley boys to secure a profit and reduce the bribe costs.[88] In Libya, girls are bought and sold outright for each stage and then have to pay back the 'debt' to the trafficker—irrespective of what the girls themselves or their parents paid at the outset. Alternatively, the money man system continues, where the traffickers only organise transportation, and the girls are not bought and sold, between destinations. The accumulated debt for the whole journey is typically USD 25–30,000 for travel to Dubai, and EUR 30–70,000 for travel to Europe. When the girls are presented with these prices in the recruitment stage, they tend to believe that the prices are in Nigerian naira, as they are often uneducated and have no concept of currency differences, or they may be unaware of how little profit they will retain. Once the madam takes her cut of the earnings, the girl is left with very little to pay down her debt. Either way, they are rarely conscious that it will take at least three years to pay off the debt.

A Changing Market

Already in 2005 most of the current key features of the Nigeria case were observable in Norway, a country that has not been considered one of the major destinations for Nigerian women and girls. They began arriving in large numbers in Norway in the autumn of 2004. One year later, Jørgen Carling observed that an increasing number of the girls were aware from the start of their journey that they would be working as prostitutes, although the circumstances in which the prostitution would take place would come as a surprise for many; that once they had paid their debt many would become madams themselves; that some travelled by air using fake documentation and others overland across the Sahara and being smuggled into Europe by boat; that many were stranded in North Africa, failing to continue their journey; that most of these women hailed from Edo State; that the recruitment involves the role of the family, recruiters, the pact, the traditional priest, the deities and the shrine, the fear of going mad if they break the pact; that the women signing agreements have no understanding of currency differences between the naira and the euro; that Turin has a key role in the arrivals in Italy and that Italy is the key destination country in Europe; that Agadez has a key role, but at that time also Gao and Kayes in Mali; and that Nigerian organised crime groups are typically organised as a network and are consequently able to quickly regenerate if a cell is taken out.[89]

The expansion of the overland trafficking route has had consequences for the dynamics of the business. While criminal networks in Nigeria have become more ad hoc in response, Niger has shifted in the opposite direction. Niger was previously very open; as such, it was an important migratory hub and the country was well equipped with hotels and transporters to facilitate the movement of West Africans to Libya. For Nigerians, it was more controlled—while they would rely on local transporters, a Nigerian would be posted at each crossroad to manage migration, particularly for girls being trafficked into sex work. They would also operate 'connection houses' along the way at key hubs.

In 2015, the Nigerian government introduced an anti-smuggling law in response to deaths in the desert.[90] The free movement allowed throughout the ECOWAS zone was subsequently restricted north of Agadez towards the Libyan border. As a result of the law, legitimate transporters became less involved in the movement of people in this area because it had been criminalised. This in turn opened a space for criminal groups that were willing to take the risk, for a higher price, on more dangerous routes and with more sophisticated vehicles. For girls being trafficked, this increases the price and the likelihood that they will have to work along the way, or the time to pay down their debt will increase. As of 2018, there were reports of brothels in Niamey, where Nigerian women were working to raise funds for their journey.

Although Libya was initially an open route to the Mediterranean, increasing lawlessness has made this part of the journey the most dangerous. Aside from the pressures discussed earlier, once the girls begin their journey, they are largely free to change their mind until they arrive in Libya. Once inside Libya, they are at the mercy of the traffickers, who will not facilitate their transport until they are satisfied that their expenses will be covered. These expenses are arbitrarily defined, so the girls end up de facto in a slavery-like condition. Their captors say the girls can leave at any time, but without the protection of traffickers against other traffickers, corrupt police, or militia members, the girls enter a lawless environment where they are all but guaranteed to suffer extreme hardship or death. The growing saturation of the European market, and the transporters' realisation that they can make more money the longer the girls are en route, has also resulted in extended stays in the country, with many girls becoming trapped in Tripoli.

Because the situation changes in Niger and Libya, these countries are addressed in the following two chapters.

3

NIGER

THE EDGE OF THE ECOWAS FREE MOVEMENT ZONE

Rune Henriksen

Niger is strategically located at the southern end of the Sahara, connecting the Sahel with North Africa and West Africa with Central Africa. The country is poor and lacks basic infrastructure, such as electricity and roads. In terms of European partners, Niger has particularly close relations with France, as well as Spain, Germany, and Italy.

Niger's security situation has several separate dimensions. On the one hand, it is a relatively stable country, with good relations with the West. However, its borders are threatened by the spill-over of different kinds of conflicts. From Mali, the threat is political, as conflicts between the Mali government and marginalised tribes could spill over the border, which has been exacerbated by the jihadist offensive in the region since 2012. Boko Haram is a military threat in the south-east, and the instability in Libya could spill over from the north, where various militias sponsored by outside countries as well as by the major power groups inside Libya fight over territory and the attendant smuggling flows. This area also has a jihadist presence.[1]

These spill-over risks are not helped by extremely porous and unpoliced borders, where there is a 30-kilometre wide zone on both sides of the border with Mali and Burkina Faso, which is essentially a free-for-all for smugglers of all manner of contraband. In addition, the presence of Islamic State's Adnane Abou Walid al-Sahrahoui, the Islamic State's Grand Emir for Sahara, is a long-term threat in the Mali, Burkina Faso, and western Niger region.[2]

Finally, migration is also a threat to stability due to expectations in the north of continued revenue from the increased flow of migrants, and thus money, which generates much more income than both weapons and drugs.[3] Local authority figures are deeply involved in the smuggling and will not give up this income without realistic compensation. The criminalisation of this smuggling by the Niger central government walks a fine line between sufficient enforcement to change the routes and thus reveal progress vis-à-vis the EU. However, a total and effective crackdown on the smuggling is too risky since the stability in the north between the central government and Touareg in particular is predicated on effectively leaving them to continue their smuggling activities.

In terms of migration flows, Niger is both a source and transit country. A large number of people travel through it, from West Africa in particular. In 2016, an estimated 300,000 people passed through Niger, which dropped down to about 60,000 in the following year.[4] The drop in 2017 should also be seen against an average of 100,000 people per year since 2000.[5] The decline indicates that some of the countermeasures, such as Niger authorities arresting 100 traffickers since 2016 and confiscating large numbers of vehicles, are having a positive effect.[6]

Arrival numbers in Italy dropped from 181,436 in 2016 to 119,130 in 2017.[7] Since the number of people inside Libya is unknown, the arrival numbers in Italy are one of the few gauges of the size of flows. In April 2018, IOM detected 4,758 people entering Niger, which matches the 2017 average of about 60,000 per year, and 6,056 people leaving, albeit limited to the two observation points at Arlit and Séguédine in the north; 92 per cent of these were travelling in private vehicles, buses, or trucks.[8] According to their own reports, 88 to 93 per cent travel for economic reasons. Only 2 to 3 per cent cite war, conflict, or insecurity.[9] The top nationalities leaving Niger in mid-2016 were from Nigeria, Niger, Gambia, Senegal, and Côte d'Ivoire.[10]

The security situation in Libya has deteriorated dramatically since 2011—people are consistently exploited and abused, and because of the increase in violence many are returning to Niger from Libya by road. Libya used to be a relatively safe destination for seasonal work, and like Algeria it was a final destination for many from Niger. People from Nigeria, Senegal, and Gambia, on the other hand, usually have Europe as their destination.[11]

Anti-trafficking and Anti-smuggling Efforts

In 2010, Niger established Agence Nationale de Lutte contre la Traite des Personnes (ANLTP), an anti-trafficking agency, following the passing of an anti-trafficking act in the same year. In October 2013, people smugglers had left ninety-two migrants, almost all women and children, to die in the desert.[12] This caused outrage in Niger, and on 11 May 2015 public pressure led to Niger's parliament passing the 2015 Anti-Smuggling Law, which criminalised people smuggling. There has been a great deal of confusion over how to enforce the law, such as distinguishing between smuggling and trafficking.[13] The authorities in Niger do not have the resources to quickly determine if people in the large flows of migrants are travelling on their own accord or are being exploited.[14] Since the legislation was passed, new actors have provided resources for countering smuggling, but less so for taking care of trafficking victims.[15] Meanwhile, international agencies like IOM are assisting government agencies by sensitising, capacity building, and building national referral mechanisms.[16]

However, the deaths in the desert have continued. In the first half of 2015, at least thirty-three migrants died in the desert.[17] In June 2016, thirty-four migrants who had been abandoned by people smugglers were found dead in Assamakka, near the border with Algeria.[18] In June 2017, fifty-two migrants were found dead, also abandoned by smugglers, near Séguédine.[19] Such incidents are partly attributable to the more dangerous routes taken by smugglers to avoid being caught, and by the willingness of smugglers to discard their passengers in the desert if they perceive a risk of getting caught. Until August 2017, Niger authorities and IOM together saved at least 1,000 migrants who had been left to die in the desert.[20]

In August 2016, the Niger government began implementing the law that criminalises the transportation of migrants north of Agadez.[21] The motivation for implementing the law came from inside Niger, with the public outcry from the 2013 deaths in the desert as a push factor, and from the EU Valletta Summit in November 2015.[22] According to civil society representatives, however, the criminalisation has led to more drugs and crime in Agadez and ex-migrant transporters looking to the EU to provide them with livelihoods, while the transportation of migrants has been taken over by criminals. The criminalisation of the transportation of migrants has caused considerable resentment in Agadez, exacerbated by the security situation making other sources of income, such as tourism, extremely difficult. Since the early 2000s, kidnap for ransom has reduced tourism in Niger to virtually zero.

The area north of Agadez is divided territorially between the Touareg and the Toubou. The Touareg make up 10 per cent of Niger's population and control the approach to Algeria, around Agadez and Arlit. Many of the Touareg gained military experience under Gaddafi's pan-Arabic Islamic Legion in the 1970s. This experience came into play in the two Touareg Rebellions in 1990–5 and 2007–9, where demands were made for political representation and a share of the profits from French uranium extraction in the Arlit area. The government's solution was to co-opt Touareg leaders and give them state positions while also paying militants. Although this helped make the situation more stable, the government has paid for this by accepting senior authority figures in the north being heavily involved in drugs, weapons, and migrant smuggling. Given the security challenges raised above, the predominant focus of the government is to preserve internal security, and that means not rocking the boat too much in terms of interfering with the migrant smuggling.[23]

The Toubou are only about half a percent of the population of Niger, but they wield strong influence in the area where migrants go north from Agadez and into Libya through Tummo. For both these tribes, smuggling is a way of life, partly because there is no other work for them in the area now that tourism is no longer an option.[24] The tribes are not in open conflict, but they are competitors, and smuggling follows ethnic alignments, with routes divided between the tribes. There is also a significant intergenerational conflict line in both tribes between older traditional leaders and younger smugglers who have recently returned from Libya.[25]

A significant upscaling of international projects has been aimed at compensating for these tensions, but people in the north say they see little effect, arguing that most of the resources go to Niamey. Further, many elements of the EU Action Plan against migrant smuggling are security measures designed to police the borders. These measures enforce the 2015 anti-smuggling law with heavier sentences and fines for people smuggling, including seizures of vehicles. Transportation operators are targeted as enablers and facilitators. In the law, these actors are given an entire chapter, although little is being done to the bus companies by way of enforcement.[26]

The transportation industry is one of the country's few non-agricultural industries, and many people who are employed in bus companies and as drivers of cars and vans in the north belong to the segment of former insurgents turned tourism operators turned bus and car drivers for migrants. In Dirkou, for example, 60 per cent of eighteen to twenty-five year olds work in migrant transportation. They work in the parallel informal economy, and there are risks involved in disrupting it.[27]

What exists in the north of Niger is effectively a semi-permanent truce between disaffected tribes and the government, where old smuggling traditions are allowed to continue as well as high positions given to leaders in return for stability. Today, these senior tribal figures are sponsors of the democratic government and hold key roles as advisors to President Mahamadou Issoufou. The government is extremely reluctant to deprive them of their income and risk upending a tenuous unofficial compact.[28] It has been suggested that the enforcement is finely balanced between allowing the government to receive money from the EU because they are doing something[29]— and indeed the flows have reduced—while simultaneously allowing the smugglers to continue, albeit in a more circumscribed, professional, and discreet way. This reinforces the stature and power of the key co-opted leaders who can take a cut from the smuggling using the enforcement as income and a stick to force compliance and sharing of profits. Such an approach also drives up prices of individual travel legs and reduces competition, keeping prices high. The large flows lowered the threshold to take part in smuggling, which in turn lowered prices.

Agadez

Agadez is a region with a population of about 500,000. The local people are frustrated because the criminalisation of migrant transportation is depriving them of an income, and they want compensation from the EU. Bus companies, for example, are losing 60 to 70 per cent of their income. In Agadez, 60 per cent of migrants are Nigerians, with an even split between men and women. The women pay with sexual activities, like in Niamey, and are generally left alone by the police. The men often work in slave-like conditions.[30] Upon arrival in Agadez, the migrants, whether they have valid travel documentation or not, must use illegal means to travel farther, since facilitating their travel has been criminalised and enforced since August 2016.

In Agadez, the migrants then rely on an organised network of facilitators, which is led by a *passeur* (guide) acting as the overall coordinator. The *passeur* employs *cokseurs* (middle men), who approach migrants and recruit them for the onward journey, initially putting them into nationally divided ghettos, controlled by ghetto bosses who charge for and arrange accommodation outside Agadez.[31] These ghettos used to be in the town itself but have now been pushed out into the suburban areas.[32] From here, they are taken into the desert by drivers in all-terrain vehicles. At each leg of the journey, they are introduced to new *cokseurs* and ghetto bosses who put them on new car journeys. In 2007, there were twelve travel agencies in the area, but that figure had risen to seventy smuggler ghettos by 2013.[33]

For the migrants, the criminalisation has meant more dangerous routes circumventing Agadez and hence more risk. For example, migrants that fall off a truck full of people crossing the desert will not be picked up. Smugglers who are used to smuggling guns and drugs are happy to transition into smuggling migrants, but there is little movement from smuggling migrants and going into guns and drugs. The routes used by smugglers change every day.[34] Police officers are unable to counter the smugglers as they lack basic necessities like fuel and all-terrain vehicles, whereas the people smugglers have the latest Toyota Tundra vehicles that are able to travel off-road.[35] The military budget for fuel and supplies, for example, often disappears in Niamey, and the military in turn uses illegal taxation in part to fund its operational costs, effectively making the smugglers and migrants fund fuel for the military outposts.[36]

Migrant women spending time in Agadez or Dirkou often end up in prostitution. When they talk to IOM, they often initially say that they are voluntary prostitutes, but then when they are in shelters the story changes, making it hard to ascertain the truth. There are some patterns in the trafficking going through Niger. In early 2018, the trend was children begging internally in Niger. Domestic servitude victims typically came from Niger or Nigeria, while sexual exploitation victims largely come from Nigeria.[37] Generally, for migrants from Niger, women and children from south-west Zinder all go to Algeria, for historical reasons. Those who come from Tahoua generally go to Libya.[38]

Travel is made easy up to Agadez because of ECOWAS visa-free travel. Visa free does not mean document free, and migrants need proof of entry, such as a stamp in their passport. They have ninety days to stay in Niger from the date of entry, which is enforced by the Niger border agency Direction de la Surveillance du Territoire (DST).[39]

Nonetheless, in practice many migrants travel without valid documents. This is facilitated by bus companies taking migrants into Niger from Benin, Burkina Faso, or Nigeria who may stop before a border crossing and drop off the migrants so that they can use taxies to cross irregularly and then get picked up by the buses again after the crossing.[40] There are several police checkpoints, originally put in place as counterterrorism measures, both on the border crossings and between Niamey and Agadez. The cost of crossing these checkpoints is often included in the bus ticket. These checkpoints exemplify institutionalised corruption and feature set prices for crossing, such as USD 65 for migrants with valid documents and USD 130 for those without.[41] The same practice takes place all along the Niger border, where a typical fee of EUR 200 is charged per migrant. The border officials are closely entwined with the smugglers, often belonging to the same tribe.[42]

In 2016, trucks would leave Agadez on Monday evenings with 1,000 to 3,000 migrants. If someone fell off a truck, nobody would stop. By early 2018, this situation had changed and there were national guard and police checkpoints all around Agadez, controlling migrant travel. About twelve to fifteen small networks, with forty to fifty smugglers using about seventy cars, have been arrested and seized for people smuggling.[43] The smugglers in turn circumvent the checkpoints, or drop the migrants off to let them walk through the checkpoints and pick them up farther along the road. These networks have connections to Gambia, Senegal, and Guinea Bissau, where many of the migrants originate. Although law enforcement efforts led by Niger, and assisted by European nations, have been ongoing for over a year, they have been hampered by a reactive rather than proactive operational approach.[44]

A further complication has been the engagement from the legal and law enforcement agencies.[45] In cases where arrests have been made, the local authorities have not had sufficient capacity to process smugglers through the legal system, leaving them in jail without charge or trial, which violates rule of law principles and antagonises the local community. That only Toubou have been arrested has reinforced the resentment, because the local leaders in Agadez are Touareg. The local resentment at one point became so serious that inhabitants nearly overran the police station in Agadez where the seized vehicles were located and threatened to burn it down.[46]

Up to Dirkou, the travel is in convoy with military escort, which is a tradition going back to the Touareg Rebellions. From Séguédine, the convoy is protected by the French and Niger garrisons in the area.[47] A perhaps unintended consequence of this practice is that it routes migrants through areas that are controlled by the military, which has further institutionalised the security agencies' corrupt practice of illegal taxation of the migrants. In Dirkou, different security agencies were bickering so much over who had a right to which illegal taxes that the mayor had to intervene and arbitrate. Smugglers responded by circumventing Dirkou and then the same thing happened in Séguédine, which is effectively the last border post on the Nigerien side. At Dao Timmi, about one-fifth of smugglers are willing to cross a minefield to avoid taxation.[48] As Fransje Molenaar puts it: 'This serves as an important reality check for policy makers that expect the Niger security forces to be able to police the desert effectively.'[49]

North of Agadez, the route goes north-west to Arlit, where extensive mining operations are based, and onwards to Tamanrasset and the Assamakka border crossing into Algeria, about five to seven days after leaving Agadez (see Map 2). This area is controlled by Touareg. Or the migrants travel north-east through Séguédine, past the garrison in Madama and through the Tummo crossing into Libya, eventually arriving in Sabha. This route is controlled by the Toubou.[50]

Many migrants who travel these routes do not intend to go to Europe. Instead, they are part of old circular regional migration patterns. Traditionally, people from Niger have gone to Libya to work, although the risks of violence are much higher given the current lawlessness there. But many still go. The problem with the larger flows is that they involve a vast number of migrants who are not simply smuggled but experience some form of exploitation. As they enter Libya, they lose all control and shift even further along the spectrum between people smuggling and human trafficking to become trafficking victims.

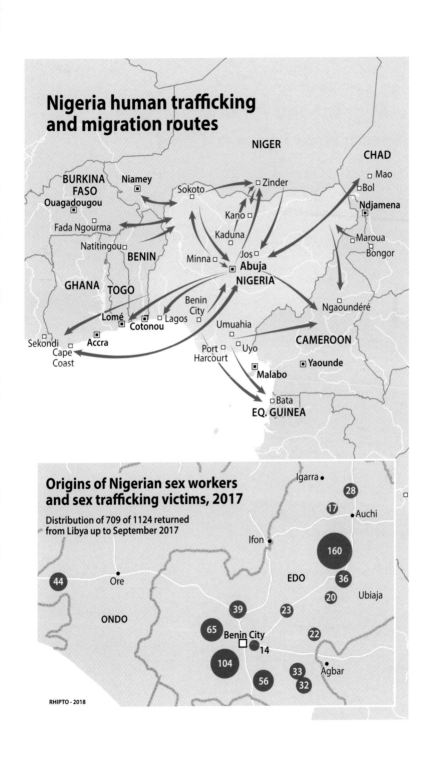

Nigeria human trafficking and migration routes

NIGER

CHAD

BURKINA FASO
Ouagadougou

Niamey

Sokoto

Zinder

Mao
Bol

Ndjamena

Fada Ngourma

Kano

Natitingou

BENIN

Kaduna

Maroua
Bongor

GHANA

TOGO

Minna

Jos

Abuja

NIGERIA

Lomé

Benin
City

Lagos

Umuahia

Ngaoundéré

Cotonou

Sekondi

Accra

Port
Harcourt

Uyo

CAMEROON

Cape
Coast

Malabo

Yaounde

Bata

EQ. GUINEA

Origins of Nigerian sex workers and sex trafficking victims, 2017

Distribution of 709 of 1124 returned
from Libya up to September 2017

Igarra

28

17

Auchi

Ifon

160

44

Ore

EDO

36

20

Ubiaja

39

23

ONDO

65

Benin City

22

14

104

33

Agbar

56

32

RHIPTO - 2018

Migrant and trafficking routes from West Africa to Libya

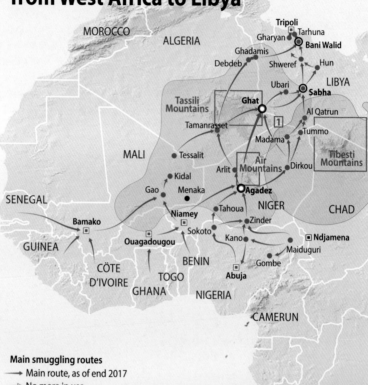

Main smuggling routes

→ Main route, as of end 2017

⇒ No more in use

● Transit point

○ Main hub

◎ Main hub disputed by different forces

▯1 Area of strategic importance for traffic movements

1. Salvador Triangle

Ethnic group presence

▢ Toubou

▢ Touareg

RHIPTO - JANUARY 2018
Source: IOM, 2014; UNHCR, Mixed Migration Trends
In Libya, 2017; United States Institute for Peace,
2014; Norwegian Center For Global Analysis, 2017

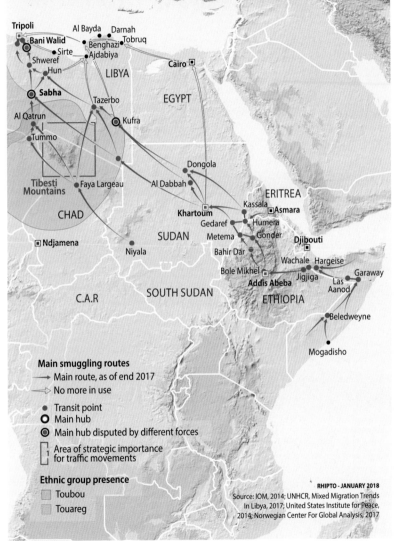

Migrant and trafficking routes from East Africa to Libya

Main smuggling routes

→ Main route, as of end 2017

⇢ No more in use

● Transit point

○ Main hub

◎ Main hub disputed by different forces

▯ Area of strategic importance for traffic movements

Ethnic group presence

▢ Toubou

▢ Touareg

RHIPTO - JANUARY 2018
Source: IOM, 2014; UNHCR, Mixed Migration Trends
In Libya, 2017; United States Institute for Peace,
2014; Norwegian Center For Global Analysis, 2017

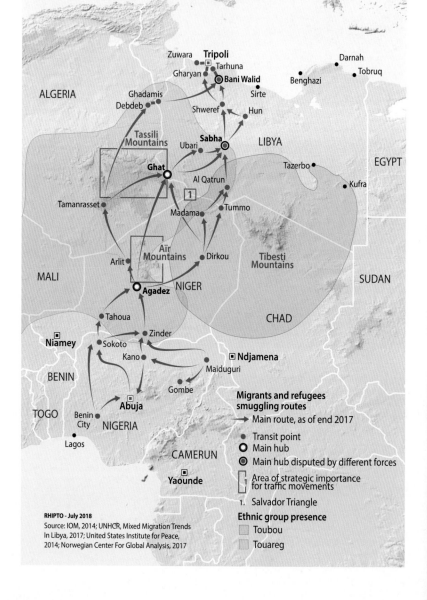

Migrant and trafficking routes from Nigeria to Libya

Zuwara **Tripoli**
Tarhuna
Gharyan ◉ **Bani Walid** Darnah
Benghazi Tobruq

ALGERIA Ghadamis Sirte
Debdeb Shweref Hun

Tassili
Mountains Ubari **Sabha** **LIBYA**

Ghat Tazerbo **EGYPT**
Al Qatrun Kufra

Tamanrasset 1

Madama Tummo

Aïr
Mountains Dirkou Tibesti
Mountains **SUDAN**

Arlit
MALI **Agadez** **NIGER**

Tahoua **CHAD**

Zinder
Niamey
Sokoto
Kano **Ndjamena**
BENIN Maiduguri

Gombe **Migrants and refugees
smuggling routes**

Abuja → Main route, as of end 2017
TOGO Benin
City **NIGERIA** • Transit point
Lagos O Main hub
CAMERUN ◉ Main hub disputed by different forces

Yaounde ▯ Area of strategic importance
1 for traffic movements

1. Salvador Triangle

RHIPTO - July 2018
Source: IOM, 2014; UNHCR, Mixed Migration Trends
In Libya, 2017; United States Institute for Peace,
2014; Norwegian Center For Global Analysis, 2017

Ethnic group presence
▢ Toubou
▢ Touareg

4

LIBYA

LAWLESSNESS AND ARMED GROUPS

Rune Henriksen

The primary obstacle to stability in Libya is the proliferation of militias and power blocs at the level above the militias. With so many actors, in large measure well armed and funded, it is difficult to foresee a credible path towards stability. Indeed, Libya currently has an extraordinarily complex web of non-state armed groups at all levels, ranging from local militias to large quasi-governmental power blocs. Their agendas cross from criminal gain, tribal loyalty, religious devotion, ideological commitment to the revolution, and pure instrumental fighting for power beyond their current realm. This picture is further complicated by the existence of three main political groups with their own governments.[1]

In all three political blocs, the political authorities are at the mercy of militias who provide the manpower and constitute the real power, which is based on armed strength. Militias influence agendas within the political blocs, but the political blocs are unable to control the militias. There is not one single example of any political bloc with even regional legitimacy having been able to demobilise or fully control a militia since 2011. Law enforcement and any nascent justice apparatus are completely dysfunctional, having been replaced by militia rule. The

51

violence in Libya is of a high intensity. A significant proportion affects civilians, but most of the fighting is between armed groups. According to numbers from the Armed Conflict Location & Event Data Project (ACLED), analysed by the African Centre for the Constructive Resolution of Disputes (ACCORD), conflict-related deaths numbered 2,705 (including 760 civilians) in 2015, 2,870 (including 604 civilians) in 2016, and 964 (including 350 civilians) in the first half of 2017. This compares with 10,204 in Syria (according to the Syrian Network for Human Rights; SNHR) and 1,662 in the first half of 2017 in Afghanistan (according to the United Nations Assistance Mission in Afghanistan; UNAMA).[2]

A significant international element also pervades the picture, with a proxy war between Turkey/Qatar and UAE/Saudi/Egypt and featuring interference from Chadian and Sudanese insurgents, and with the migration flow into Italy as well as international counterterrorism concerns. All these fault lines manifest in different and constantly shifting ways in Libya's three main regions.[3]

North-western Tripolitania was characterised by fierce fighting between Gaddafi loyalists and *thuwwar* (revolutionaries) in 2011. In the east, in Cyrenaica, it was comparatively quieter at that time. Later, the fault line was between Islamists and security forces in Benghazi and Derna, for example, which self-appointed Field Marshal Khalifa Haftar exploited in his rise to power. Haftar campaigned on strengthening the armed forces and giving them 'dignity' while fighting Islamists, thus naming his campaign Operation Dignity.[4]

In the southern region, in Fezzan, the fighting came later, and here militias and military councils were more divided along ethnic and tribal lines, such as Arabs versus Toubou, with competition over oil fields and smuggling routes. In late 2017, fighting between the Haftar-led Libyan National Army and the UN-recognised Government of National Accord took the form of competition for local alliances.[5]

The Misrata Third Force was aligned with the Awlad Suleiman tribe and the Touareg, while Haftar was allied with the Toubou. But there is also an international element in the south. For example, in December 2016 Haftar attacked the Misrata-allied Chadian insurgent group Front pour l'alternance et la concorde au Tchad (Front for change and concord; FACT). FACT is a splinter group from the Chadian Union of

Forces for Democracy and Development (UFDD) insurgent group, operating in Libya. Haftar is allied with Chad's President Idriss Déby. Haftar is also supported by Sudanese opposition group the Justice and Equality Movement (JEM), which operated with Qaddadfa tribes against Awlad Suleiman tribes in Sabha in November 2016.[6]

In the background is all the major actors' knowledge that the EU is watching, wanting to incentivise those who can stop the migration flows into Italy, in return for recognition and resources. This was already attempted by Italy in Sabratha, which resulted in an escalation of local conflicts and shifting of flows further east. Likely as a result, in early 2018 a Toubou brigade from Qatrun moved to close the Niger–Libya border.[7]

And there is another international element in the Fezzan. Four militias comprising a total of seven groups are supported by foreign actors. Each foreign actor has one militia. Qatar and Turkey, for example, have one each. These militias may combine to form a coalescing threat, which will further entrench the stalemate in Libya, making the politico-military terrain similar to Mali. These developments constitute the power blocs within which armed groups and smugglers navigate migrants through Libya.[8]

All three main migration hubs—Sabha, Bani Walid, and Kufra—are subdivided between different armed groups, with constantly disputed boundaries. They have not consolidated under the control of one strong actor. In Sabha, for example, there has been fighting between Toubou, Qaddadfa, and Magarha armed groups against the Awlad Suleyman armed group. In Kufra, there has been fighting between Arab Zawiyah and Toubou armed groups.[9]

Incomes to Armed Groups in Libya

In terms of income to smugglers, Nigerians and Libyans combined, the average price for travel through Libya is USD 300–500, and an additional USD 200–250 for the departure from the coast. These amounts are likely to be conservative because they refer to migrants in general, whereas the women and girls are often kept for extensive periods to work off inflated debts. Nonetheless, the amounts give an indication of the scope of money involved. An estimated 143,000 to

300,000 migrants passed into Libya from the western route through Algeria and Niger in 2016. About 43,000 arrived on the eastern route via Kufra, 186,000 of whom arrived in Italy in 2016. The total revenue for armed groups and smugglers for the facilitation of migrants was USD 88.6 million to 235.8 million. This amount is based on detailed calculation of separate price levels for different legs of the journey and the estimated numbers of people travelling along these routes.[10]

The eastern route via Kufra is largely controlled by Toubou tribes, whereas the western route is split between arrivals from Touareg-controlled south-east Algeria via Tamanrasset, Ghat, and Ghadames, or Niger via Tumu, which has been a traditional demarcation line between Toubou and Touareg (see maps 2 and 3). All flows join up in Sabha, making the town extremely contested between tribes. Sabha has mixed control, with the farms in the south-east and the Mahdia and Hay Nasser neighbourhoods controlled by the Toubou. The middle areas, Hay Abdelkefi, Shuhada, and the Al Fateh area, are controlled by the Gaddadfa. The Magarha control the Al Waresh area north of town. The south-western Manshiya area is controlled by the Awlad Suleyman. Since control in Sabha is fragmented and constantly fought over, it is nearly impossible to assess incomes there, other than to assume they do not go to one group to the exclusion of others.[11]

Departure points on the coast are all in the north-west, about 50 kilometres east and 70 kilometres west of Tripoli. The presence of isolated beaches is a key ingredient for what makes it a departure hub. Sabratha is the main departure point, which partly explains the fighting that has gone on there. Garabulli is the second busiest departure point, with less busy ones at Zawiyah, Gargaresh, Tajoura, and Ghimna.[12]

The smuggling transactions to do with departures are administered by the smugglers some kilometres into the interior, away from the coastal highway, which they prefer to avoid. Migrants are kept in safe houses until boats are ready to take a sufficient number and conditions are right for doing so.[13]

Migration / Trafficking

While the distinction between smuggling and trafficking is blurred in Nigeria and Niger, it clearly turns into trafficking in Libya, certainly for women and children. As with the beginning of the route, Nigerians have traditionally controlled the movement of Nigerians, particularly women being trafficked. However, increasing lawlessness in Libya has meant that Nigerians have had to rely much more on their Libyan counterparts for access to routes and protection along them.

The perpetrators of the trafficking in Libya also refer to themselves as facilitators, like the smugglers at the earlier stages, and they are largely Nigerians and Libyans who divide responsibilities between them. The Libyans control the ground and have the ultimate say over the terms and conditions of the trafficking, but they prefer to leave the Nigerians to do most of the work—especially the direct involvement with the trafficking victims. 'Libyans' in this context refers to smugglers working with whoever is the dominant militia in a given area of Libya. Since there is no credible state authority in Libya, the militias are in control, and they vary from local ragtag community clans to large conglomerations of thousands of men. Some of the militias are structured around ethnic groups or tribes who control a given area. These militias extract a sizable income from the movement of people that funds their other activities.

Historically, Nigerians have been renowned for the control they exercise over trafficking from source to destination. Because of the threat of violence from Libyan militias, Nigerian smugglers must comply with their demands. As a consequence, the conditions of transportation are far from what is expected by the girls, partly because they have never been told the full story, but partly because the Nigerians have far less control in Libya.

The Libyans who control transportation and protection usually own the brothels and assembly houses where migrants are held and take a large share of the income they generate, even if Nigerians are running the actual houses. Protection expenses paid to Libyans can constitute as much as half the income made by Nigerian smugglers. As in Niger, transportation is always done by locals but paid for by Nigerian smugglers and with Nigerians present at each hub.

Nigerians are in charge of facilitating transport and logistics, including the housing of the girls and distributing them to the brothels. The brothels tend to be run by Nigerians but owned by Libyans. In other words, Nigerians control large segments of the smuggling chain but are at the mercy of Libyans, as explained by a Libyan:

To settle any smuggling job like to run a transit house for migrants, or a prostitution house, they need: a Libyan partner or a local Libyan protection, they are not allowed to run cars or trucks: all the transport must be made by Libyans, and the same for the transport to Italy … Nothing can happen if they are not authorised by us and they cannot transfer any migrant from here to there: this must be done by Libyans with drivers who work in specific areas, according to specific tribal areas of influence agreed by Libyans among themselves.[14]

The division of labour as well as the power discrepancy between Libyans and Nigerians is also reflected in the gangs that control migrant camps, where prostitution and slavery is widespread. Actual camps can be controlled by Nigerian armed gangs, but the surroundings are controlled by Libyans. The Nigerians pay the Libyans well to be allowed to operate:

We have strong interaction with Libyans, they know everything that happens. We rent the place from them, they provide protection from other Libyans and police. Libyan smugglers are the only ones authorised to transport migrants to Tripoli, Al Shwayrif or Bani Walid. Girls know nothing about Libya, so need us when they come. It is the same all the way.[15]

The farther north in the smuggling chain the more of the activities are controlled by Libyans, and the Nigerians have comparatively less say. This is reversed in the south, influenced by the strong degree of Nigerian control over the supply side and on facilitation through Niger. The smugglers in Sabha typically have connections to Niger and even to Nigeria. In the north, the smugglers in Sabratha, Garabulli, or other coastal launch points have connections to Europe. Both northern- and southern-based smugglers necessarily have connections into the interior: 'Libyan transporters call from the border, wanting my services,' says a Sabha-based Nigerian smuggler. 'They send them to me and I pay them. I get calls from Nigerians in Kano or Lagos, prepare me for arrival of a certain number. My boss confirms and we move.'[16] Fragments from interviews with smugglers suggest there are highly placed Nigerians who have connections all across the chain, and also into Europe. But their presence is not essential for the integrity of the smuggling chain.

Since the autumn of 2017, the number of migrants has reduced markedly. Nonetheless, the numbers are such that a single smuggler can be involved in moving 1,000 migrants in a single month. Another smuggler engaged in transportation operating in Tripoli says he and his friends turn over about 150 migrants per month, distributing them to brothels or other smugglers, or sending them to Italy.[17] The main way stations with assembly houses and brothels are in Sabha, Al Shwayrif, Bani Walid, and Tripoli's Gargaresh neighbourhood.

Even when the price for the entire journey has been agreed in advance, girls are bought and sold along the way, and they have to earn funds to cover expenses such as food, accommodation, transportation, and protection, which are paid to the smuggler who has purchased them at a given stage of the journey, plus his profits. The work can be menial labour but sooner or later turns into prostitution for all women and girls. In theory, the prostitution is voluntary, but in practice it is forced:

> Sometimes girls refuse to work in prostitution, so they end up working as cleaners, for example in the Libyan houses in the morning, and come back to the house in the evening, but the income is so low, and I make clear that it is not worth it for me to protect them for the little money they bring us, and bad things can happen to them without our protection. After bad things happen they come back to us. We give them protection. Once they are in Libya, without us they will be finished in a few minutes.[18]

According to some sources, the girls and women do not keep any of the profits from their sale from one smuggler to the other. Instead, their debt restarts for every leg. This makes the journey extremely slow, as well as brutalising and dangerous. The smugglers in Libya do not know the details of the deal the girls or their family have made back in Nigeria. Regardless, those arrangements are void as soon as the girls arrive in Sabha. The girls have usually not paid anything for their journey up until that point. But as soon as they arrive in Sabha they lose all control over their situation and are locked into a series of slave-like conditions.

In some cases, a girl's entire journey is controlled by a madam based in Italy who has ordered her. These girls also remain prisoners in Libya until the madam pays for the next leg of the travel to Italy. In order to safeguard herself, the madam does not pay everything in one transaction, especially in case a girl dies or gets 'damaged' during the trip or while in Libya.

When the madam pays, the girls are liberated and brought to the beach to leave Libya promptly. The madam has interests in paying as fast as possible because of the running costs of the girls staying and eating in the connection houses and, at this stage, the entire economic responsibility of the girls falls on the madam. Naturally, the madams do not have unlimited money, so, from time to time, they cannot pay the connection manager. In that case, the connection manager sells the girls who were destined to that madam, thus exploiting the trading potential of the victims to the greatest extent.[19]

The smugglers all say the same thing: that the girls can leave at any time, as soon as they have paid their debt. Yet, without protection, the girls are effectively left to be abused or killed, so the choice is only a sham, even when they have paid their 'debt'. A Tripoli-based Nigerian smuggler explains: 'At that point she needs to pay me back her price [LYD 3,000/USD 2,190], including my profit and the expenses, or I will keep her, but I can sell her to another person for the price I like.'[20] According to another Libyan smuggler:

> If the women become sick or crazy [the Nigerians] throw them away like trash. Sexual violence is normal for the Nigerian women. They come here for the money … Some of my drivers sometimes deal with them and they say they [the girls] do not know nothing about anything. For them they are just like walking on the moon and they think they are going to paradise in Europe.[21]

When the girls are kept in temporary houses, or in brothels, they are usually controlled by Nigerian women who manage the girls directly on the Nigerian smugglers' behalf. These women will sometimes treat the girls and women more harshly than the smugglers themselves, according to the smugglers.[22]

One Sabha-based smuggler would keep ten to twelve girls in Sabha and the same number in Agadez. They would be owned by him, and he would rent them out to brothels, retaining 40 per cent of their earnings with the rest going to the brothel.[23] Another smuggler active in purchasing girls and distributing them to brothels around Tripoli would handle about thirty girls per month at the start of 2018. He would typically pay about LYD 7,000 (USD 5,000) per girl.[24] As prostitutes in Libya, the girls could earn about 30 LYD (USD 22) per customer at a rate of ten to twenty customers per day. The girl keeps half and pays the other half to the smuggler. But the girl's share is down payment of her 'debt' to the smuggler.[25]

Who are the Smugglers?

There are hundreds of Nigerian smugglers in Libya[26] who consistently say they are in the trade because of the good money. Many of the Nigerian smugglers have been car mechanics before, early in their time in Libya. The smugglers' only worry is other armed groups, or police, interfering with their business. In some cases, girls are taken by groups that the smugglers pay protection money to, and the smugglers have to pay ransom money to release them. Generally, the best compensation against these risks are experience and connections. Many of the smugglers have been involved in the work since before the 2011 revolution. After the revolution, the market boomed, and more people became involved:

> Everybody wanted to go to Libya because the borders were opened, and smuggling boats were so available on the Libyan shores of Sabratha, Zuwara and Garabulli, so most of the Nigerians who could make it to Libya were making it into Italy and Europe as well.
>
> You will understand this was like a dream for Nigerians and Africans in general. And for us in the business it was wonderful: we were able to put our own people in the strategic points of the smuggling in Libya and in Niger, and run our own houses in an open way everywhere in Libya, which means that our network in Nigeria was extended to Niger and Libya.
>
> This means that we were able to connect directly with our correspondents in Europe and create a bridge in which in a few days you could send a person without any document from Nigeria to Italy and have it received there by other operators connected with the local society who could distribute them in the rest of the world. We became like a travel agency.[27]

Before the revolution, smuggling was a more high-skill activity where smugglers needed to maintain a low profile and have access to the Libyan security service.[28] Today, the smugglers come from very different backgrounds. One Libyan smuggler has a government job, but argues it does not pay well enough, so he also does smuggling. One Nigerian smuggler who failed to reach Europe as a migrant described his choices in the following way: 'In the Libyan environment there is no great choice for us: you can work very hard for little money, or you can be jobless and desperate, or you can become slave or kidnapped somewhere, or you can become crazy, or invalid, or you can die.'[29]

Among Libyan smugglers, Nigerian smugglers are reputed for being ruthless against their own women but respectful to the Libyans. The Nigerians are seen as organised and effective but brutal, often killing Nigerian migrants, but never Libyans.[30]

The entry point into the business is the opportunities that come with a constant stream of new arrivals who know nothing about how to safely navigate Libya's lawlessness, so they can easily be exploited. Most of the smugglers involved in prostitution have specialised in this field, from the more general field of smuggling migrants, because there is much more money in it, by a factor of at least fifteen.[31] Given some familiarity with the smuggling chain, and the constant stream of arrivals, the next requirement for a facilitator is to buy protection from Libyans:

> Nigerians in general are connected with organisations outside Libya: they are connecting with networks in most African countries and Europe and I heard for sure that they can send their girls to the Arab Gulf countries from Italy, such as the United Arab Emirates and Qatar for work. The Libyans provide all the services, such as transportation, shelter and protection of the Nigerians.[32]

Interviewed smugglers indicate that there is a separate network involved in trafficking underage girls through Libya. Young girls spend no more than two to three days in Sabha, and they are escorted by Nigerians who follow the transports with GPS and satellite phones with constant updates. A much higher degree of supervision is involved in these transports compared with others. These girls are handled by experienced Nigerian women inside Libya. From Tripoli, they are transported to Europe by private boats. European groups are involved in monitoring the progress of the journey through Libya, which typically takes no more than ten days.[33]

A controversial case from Italy involved an underage girl who was imprisoned for eight months in Libya while waiting for the madam to pay for her trip to Italy. After several months in Tripoli, she was 'freed' (bought) by a man who brought her to Italy with him on one of the many inflatable rafts leaving Tripoli. Upon disembarkation, he forced her to claim she was of age and marry him. In that case, the assessment procedure and identification was done incorrectly, and they were sent to the same hosting centre and identified as a 'family unit'. He forced her to work as a prostitute right outside the centre. After a while, the police identified her and brought under protection in Catania. He was arrested but accused only of exploitation of prostitution and sexual violence and sentenced to two years in jail. The girl did not accept protection and escaped from the hosting centre. She still works as a prostitute on the Catania–Gela highway.[34]

What is the Degree of Organisation in the Smuggling Networks?

The degree of organisation in the various smuggling networks varies, and this is compounded by different interpretations of what 'organised' entails. All the smugglers are members of a loosely connected network at a minimum, though this is not usually hierarchical or formalised in any way, but more for their own protection.

In some cases, there is much more organisation. One smuggler said he was a member of an international smuggling network comprising Nigerians and Libyans, with a network leader based in Sabha, who overlooks nearby Murzuq and Qatrun, is connected to Nigeria and Agadez, and who has other Nigerian bosses over him. All the smugglers have collaborators, either trusted friends or family. All of them pay bribes or protection money to whoever is in control of the terrain where they operate, and to any police force of relevant strength, whether in Nigeria, Niger, or Libya.[35] A Nigerian smuggler based in Sabha explained:

> Of course, to run this business in three different countries cannot happen unless you are connected and 'authorised' by other main players in the traffic, mainly Nigerians, and relevant people in Niger and Libya who will be your partner and take a share. Plus, you have to pay the police and in Libya you must be connected with a local militia.[36]

Few smugglers think of themselves as part of an organisation in the hierarchical sense, yet every smuggler is connected to other facilitators by necessity. Some smugglers only facilitate accommodation and transport in a section of Libya, while others monitor the migrants from point to point and are involved in the facilitation over greater distances, including from Nigeria via Niger, and into Europe. All of them concede there are rules that must be observed: 'Our world is organised and has its own laws.'[37]

Sabha: The Turning Point Where Smuggling Turns into Trafficking

Trafficking starts in Sabha, where the smuggling activity is controlled by Libyan families who are well known to all involved. The traffic from the Niger border through Al Qatrun into Sabha is controlled by Toubou tribes. From Sabha to Shwayrif, the flow is controlled by the Magarha tribe, and from there to Bani Walid it is controlled by members of the Warfalla tribe. Tribal members from these respective areas control the transport.[38]

Sabha is the point where the girls enter a lawless territory, where they not only need advice about how and where to go but are completely dependent on protection, as well as money to pay for onward travel, or even return should they want to do so.

It is increasingly common for people to come from Europe all the way to Sabha to buy girls, and select them at an earlier stage, cheaper, and to ensure that the girls are not too damaged by the time they come to Europe. These people from Europe pay for the girls and also front the cost of having them shipped to Europe from Sabha.[39]

In Sabha, the Qaddadfa and Magarha tribes provide housing for migrants. They are landowners and do this in association with the Nigerian gangs. An increasing number of armed Nigerians are in control of day-to-day activities in Sabha, with the Libyans simply supervising and being paid.[40] But farther north, both in the desert and the more northern hotspots like Shwayrif and Bani Walid, Nigerians are only facilitators without any power. Only in Tripoli or the northern locations do they manage some facilities, like brothels and assembly houses, but without weapons and under close supervision by Libyans.

In the Abdulkafi district of Sabha, a camp is controlled by a Nigerian armed gang. The leaders pay a large amount of protection money to Libyans who control the surroundings. Nigerians sell alcohol and drugs to wholesalers in the camp, which contains several brothels, and there are also internal rivalries between the gangs. The camp also has a detention centre for women and girls, with about 300 at any given time. The detention centre has an associated open slave market, where the women are sold without any agreement or prospect of release, and according to one smuggler are subject to rape, beatings, and torture.[41] In addition, there is a secret prison where people from Mali, Burkina Faso, and Niger, for example, are locked up and released only after they or their families pay ransom. These activities are all run by Nigerian gang leaders.[42]

The shifting dynamics in Libya, from being an open door to Europe to becoming a violent and anarchic environment, where militias vie for control and revenue, has put migrants, and particularly trafficked women, at increased risk. They are being held for longer in Libya to increase the profits generated for Libyan and Nigerian smugglers, unless madams or other European groups travel to Sabha to expedite their travel. Because previous agreements are disregarded in Libya, it increases the cost and length of exploitation experienced by trafficked women.

5

ALBANIA

FROM LOVERBOYS TO A BETTER LIFE

Anne-Marie Barry

Albania is often viewed as a source country for women and girls trafficked into sexual exploitation. As the origin of the 'loverboy' method—where young men seduce women and then take them abroad for exploitation—Albania is often considered to be the most prominent source country, dominated by the Albanian mafia, which is infamous for its violent tactics. However, these assumptions are not borne out by the reality, as the movement of people has historically been less organised and more ad hoc. Consensual people smuggling has become more organised and business-like, but it is mostly separate from coercive trafficking.

Human Trafficking from Albania to the UK

Albania is country of origin to some of the largest numbers of potential victims going through the UK National Referral Mechanism (NRM) for human trafficking and modern slavery. In 2017, Albanians were the second largest cohort after British referrals, with 777 being referred to the NRM.[1] Most of these cases involved women reportedly trafficked for sexual exploitation.[2] However, there have been no prosecutions of Albanian nationals for human trafficking and modern slavery in the UK, and the 2017 National Crime Agency (NCA) Strategic Assessment found that 'Romanian and British offenders are predominant'[3] in this type of crime, with drug trafficking and distribution being the most 'significant threat' posed by Albanian organised crime groups. This undermines the assumption that the Albanian mafia controls human trafficking.

With respect to potential victims of trafficking from Albania, questions have been raised about the adequacy of the NRM system, with suspicions of 'sold stories', or fake accounts of trafficking fed to migrants and used to assist asylum cases,[4] or the use of corrupt interpreters or legal firms in the interview process. Despite such large numbers of referrals, authorities have received little intelligence that explains the extent and organisation of human trafficking from Albania to the UK. The connection between Albanian women and human trafficking has long received media attention and has re-emerged in the UK as a result of the large numbers of women being referred, despite a lack of evidence to support many of these accounts. The referral numbers only represent those who voluntarily agree to be put through the system as 'potential' victims who may not be conclusively deemed victims.

Police forces in the UK cite intelligence gaps and a 'thirst for knowledge about Albania because there is a belief that this criminality is really affecting us,' acknowledging this is 'more so around the drugs and firearms element, but no doubt there'll be some trafficking sat around some of that'.[5] The NRM claims for Albanians are varied but many follow a similar trajectory—the site of exploitation is frequently reported to have taken place in other European countries, such as Italy and Belgium, where women may have been taken by a boyfriend and sold into a gang before escaping to the UK. Very few Albanian women will fly straight into the UK and are instead smuggled in by their traffickers or the large numbers of smuggling agents and groups providing services from Belgium, the Netherlands, France, or Spain. The rates of 'positive conclusive grounds' decisions, where individuals are confirmed as victims, is around 35 per cent with the referrals of Albanian nationals. But as referrals increase, so too does the lack of detailed information on individuals. The reasons are manifold: fear of the perpetrator, lack of awareness due to being passed around by multiple traffickers, fabrication of stories, or seeking to avoid causing the perpetrator any trouble as they feel they are in a relationship with them.[6]

Trafficking of Albanian Women: 1990s to the Present-day

The trafficking of Albanian women and children out of Albania and into Western Europe peaked in the 1990s. While numbers are contentious, some estimates reach as high as 100,000.[7] This involved the large-scale deception and coercion of young women, from around the age of fourteen, who were promised marriage and jobs, or even kidnapped, to be sold into prostitution, mainly in Italy and Greece.

Major economic and social turbulence characterised Albania in the 1990s. The period entailed the transition from communist isolation and a centralised economy, the collapse of the Pyramid (Ponzi) Schemes in 1997, and the effects of the Kosovo War. Crime flourished due to the instability these changes created, and the trafficking of young women quickly became a core activity of Albanian criminal groups.

Trafficking required little capital, and young women and their families were easy prey with the promise of marriage, work, and a life in Western Europe. It was within this rise of large-scale migration, sex work, and human trafficking in a context of increasing individual freedom and opportunity that the desire to make quick money emerged. Nicola Mai sees the sudden emergence of criminal behaviour among Romanian and Albanian gangs as attributable to the 'post-communist individualist and utopian interpretation of capitalist modernity and democracy, together with the vanishing of communist economics and ethics'.[8] Albanian criminal groups quickly became associated with fast cars and luxurious lifestyles.

The large-scale movement of women into Europe for exploitation has since changed, and there has been a significant decline in the number of women being trafficked from Albania into Western Europe, though cases still remain in which women are taken by 'boyfriends' into European countries and then pushed into sex work, or even falsely promised jobs as dancers in countries as far as Dubai.[9] The overall pattern of decline in trafficking to other European countries, however, is thought to be true for the wider Balkan region in general.[10] Domestic trafficking within Albania still remains a significant issue, with women and girls being exploited in the country's cities and coastal towns during tourist seasons.[11]

Despite the large numbers of Albanian women and children trafficked during the 1990s, traditional 'hotspot' countries currently see limited numbers of Albanian women either engaged in sex work or receiving support from anti-trafficking services. The extremely small number of Albanian women in the anti-trafficking support shelters and assistance programmes in Italy, the Netherlands, Belgium, and France could be understood in a few different ways: human trafficking may not be occurring anymore, trafficking may be occurring 'indoors' in apartments and private residences, or women may not be seeking out shelters because they do not see themselves as having been trafficked or do not want to be seen as having been trafficked. In areas of Germany where there are relatively large numbers of Albanian sex workers, most do not seek assistance from 'support' agencies and are said to be working with relative autonomy.[12]

Changing Tactics of Albanian Trafficking Organised Crime Groups: The Case of Italy

Albania and Italy have longstanding links with each other, as migration from Albania to Italy dates back to the fifteenth century and re-emerged after 1991 amid the collapse of communism when Italy, after Greece, became the second most important destination for migrating Albanians throughout the various crises of that decade.[13] The Albanian community is now 'one of the most deeply rooted communities in the Italian territory', with regularly residing Albanian citizens numbering nearly 500,000 in 2016.[14]

The largest section of the Albanian diaspora in Italy is settled in the northern region, particularly the Tuscany and Lombardy areas.[15] As such, these areas became 'hotspots' for Albanian organised crime from the 1990s. However, the same pattern seen in other European countries occurs in Italy too. While there are still Albanian sex workers in northern Italy, there has been a marked decline in their number since the 1990s. A legislative decree, 'Consolidated Act of Provisions concerning Immigration and the Condition of Third Country Nationals' (1998)[16] may have contributed to this development. This legislation stipulated heavier sentences for those involved in trafficking, increased protection for trafficked women, and made it easier for women to report traffickers to the authorities. According to a law enforcement official in Turin: 'The Albanians realised it was not as profitable as before and women started to escape.'[17] It has also been suggested that the act merely pushed Albanian organised crime groups towards northern Europe.

Another development is that improved living conditions and integration into the country may have made women less drawn into criminal networks. Albanian women dominated the foreign sex worker population in the 1990s, but a 2009 survey of 2,000 street-based sex workers in the Lombardy area of Italy found that the numbers of Albanian women were much smaller than Romanian or Nigerian women, accounting for only 11 per cent of the on-street sex workers and only 6 per cent of those asking for assistance.[18] The survey also found that women were less coerced and deceived and more aware than ever that they had come to Italy to work in the sex industry. Most appeared to be engaged in a negotiating relationship with their pimp, a reciprocal relationship in which women were offered assistance and their managers received a cut of their pay. Albanian criminal networks involved in the management of prostitutes or in the trafficking of women are now managing women of multiple nationalities (a pattern found in many European countries) in addition to Albanian women, including Romanians, Moldovans, Ukrainians, and Bulgarians. Most female sex workers currently based in northern Italy, as in many other European countries, are Romanian. While Romanian pimps will only manage Romanian sex workers, Albanian pimps will manage multiple nationalities, and marriages between Albanian men and Romanian sex workers are now increasingly common, both in Italy and other EU countries. In some cases, Romanian girlfriends are involved in the Albanian prostitution rings and act as recruiters of sex workers from their home country. Collaboration between Romanian and Albanian criminal groups is also becoming well established, as well as conflicts between the groups in certain areas of the cities.

Albanian organised crime groups are becoming more sophisticated and business-oriented. In the 2000s, Albanians began 'renting out' streets or 'spots' to Romanian groups to use for the prostitution of Romanian women. These include the Milan area, where direct Albanian management is thought to be only 20 per cent of the total.[19] While Romanian groups deal with the logistical arrangements, the Albanian organised crime groups take on a less visible, managerial role. Albanians have become much more heavily involved in drugs trafficking and distribution, with management of prostitution less of a priority as their criminality has increased in sophistication: the Italian National Anti-Mafia Directorate of 2017 highlighted a 'leap in quality' in the operations of Albanian organised crime groups in relation to drugs distribution, in which they are no longer 'salesmen' on the streets, but suppliers.[20]

There has, however, been a slight increase in the number of Albanian sex workers being trafficked into northern Italy since 2017, with younger, more vulnerable women composing one group, and another group described as older women who have a higher degree of freedom and independence and who have come into contact with criminal groups after losing their jobs. Both these groups have been able to 'assimilate' into the established sex worker networks. This increase in women who are seeking out criminal networks to engage in sex work highlights the complex question of coercion versus choice when discussing human trafficking.

Anti-trafficking and the Sliding Scale between Choice and Coercion

The legacy of the 1990s has perpetuated the assumption that all Albanian women engaged in sex work are victims of human trafficking. While there still are, and probably always will be, cases of women being trafficked for sexual exploitation, the issue draws attention to certain areas of the anti-trafficking movement that conflate prostitution with trafficking and assume that all foreign sex workers are working under force, dismissing the individual decision-making process exercised by women, or the underlying drivers that lead them to move into sex work. This stereotype can often be seen in media reports about trafficked Albanian women. Julie Vullnetari describes this stereotypical figure as an 'innocent, naïve, young, uneducated village girl, often of Roma origin'. This, however, is 'far from the reality of the complex continuum of age, education, social class, geographical background, consent for migration and participation in sex work'.[21]

There are women from Albania who, rather than having been deceived and coerced, now view prostitution as an 'opportunity' to travel to Greece and Italy to earn money as sex workers, for periods as short as one weekend.[22] Similarly, many Albanian women working as sex workers in Germany assert that they have chosen to be sex workers and that they cannot sustain the alternative option of returning to Albania, where job opportunities are few and work is extremely low pay. Moreover, with visa restrictions in Europe making legitimate work difficult to obtain, some women have come to view sex work as the only option to earn a decent living.

The reasons behind women's decisions to enter sex work are multifaceted. In John Davies's study *My Name Is Not Natasha*, in which Albanian sex workers in France were interviewed in the late 1990s and early 2000s, it was found that after the nature of coercive trafficking networks became known, the numbers of women entering sex work reduced, but a certain cohort of women used sex work as a strategy: 'The deception started from 1990 and lasted perhaps until 1995. From 1995 until now all new girls are not deceived but they want to do this work themselves.'[23] The study showed how many socially excluded divorced women 'began to use the trafficking networks as a mobility strategy in pursuit of migration goals beyond prostitution', with migration and sex work being used to achieve social rehabilitation through marriage to a foreign man.[24] As a strategy to avoid stigma, women were seeking out prostitution rings and gaining 50/50 contracts with their pimps. Stigma not only affects divorced women in Albania but also women who have already been engaged in sex work and thus find any sort of re-integration into their home community impossible. Women may therefore seek out networks to be re-trafficked, restarting the trafficking cycle. For many of the women trafficked in the 1990s, their associations with sex work have hampered their ability to rehabilitate and break the cycle.

In many cases, however, the women voluntarily enter into sex work to earn some cash, and from there their involvement increases.[25] An agreement to engage in sex work often turns into a situation involving violence and coercion, which undermines the initial consent. In the case of Albanian sex workers in Belgium, it has been reported that 97 per cent of Albanian girls know why they are going, but they do not anticipate the violence[26] employed against them. Threats are made against women in relation to their family, with attendant stigma surrounding their involvement in sex work. Many concede that 'Albanians are distinguished by the violent methods they employ.'[27] Several interviewees have remarked that violence by partners or 'pimps' is still a significant issue, as was also reflected in the UK Home Office's 2018 fact-finding mission in Albania,[28] which found that gender-based violence and domestic abuse is still a significant issue in the country. Several serious cases have been prosecuted involving women in various European countries, where women are coerced into sex work, with many involving the 'boyfriend' or 'loverboy' deception and manipulation methods, where threats against family are common.

The stigma associated with sex work may lead to exclusion and trauma. Even though Albanian women may not fall into the often-restrictive category of 'trafficked victim', their experiences may still have a negative impact on their lives. On the other hand, many Albanian women, as is the case with women and men of all nationalities, are pulled into sex work to improve their economic prospects, or pushed by a lack of opportunities for lucrative work in their home countries or for legal routes to work in destination countries. Extremely restrictive visa requirements as well as few options for well-paid work in Albania for women are more commonly associated with the decision to engage in sex work than kidnappings, coercion, and deception. This lack of any prospects opens opportunities for pimps, deceitful 'loverboys', or even gangs to perpetrate trafficking. As a sex worker in Davies's study asserts: 'It's all about papers and money … with papers and money you are free to go somewhere and start again, without them you are a prisoner.'[29]

Structure of Human Trafficking Organised Crime Groups

According to the UK's National Crime Agency, the groups involved in modern slavery in the UK, regardless of nationality, are 'small with limited hierarchies, although larger, more structured groups exist'.[30] Those engaged in human trafficking throughout Europe are also thought to be small-scale, ad hoc networks. However, in the case of Albanian organised crime groups, personal and established links throughout Europe and beyond make their international footprint extensive. The ethnic Albanian diaspora has played a crucial part in connecting Albanian traffickers internationally. In one case, a Ukrainian family sold two sisters to a Russian criminal group, which brought them to France to work as prostitutes. In France, they were bought by an Albanian group that then moved them to Kenya to work as prostitutes for the expat community, before bringing them back to France to work again. This group also had a strong connection to Italy.

Poly-criminality is another significant feature of Albanian organised crime. In the hierarchy of criminality, crime groups usually begin with human smuggling and exploitation, or the management of prostitution, before moving into drugs and weapons smuggling and distribution. The management of sex workers typically remains a significant part of their criminality, but prostitution is usually not the main focus for large organised crime groups.

Human trafficking of Albanian women is not usually conducted by well-organised criminal networks. In many cases, the groups are small scale, with relationships based on blood, friendship, or territorial ties. The structure still appears to be based upon what Ivana Markova calls 'reciprocal solidarity', as opposed to hierarchy, and in human trafficking cases, the 'loverboy' technique is the most frequently cited in all of the interviews and research into the methods used by perpetrators. The main method of trafficking is a marriage with a fiancé, taken for a better life, and then told they need to go into prostitution to pay bills and other various methods of manipulation: 'It's psychological coercion, and most of the time it is small scale and not very well organised.'[31] In one successfully prosecuted case, an Albanian male recruited two women who were in a vulnerable economic position and who had no male figures within their family. They were both told that they were his wives and taken to Italy by bus. They were passed to another Albanian in Italy where they were then forced into prostitution. The brother of the man trafficking these women into Italy was also trafficking a woman in France. In Belgium, there have been several cases involving

Albanians and Kosovar Albanians, but these have been small scale, involving brothers or half-brothers. Loverboy tactics were used to target two girls who had run away from a youth centre, for example.

For larger Albanian organised crime groups, human trafficking and prostitution is a secondary activity. Johan Leman and Stef Janssens also found this when they studied police files with cases of Albanian people smuggling and human trafficking networks in Belgium from the mid-1990s to 2005. They concluded that the Albanian people smuggling and human trafficking business seemed to be small in scale, not hierarchically organised, and more or less chaotic most of the time.[32] They describe this type of Albanian organised crime as being characterised by an entrepreneurial culture, with a patriarchal society that exploits women. The smuggling also has a clan-based structure but is limited and reactive, rather than well organised and deliberate, and characterised by 'disorganised organisation'.[33] Enzo Ciconte concurs: 'Albanian crime is a tangle made up of many small groups, people linked to each other.' Along with the use of such techniques as coded language,[34] it is this organisation—which is based on trust, solidarity, and small groups linked internationally—that makes Albanian organised crime groups difficult to investigate.[35]

A History of Migration: The Role of Family and Social Networks

Rather than coercive sex trafficking, a more recent trend in the movement of Albanians is the involvement of unaccompanied minors. Concern has grown for the safety and wellbeing of the thousands of Albanian minors seeking asylum in EU countries. In 2014, the UK received 632 applications from unaccompanied asylum-seeking Albanian children (there was a significant decrease in 2017).[36] Germany and Sweden have also experienced this phenomenon, and UNICEF and ECPAT UK have highlighted the risk human trafficking poses to these minors. It is known that, in countries such as Germany, Italy, and Belgium, family members are facilitating movement into other European countries where Albanian citizens are able to move freely under Schengen rules, where the minors will either claim asylum and be protected as children for several years, or make the next move to the UK through the use of smuggling networks.

Illegal migration and destination choice is connected to family and region. Most of those who move clandestinely to the UK, for example, are from municipalities in the north and north-east of Albania, such as Has, Kukës, and Krumë. Has experienced a large wave of emigration in the late 1990s due to its proximity to Kosovo and thus the ability to assume Kosovan identity. Kukës is nicknamed 'Little London', as part of the population there has migrated to London. The significant networks established in the UK, the perception that there is plenty of work, and in some cases perception of a more favourable asylum system, make the extra and 'illegal' step to the UK a goal for many. There are frequent street parties in Albanian towns and cities to celebrate the migration of a child.[37]

Media sources feed into simplistic narratives of criminal networks and exploitative intentions that obscure the issues of migration as economic decision-making and the role of the family in the migratory or smuggling process. Some sources have inaccurately used terminology such as 'human traffickers' in place of smugglers when describing the facilitation of Albanian minors to the UK.[38] International migration is a core constituent of Albania's social, political, and economic life. The idea of *kurbet*—travelling long distances in order to support the family in the home country—dates back to the Ottoman Empire, where migration occurred up until Hoxha's repressive rule.

The number of emigrants exceeds the number of households.[39] Mass emigration intensified during the post-communist period of the 1990s, reaching peaks in the midst of the opening of the country and the transformation and turmoil within the economy. The collapse of pyramid saving schemes and the Kosovo crisis exacerbated the movement in intense peaks. While there are no reliable figures on the number of Albanian citizens who have left the country since the 1990s, the Albanian government has estimated a figure of over one million,[40] or around one-third of the country's workforce.[41] This makes Albania a country of origin with one of the largest migration flows in Europe. The 2000s also saw an increase in women migrating.[42]

Despite improved economic and political stability from 2000 onwards, large numbers of Albanians still seek to migrate. A 2016 survey showed that 56 per cent of Albanians wanted to emigrate from Albania, and surveys have shown that schoolchildren in Albania would like to emigrate either legally or illegally.[43] This makes Albania only second to Sierra Leone and joint with Haiti as the country with the highest number of residents who wish to leave.[44] The survey attributes the desire to leave Albania to chronically high unemployment. Clearly, economic issues within the country drive migration, but our research shows that the role of established networks were one of the biggest drivers for Albanian minors in making the additionally difficult step of moving clandestinely to the UK, specifically with the idea of getting a job, or in some cases connecting with a criminal network and engaging in drugs distribution or trafficking. All interviewees asserted that young males moving to the UK did so because they had networks there. Indeed, they would not be sent to the UK by their families if they did not have connections. The move to the UK may not only be a result of a widely held perception of good work opportunities or opportunities for asylum but may also result from the existence of a network in the UK. The role of networks is therefore crucial in understanding Albanian migration. The role of the networks calls into question efforts to curb migration, as they resist preventative measures aimed at targeting people smuggling networks or creating opportunities for would-be emigrants in country. International migration now 'plays a key role in household-level strategies'.[45]

The role of networks in facilitating migration has been studied extensively. As Marco Stampini, Gero Carletto, and Benjamin Davis have recognised, 'the growth of networks, combined with a transformation of the socioeconomic context may result in migration flows being explained mainly by networks and no longer by the conditions that had originated them, such as individual or household characteristics'.[46] This is the reason behind the increasing movement of young Albanian males and the rise in the relative number of migrants from Albania being women, almost equalling men.[47] Much emphasis is placed on the inaccurately termed 'traffickers' and criminal organisations who deceive and coerce Albanian teenagers. But the pull of the idea of success in the UK, and the embedded networks, means that families are part of the facilitation, and migrants are seeking out smuggling services themselves.

Some may use false identity in the UK to access work, such as Bulgarian or Italian documents. But for many, the lack of legitimate and thus adequately paid employment means that the only option is to become involved in criminal activity, such as drug dealing and distribution. Many may be aware when they enter the UK that they will become involved in this kind of criminal activity, but their status as minors makes this 'consent' irrelevant, and they could be considered victims of human trafficking if it is found that their labour is being exploited by others. As minors, they are more vulnerable to false promises and the lure of the luxurious lifestyle that criminal activity can be shown to bring them. Many Albanian minors are entering the United Kingdom National Referral Mechanism (UK NRM) as potential victims of labour exploitation and forced criminality.

The use of the asylum system as a strategy for Albanian nationals is well known throughout Europe, and families as facilitators is central to this, with families trying to gain refugee status on economic grounds:

> Compared to the 1990s, when people risked their lives during their travel, this way of migrating does not present considerable risks to the life and safety of those involved. However, officials at government level speak about the role of smugglers in facilitating it, albeit little evidence is available to support this argument.[48]

This migratory phenomenon and the deep-rooted desire to migrate, whether clandestinely or otherwise, has been the case for Albanians throughout their history of migration. It has operated differently from sudden refugee movements, which calls into question the utility of using border controls to address the issue. Indeed, migration reduction policies are likely to be less effective when networks have developed or engrained patterns of repeated migration are established. Many interviewees attributed criminality and the boom of smuggling networks to the restrictive visa regulations imposed by the EU and even more so the UK. Senior members of law enforcement, traditionally associated with border controls and criminal justice approaches, agree. As Stampini, Carletto, and Davis assert, 'legalising migration not only reduces the exploitation of migrants, but also, paradoxically, may facilitate their returning home, as illegal migrants are often unable to leave the destination for fear of not being able to get back'.[49]

Indeed, an analysis of the impact of the visa liberalisation regime for Albanian movement within Europe found that, rather than 'opening the floodgates' for Albanian migrants to move and settle permanently in European countries, visa liberalisation actually increased movement back to Albania after the migratory goals had been achieved. The study also showed a reduction in overstaying after the visa liberalisation regime was introduced: 'Before [visa liberalisation] many irregular migrants did not return home, even without a job, due to fear that a return home would mean a never ever possibility to enter Schengen area again.'[50] It also meant less business for people smugglers as migrants are given a short-term opportunity to try to gain opportunities or work permits in the EU.

Document Fraud

Since 2010, Albanians have been granted visa-free Schengen access to countries in the EU. The most common way of remaining in EU countries illegally, therefore, is through over-staying the three-month access period, through claiming asylum, or by using false documentation. Albanians will always leave Albania using genuine documentation as there are extremely harsh penalties if caught leaving the country on forged or false documentation. Migrants who intend to stay illegally in EU countries consequently travel into the Schengen area and then get false documents, or procure documents within Albania for use within the Schengen or other destination countries, such as the UK, the United States, or Canada. Most of the forged documents are produced in other countries, most commonly Italy or Greece. Italian ID cards are believed to be easily reproduced, and since Italian is widely spoken by Albanians with a strong history of migration and media influence, Albanian nationals are able to present themselves as Italian.

Obtaining false documentation is relatively straightforward due to the proliferation and increasing sophistication of the false documents produced in the EU and online.[51] Greece is a hotspot for the production of fake, forged, or stolen documentation, with many 'labs' having being discovered.[52] The networks running these labs often comprise multiple nationalities to cater for the multitude of nationalities requiring their services. Albanian organised crime groups are also heavily involved in supplying documentation that will facilitate the movement of Albanian citizens to the UK or for them to remain in the European Union. Many of the labs operated by Albanian smuggling networks are based in both Albania and Greece. In one such case, multiple document labs found in Athens provided Greek, Cypriot, and Bosnian passports for around GBP 4,000 each for Albanian migrants who wanted to fly to the UK.[53]

Travel agencies and other such legitimate businesses are suspected of being involved in the smuggling or production of fake documents. One of four such labs based in Tirana and with connections to Greece had the legitimate front of a printing shop producing promotional leaflets, whereas it was in fact creating a wide variety of 'perfect' counterfeit documents. The documents included French, Italian, Hungarian, Greek, and Romanian passports, ID cards, and travel licences. A police officer operating on the Albanian border was also involved in this network. The business also arranged travel to the UK.[54] Some networks provide documents and facilitation to the United States and Canada for up to USD 30,000, often flying through the Dominican Republic or South American countries.

One highly organised Albanian network provided new documents to migrants who had been rejected at borders within forty-eight hours. Italian top-up visa cards have reportedly been used to book travel, with requisite funds deposited as required by the smuggling network. Once migrants reach their destination, they are not required to work for the smugglers, as the honour system ensures they will repay their debt if they were unable to pay upfront.[55] This indicates that in some larger-scale networks, a significant amount of capital exists to provide the initial service, especially given that flights are often re-booked for the migrant when there is a failure to cross a border, which in turn suggests that smuggling operations are much more organised and business-like than human trafficking networks.

Albania–UK: Traditional Smuggling Methods

The traditional route from Albania to the UK involved travelling through Italy and France to Calais. However, the closure of Calais, as well as crackdowns on smuggling routes, has diverted migrants. A common route that has since been adopted goes through Germany to northern Spain, where migrants attempt to board lorries bound for the UK via ferry. Bilbao is an extremely popular route for Albanian migrants, some of whom attempt to enter on the back of lorries. At Bilbao, some have tried up to thirty times to stowaway. Most migrants at this 'Bilbao camp' are males of Albanian origin and a smaller number are migrants from Afghanistan, Iraq, and Pakistan who also use the route. The routes via Santander and Vigo are also increasingly used. Some migrants attempt the journey themselves and without the facilitation of an organised crime group. Others pay for facilitation to the port and for other services, such as accommodation and advice, and some pay extra for a 'guaranteed' service, usually involving a corrupt driver. Gangs advise migrants to board lorries during the busiest periods when there is less time for questioning by border guards.

Albanian migrants, along with many other nationalities, also attempt the crossing to the UK through the Netherlands. At the ferry terminal of the Hook of Holland (Harwich), Europoort Rotterdam (Hull) and Ijmuiden (Newcastle) ports, most migrants travelling clandestinely are Albanian. The consistent method still remains lorries or vans. There was a spurt of boat crossings in the past, including DIY boats, but this was supressed by law enforcement. Bulgarian drivers are frequently implicated as drivers for 'guaranteed journeys'. This is reportedly due to their being susceptible to corruption owing to the extremely low pay in their sector.[56] A variety of methods can be used to 'fake' a passenger, such as documentation for a migrant who is listed as the second driver of the lorry, or even cases of migrants dressed as priests.[57]

Some Albanian smuggling networks are large, with connections in Belgium, the Netherlands, France, and the UK. In many cases, it is believed that family members contact smugglers in Albania to arrange the transport for between EUR 3,000 and 6,000. Migrants can pay for a cheaper service and a more expensive 'guaranteed' way in which the driver is complicit in the smuggling arrangement. The migrants are sometimes advised to destroy their passports and claim to be minors if intercepted by police along the way. In this way, they will be given protection rather than repatriated.

The sum for the transit to the UK is sometimes paid in Albania before departure, and at other times transferred after a successful journey. Part of the package involves overnight accommodation in certain hotels or apartments managed by other members of the network. There are particular hotels in Brussels and Ghent, as well as private accommodation, that are used by migrants to stay before being smuggled to the UK.[58] During the night, the migrants are taken to carparks along the motorway in Belgium and loaded into trucks. Others are taken to the Netherlands to make the crossing from there. In some cases, refrigerated trucks are used, which are more dangerous than normal trucks but recommended as there is a lower risk of detection. In other cases, migrants are put into the boot of a car. Where travel is organised with collaboration from Kurdish smugglers, who control sections of the smuggling route, the travel agencies in Albania receive the full payments from the Albanian migrants and their families and facilitate payment to the Kurdish smugglers through networks based in Belgium. Otherwise, the agent in Albania will tell migrants to deposit their payment into a Belgian account—the account may be that of another accomplice or sometimes in the identity of other people waiting to be smuggled. The money will then be taken out by the owner of the account by the accomplice or migrant and given to agents.

Albanians have also worked with Czech smuggling gangs to transport Albanians to the UK. This involved a network based in the UK. Albanians arranged the migrants' travel, and the Czech drivers filled the vans in Belgium. In Belgium, many hotels and safe houses were used. In these cases, a 'deposit' was paid first in Albania and then the remainder was paid on successful completion of the journey. In another case, an Albanian group in Albania made all the arrangements with a network in the UK. The group determined the route, collected money from the families, and paid the drivers, with two members specifically recruiting lorry drivers in poor areas between Belgium and the UK who were thought to be more easily bribed. The members of the smuggling gang would never cross the border with the smuggled people, transferring the risk to the van driver while travelling separately before meeting with the driver and the migrant in the UK, where cash payment would be made to the driver.

Albanian citizens are one of the biggest customers for the smuggling route to the UK, but Albanians only comprise a portion of the various nationalities operating along these routes. Other nationalities have now become dominant, such as Indians and Pakistanis. Until 2005, Albanian smuggling groups controlled a crucial part of the smuggling route between Belgium and the UK.[59] An Indo-Pakistani network subsequently took over the route, and consequently a lower price was offered to migrants being smuggled from India to the UK as a result of the Indo-Pakistani network cutting out the Albanian part.[60] Many of the cases currently being investigated from Belgium to the UK involve Kurdish gangs. Iraqi Kurds bought a carpark from Albanians along the E40 (which extends from west Germany through Belgium to north-east France) in 2014. This is another example of Albanians acting as owners of criminal territory that is leased out or bought by other smugglers. Albanian groups are still present along some carparks on Belgium's E40, which are used to pick migrants up in lorries and trucks. In some cases, smugglers encouraged people to go to the UK, claiming that it was easier to seek asylum in the UK than in Belgium or the Netherlands.

Funds for people smuggling are often transferred using hawala banking, where funds do not pass through Belgium but the UK, and released in the country of origin when successful. Communication is usually over the encrypted apps Viber, Skype, and WhatsApp to prevent wiretapping, as well as draft email messages. Money remittance agencies are also used, with amounts always up to a maximum of EUR 2,000. Senders will use different identities to transfer the money, and those receiving it get commission depending on what they took out. In one case, a smuggling group used a pizza delivery firm in Belgium to receive and courier the money for a commission.

The 'Albanian Mafia' and Human Trafficking

People smuggling is low on the status hierarchy of organised criminal activity for Albanian organised crime groups, and human trafficking appears even lower. Drugs and weapons are the predominant crime type for more sophisticated groups, and human trafficking has been used almost exclusively as a gateway crime to build capital to allow low-level criminals to become involved in higher-value commodities. The sophistication and interconnectivity of Albanian crime groups has led to the term 'Albanian mafia'.

The Albanian mafia is multifaceted and spread throughout the whole of Italy. They used their initial investments from human trafficking and now have negotiations with other mafia based in Italy. Albania's location has been strategically advantageous, and as Ciconte asserts, Albanian criminals were lucky to be at the centre of the passage of migrants desperate for a new life. Weapons and drugs could also be transported on the same boats. The Albanian mafia has no qualms about any type of trafficking—drugs, guns, cigarettes, people. According to some law enforcement agencies, Albanian organised crime groups are involved in so many different activities that human trafficking is relatively peripheral and therefore not prioritised overall in terms of Albanian organised crime.[61]

In the Milan area, the Albanian mafia works with Turkish gangs, who are historically suppliers of drugs to the Italian and Albanian mafias. A relationship has been built between Turkish and Albanian groups to transport Albanian drugs. The Albanian organised crime groups have also created business relationships with members of Cosa Nostra and 'Ndrangheta.

Much research shows that the Albanian mafia rests on a family structure. The family, kinship, and clan relationships, or those cemented in the villages or communities, result in trust, reliability, and reduced risk of betrayal. The *Kanun*—a traditional set of laws that regulate discipline and provide rules to be followed in relation to honour, revenge, and duties—is sometimes attributed as being the ideological source of the Albanian criminal structures, and it is still said to be observed as a justification for blood feuds, particularly in northern Albania.[62]

According to Italy's 2017 Anti-Mafia Report, the three main foreign organised crime groups operating in Italy are Albanian, Romanian, and Moroccan.[63] However, the main groups reportedly involved in modern slavery and human trafficking are Romanian and Nigerian first, and then Albanian. The report again notes the presence of partnerships among Albanian and Slavic groups for drug trafficking and sexual exploitation, as well as between Albanian and Italian organised crime groups such as the 'Ndrangheta and Sacra Corona Unita.[64]

Albanian Organised Crime and Human Trafficking: The Risk of 'Albanophobia'

With large numbers of Albanians migrating and settling in European countries, negative associations continue to pervade popular discourse. Albanians have always been stigmatised, as Russell King asserts, 'for their alleged close association with criminality, and moral degradation, in particular with drug smuggling, violent behaviour and prostitution'.[65] In the UK, as in other countries, cocaine and marijuana trafficking is dominated by Albanian organised crime groups. However, the disproportionate media coverage on 'Albanian gangs' threatening the UK, following an NCA Threat Assessment, showed other nationalities to be just as dominant. This reaffirms the negative associations of Albania and suggests that 'Albanaphobia' and association with organised crime is still alive.

The high numbers of Albanian women entering the UK system as potential victims of modern slavery have helped this threat to re-emerge in the public imagination. Similarly, the representation of human trafficking as highly sophisticated organised crime and Albanians as highly sophisticated organised criminals also bolsters this image of Albania. 'Organised crime' has always dominated discourse around human trafficking and modern slavery. Fallacious but popular and oft-repeated statements asserting human trafficking to be the 'fastest and most profitable crime in the world'[66] are an attractive way to characterise what is a complex continuum of social and economic issues. Traffickers are often portrayed as highly organised criminal actors working as part of large and sophisticated networks. But on closer scrutiny, the trafficking of Albanian women appears less a sophisticated and professional enterprise and more ad-hoc, since exploitative conditions often occur through a relationship with the male, which, as one interviewee comments, then 'turns into something bigger'. The women no longer appear as 'ideal victims', nor do the males fit the category of 'ideal trafficker'. As Minna Viuhko asserts in her own study of traffickers in France, 'trafficking operations and actions can be very well organised and systematic without being organised by professional criminals and/or by members of [organised criminal groups]'.[67]

6

VIETNAM

GROWING THE ECONOMY THROUGH THE EXPORT
OF MINORS

Anne-Marie Barry

The trafficking and exploitation of Vietnamese nationals is well documented within the context of women and children being moved within South East Asia and beyond for the purposes of sexual exploitation, domestic servitude, and forced marriage.[1] Exploitative working conditions have also been strongly associated with a number of guest worker and temporary labour programmes in surrounding countries, which are often unregulated and managed by unscrupulous agencies.[2]

Vietnamese migration to the United Kingdom has become widely associated with human trafficking or 'modern slavery' within the country's mainstream media and the anti-trafficking or child protection services.[3] According to the UK Home Office, Vietnamese organised crime networks 'recruit and transport Vietnamese nationals, especially children, to Europe—particularly the United Kingdom and Ireland where victims are often subjected to forced labour on cannabis farms'.[4] Exploitation in nail bars, and to a lesser extent sex trafficking, is also deemed to affect young Vietnamese migrants, and in 2017, Vietnamese nationals comprised the third largest overall national group

85

and the second largest group of minors entering the National Referral Mechanism (NRM) as potential victims of modern slavery.[5] However, the often alarming and simplistic narratives that create automatic associations between Vietnamese migration and coercive 'slavery' and highly organised crime[6] are complicated by research suggesting that the migratory experience of Vietnamese migrants is complex, and the line between trafficking and smuggling, migration, and exploitation in the movement is extremely blurred.

Vietnamese Migration to Europe and the UK

Vietnam has a long history of both forced and voluntary international migration. Migration has continued over recent decades and much research shows that the main drivers for this flow are economic. Despite rapid economic growth since the 1980s, economic inequality in Vietnam has persisted, and an increased demand for jobs combined with insufficient capital to meet that demand has precipitated a drive—encouraged by the Vietnamese government—for international migration.[7] To alleviate underemployment and low salaries, migration through labour agencies and fixed-term contracts for temporary work has boomed, and it is now estimated that around 90,000 Vietnamese labourers leave Vietnam each year on overseas work contracts.[8] This large-scale labour migration puts Vietnam in the top ten countries in the world for remittances, which in 2017 made up 6.7 per cent of the country's GDP.[9] Migration for work has therefore become integral to the country's economic growth.

Greater movement into Europe, both regular and irregular, has also been spurred on by the networks that have been built up as a result of historic migration, economic necessity, and even natural disasters. It is thought that a significant proportion of irregular migrants in Germany, for example, are from Nghệ An province—a region that has a history of vulnerability to typhoons and natural disasters (around ten per year).[10] In 2017, multiple typhoons destroyed land and affected the agriculture and fishing industries.[11] This destruction of land and produce, combined with a lack of compensation from the government, caused increased levels of impoverishment and a concomitant drive to migrate.[12]

Vietnamese migration to the UK has been occurring in phases since the 1970s, with irregular migration taking place since the 1980s.[13] Most of those migrating to the UK are thought to be from the central and northern provinces of Vietnam.[14] The UK is not believed to be one of the 'top' countries of choice for Vietnamese migrants, but there is a significant settled Vietnamese diaspora, and the number of undocumented migrants ranges from 20,000 to 71,000 (the latter figure is an estimate of those working in nail bars alone).[15]

The snowball effect of migration has resulted from an already established diaspora in the UK, from 'success stories' of other migrants, as well as the perception of the UK as a paradise.[16] Studies of Vietnamese cultural media have shown that in the narratives of many popular television programmes, books, and films, the migratory process and the concept of sending young people and children abroad to Europe to begin a new life while supporting family back home is often represented as a key to a family's financial success and status.[17] While these stories are sometimes counterbalanced with media reports describing the difficulties of life in the UK, the risk is often believed to be worth taking, since the rewards of reaching 'El Dorado' may make it worth it.[18]

Child Trafficking from Vietnam

The movement of irregular Vietnamese migrants to the United Kingdom has become strongly associated with cannabis cultivation and nail bars (the 'niche' business areas attributed to Vietnamese settlement in the UK), and in the context of modern slavery and human trafficking, with forced criminality. The high numbers of young Vietnamese being found in the often hazardous and isolated surroundings of cannabis farms, combined with a move towards statutory defence and non-punishment for those who commit criminal acts as a result of force or coercion—as consolidated in the Modern Slavery Act (2015)—has precipitated a push for law enforcement and legal bodies to treat the 'gardeners' in cannabis farms as potential victims of slavery and exploitation, before treating them as criminals.[19] Since many of these 'farmers' are considered to be minors or claim to be minors, the issue in many cases has become one of child trafficking.

In 2017, more than 300 Vietnamese minors were referred to the NRM as potential victims of modern slavery, making Vietnam the largest source country for potentially trafficked minors in the UK after British nationals.[20] Consent to exploitative conditions is irrelevant under the law on human trafficking with regard to minors, and as such, many of the individuals found in cannabis cultivation to be (or who claim to be) under eighteen are deemed victims of child trafficking and modern slavery. A great deal of advocacy is therefore taking place within the child protection and anti-trafficking community to ensure that these children are treated as such and that perpetrators are captured under trafficking and modern slavery laws.[21] Where the victim is not a minor, however, the issue of coercion and debt bondage is a complex one, as is the additional complication of many migrants falsely claiming to be minors.[22] In a further complication, many interviewees for the research alluded to the disjuncture between concepts of childhood between Vietnam and the UK, which creates varying perceptions of vulnerability and responsibility. In Vietnam, children reach adulthood at sixteen years of age.[23] Migration for work may therefore be considered normal or even desirable for many families in Vietnam who want to improve the family's prospects. Indeed, Tamsin Barber describes how migration can form an integral part of transition from childhood: 'Migration itself is an important life event, so in a sense, these young people are being urged to "leave" their childhood and transition into adulthood.'[24]

There are fears within the UK that child trafficking from Vietnam is highly organised: 'Upon arrival the children are faced with a highly organised system of criminal activity, with methods of control ranging from extreme physical brutality to debt bondage. Before they even arrive, that trap is set for them.'[25] It is believed that young Vietnamese are targeted by organised crime groups as a result of both their vulnerability and their debt burden. Children as young as ten are reported to have been put to work in the hazardous and isolated farms.[26] On being identified as a potential victim of modern slavery in the UK, Vietnamese minors are placed in local authority care, from which many abscond.[27] In suspected cases of modern slavery, individuals should be treated as minors if they declare themselves as such and there is reason to believe that they could be. Potential minors cannot be detained, and yet there is a fear that minors are being picked up by their 'traffickers', and law enforcement officials thus find themselves in a bind—which was expressed in the following way by one interviewee: 'have you lost a suspect or have you lost someone to be re-trafficked?' In the opinion of some, there is a moral case to detain in order to provide some protection if they are a minor at risk of re-trafficking.[28]

Disappearance from local authority care after an asylum or trafficking claim is a frequent occurrence in European countries. This is attributed to traffickers knowing where the minors are located, which means they can then be picked up to be re-trafficked. On the other hand, the necessity of escaping in order to enter a shelter or protective centre to go back to work where they can pay off their debt is a likely driver. The two factors may often be intertwined.

From Education Visas to Precarious Working

Migration for study is extremely common among Vietnamese students.[29] The number of self-funded students makes up a large and rising proportion of these students.[30] While many of these students study legitimately, misuse of the education visa is feared to have risen. There has been an increase in students enrolled in language colleges across the UK and in other European countries that have turned out to be either fraudulent or not attended by the student who is enrolled.[31] Similar to disappearances from local authority care, there is little understanding of whether these students are victims of larger trafficking networks, whether they ever intended to attend college at all, or whether the cost of migration is so large that finding paid work is a necessity.

Views of the situation based on these two different trajectories are being played out within agencies responding to criminal activity or to cases of human trafficking. For some—usually those who take a 'victim-centred approach' and defend or support victims of human trafficking—there is usually deception, as migrants often think they will work in a nail bar or a restaurant but end up in a criminal activity as a result of this offer not coming to fruition. In the opinion of one UK-based lawyer, a control mechanism is always there in the form of debt bondage since the cost of the journey to the UK is so high that is impossible for many Vietnamese migrants to pay it off.[32] These cases accordingly fall under the legal definition of human trafficking or modern slavery. Others, however, have become suspicious of what appear to be scripted accounts: 'when so many Vietnamese are being found and so many of their stories are vague, unfortunately cynicism kicks in'.[33]

Numerous studies and our own interviews have shown that many migrants are aware through social media and other sources of the risks associated with irregular working and the potential necessity of taking up such work. Some know that there is an option to work in cannabis cultivation on arrival in the UK. Yet for others it may be a conscious decision from the beginning, since the prospect of working illegally in 'legitimate' jobs will offer no hope of paying off the initial debts accrued to fulfil the goals of migration and expectations of the family.

Vietnamese Migration and Debt Financing

The binary of enslaved migrant under debt bondage versus illegal migrant choosing to commit criminal activity—a binary implied in the two responses to Vietnamese migration in the UK outlined above—is for the most part inadequate to understand the complexity of the experience of the individuals involved and the choices that are made to facilitate migration. It has been shown that debt-financed migration and informal credit schemes are common within the Vietnamese migration strategy, and that many Vietnamese migrants view the use of informal brokers and the adoption of multiple debts as a normal responsibility rather than a potential form of enslavement.[34] There is a grey area, as Nicolas Lainez argues, between what is described as debt 'bondage' and what is described as debt 'finance'. Julia O'Connell Davidson articulates this variation and describes debt as a strategic investment and opening to a better future in the context of migration: 'while debt can lock migrants into highly asymmetrical, personalistic and often violent relations of power and dependency sometimes for several years, it is also a means by which many seek to extend and secure their future freedoms'.[35]

There have been cases where Vietnamese gardeners on cannabis farms have paid off their debts and have been able to advance within the organisation or finance their future in the UK.[36] Conversely, many Vietnamese migrants are vulnerable to pressure as they have accumulated substantial debt. Sometimes families are involved in this pressure, having handed over deed books for properties as collateral for the initial leg of the journey.[37] Indeed, the parents of some Vietnamese minors who are discovered in the UK are often described as 'uncooperative' by law enforcement when they are informed.[38] Many Vietnamese face strong pressure to continue working in dirty and dangerous jobs such as cannabis cultivation despite the difficult and often isolating nature of the work.

Daniele Belanger addresses this grey area by alluding to the inadequacy of the concept of human trafficking, which 'needs to be reframed as a labour migration issue'.[39] Drawing on the case of overseas temporary work contracts and the role of state actors in creating conditions where exploitation may flourish, Belanger implies that the 'trafficking' label is similarly inadequate to describe the 'complex web of obligation and debts' that Vietnamese migrant labourers find themselves in and the continuum along which obligations and external factors influence their vulnerability (or indeed resilience) to exploitation. Where credit 'may be an initial source of empowerment to access geographic and labour mobility',[40] it can also lead to forced labour and coercion, and indeed elements of human trafficking can be found at different stages along the migration process.

Smuggling through Europe

In many transit countries to the UK and destinations in Europe, such as Germany, the Netherlands, Belgium, and France, Vietnamese nationals do not feature within the trafficking statistics and are primarily seen in relation to smuggling and organised immigration crime.[41] However, various cases of potential exploitation in cannabis farms or sexual exploitation have been found, as in one case of a male who was sexually exploited and forced to grow cannabis in the Netherlands.[42] In general, the Vietnamese throughout these countries are viewed as having a 'low profile' and are thus rarely focused upon. David Silverstone and Stephen Savage came to similar conclusions in a 2010 study of Vietnamese organised crime groups in the UK, deeming them to be 'under the radar' due to their closed nature and non-violent criminality.[43] Law enforcement in many countries comes across groups of young Vietnamese migrants who are travelling irregularly, but the understanding of the community and the journey of these migrants often remains a mystery as a result of the frequent disappearances and lack of disclosure of information regarding their circumstances.

The smuggling routes from Vietnam into Europe and into the UK are well established and have been described in various studies.[44] Migrants are offered smuggling 'packages' in Vietnam consisting of a cheaper, overland route via Russia, or a more expensive route involving a flight into Europe and then facilitated to France or Belgium. There are multiple agencies that can provide various routes through Europe and similarly via Russia. The Russian route is the most common and is thought to be easily facilitated as visas are easily obtained and collaboration between Russian, Chechen, and Vietnamese smugglers is well established.[45] Little is known of the conditions experienced in Russia, but it is thought that migrants can spend significant time being housed in the country to wait for the onward journey. 'Bottlenecks' occur as migrants wait for more to arrive to fill trucks or other forms of transport. Some migrants are put to work during this period in factories, often in exploitative conditions in which they may receive no pay.[46]

Almost all Vietnamese migrants leave Vietnam legally with a visa and documentation for their first step and thus Vietnamese authorities do not intercept: 'In other countries you have to prove that the purpose of your trip is genuine, but according to immigration law in Vietnam, the authorities are unable to intervene even if the suspicion is there.'[47]

The various ways to stay irregularly in Europe involve overstaying short-term Schengen visas; so-called 'transit abuse'—flying visa-free to an eligible country via a European country and losing documentation; and educational visas, sometimes for fraudulent colleges. Some Vietnamese-based travel agencies are suspected of being involved, since flights frequently include a return ticket even though the person has no intention of returning. The money for the return flight will always be paid back to the original purchaser.[48]

Many irregular migrants to the EU remain in countries such as Poland, the Czech Republic, or Germany. In the case of Germany, for example, Vietnamese comprise one of the largest groups of irregular migrants.[49] The UK is only a destination country for migrants from around four to five of Vietnam's sixty-three provinces. The snowballing effect occurs as smuggling networks based in these provinces 'specialise' in smuggling to Europe and/or the UK, and previous migrants and networks may be deemed a 'success story' since moving to the UK. The crossing from France has been the traditional route for Vietnamese migrants—indeed, a migrant camp in Angres was even nicknamed 'Vietnam City' because so many Vietnamese migrants stayed there before attempting to cross into the UK.[50]

Since groups facilitating human smuggling are prevalent across Europe, Vietnamese members of the smuggling network are posted in the transit countries and work with contacts or locals in each to help the movement across eastern or southern Europe. While an agent of Vietnamese nationality is believed to be present along the way, the Vietnamese smuggling groups are thought to use facilitators of different nationalities along the route, and the Vietnamese facilitator is thought not to be present on the final leg to the UK. On transition to the UK, either from France, Belgium, or the Netherlands, Vietnamese migrants use lorries driven by many different nationalities.

In many cases, it appears that the main facilitated smuggling takes migrants into Europe, and for those migrants who wish to continue to the UK, separate facilitators are needed. As a result, extra money is usually required for the crossing to the UK, and this is where many are said to 'get stuck' and where the potential for trafficking is suspected. Lorries along Belgian motorways or in the Netherlands and France are frequently used, and migrants enter either with complicit drivers (there may even be a second floor or wall in the lorry) or as stowaways hiding beneath the cargo of trucks, without the driver's knowledge. At this point, smuggling is usually organised by other networks working along the route. Migrants will usually travel alone and will always have a contact phone to connect them to potential employment in the UK, or they will often use networks and communities within the UK who will help connect them with work. In some cases, migrants have been advised to approach the nearest nail bar and Vietnamese community when they enter the UK.

The connection between the exploiters in the host county and the smugglers is unclear in all potential cases of trafficking for cannabis cultivation or exploitative labour. The seemingly constant flow of migrants for this type of work suggests links or collaboration between smugglers and exploiters.

Money Transfers

Western Union-type transfers may be used from EU countries and back to Vietnam, and the family of the migrant will often be responsible for the payment back to the smuggling network. In some cases, the parents of the main facilitators have been involved in collecting the money. Money may also be carried back in cash, or through legal business structures. In the UK, legal business structures such as nail bars may be used to launder the illicit proceeds of cannabis farms, and workers may move between the two. The price negotiation begins at the start of the journey, and family in Vietnam will often pay part of the costs. If the migrant reaches the UK, there will be a phone call back home and the family will pay the smugglers. It was stated that in some cases there was no debt between smuggler and smuggled, and rather most migrants will have to pay it back to their families, rather than back to the smuggler. Often families get together and will not pay everything upfront. In these cases, there is thought to be an initial payment for the ticket and visa, then the cost of the transport to Europe, and a final payment for the UK.[51]

Europol issued an alert warning for the 're-emergence' of Vietnamese organised crime groups in 2013.[52] However, very few large cases involving Vietnamese come to the agency, so they are seen as a very small caseload in comparison with other nationalities. Many members of law enforcement believe that while the smuggling routes are extremely well established and organised, they are composed of multiple networks, the business of which may depend on family and acquaintances. In the view of one interviewee: 'it's not as organised as one may think'.[53]

Cannabis Cultivation: Between Choice and Coercion

Most cases of Vietnamese migration will begin with human smuggling and, due to the complexity of the circumstances, turn into something that is less within the migrant's control, such as human trafficking and exploitation. The route to the UK can cost between EUR 2,000 and 5,000, with reports in 2017 of this leg costing up to EUR 12,000.[54] Some of those travelling find themselves facilitated into cannabis farming or being exploited, not because they are being forced to do so by a 'trafficker' but out of the necessity of paying off their significant debts. Many interviewees believed that 'the exploitation is not planned from the beginning' and that the smuggling organisations in Vietnam are distinct from the purported exploiters in the UK. While smugglers are likely to be aware of the nature of irregular working in the UK, and that the migrants may end up in a cannabis farm, 'the smugglers are selling their service; they're not going to say you could be exploited'.[55] The disjuncture between the perceptions of Vietnamese authorities and the UK authorities also complicates the trafficking paradigm. 'The labour law is different; for Britain they're trafficked, for the Vietnamese they're working.'[56] For the Vietnamese authorities, who see much of this movement as economic migration, their priority for 'trafficking victims' lies with the thousands of migrants who are deemed to have been trafficked for sexual exploitation in surrounding countries each year, so 'it's hard to see this as a priority'.[57]

However, many migrants are thought to be unaware of the difficulty of their journey and 'don't have a clue what they're getting into'.[58] The route is long and difficult, and they are often left in isolation and passed along various facilitators who may well be violent, controlling, and exploitative. Moreover, many may not have been informed about the real working conditions they will face when in the UK, and when things do go wrong, the issue of shame associated with failure to provide for the family can prevent them from removing themselves from a difficult situation. They take the decision to make this journey and do not want to be identified as trafficked victims nor talk about the difficulties of the journey or the conditions they experience in the cannabis farms: 'most males wouldn't talk about what happened to them and wouldn't want to talk about their failure. Even when conditions are bad, you need to pay the debt. When there is a lack of legal channels, you are forced to do this.'[59]

Yet in light of the historical migration to the UK and the careful planning that is often involved in the journey, the idea that all are either 'slaves' or 'willing illegal immigrants' is problematic and does not take into account the complex reality of the journey. Speaking of the migration, one interviewee asserted that migrants 'will not just go without knowing anything; they will ask which agent, what journey, and ask a lot of questions'. For another, 'the migration will continue for as long as the drivers are there'.

Many Vietnamese are willing to handle short-term difficulties in sight of long-term goals, and cannabis cultivation may be seen as preferable to the options, or lack of options, that they have back home.[60] In studies of migrants in the UK, many do not want to return, facing shame, debt, and lack of prospects, and studies of returnees back to Vietnam show that many wanted to return to the UK and would attempt the journey again.[61]

Rather than coercion and force being imposed by the traffickers themselves, the lack of ability to work legally and thus earn enough money makes it difficult to avoid the option of cannabis cultivation or other such illegal work. Several studies have shown that cannabis cultivation is an option often factored in from the beginning, and for many it may be an opportunity. In the Netherlands, Vietnamese cannabis cultivation has been established for some time, and studies on cases have found that most suspects had been legally resident and were not potential human trafficking victims. The workers 'were found to be vulnerable in some way, but had agreed to guard or operate the farm voluntarily'.[62]

However, many of the farmers in cannabis farms in the UK are found to have irregular status—potentially providing more leverage to facilitators—which could explain the higher numbers being identified as trafficked and the increased vulnerability to exploitation.

The number of Vietnamese minors being identified as potential victims of labour exploitation in the UK is significant, and it is clear that criminal groups are using the irregular status and potential vulnerability of young migrants for their own benefit. However, in Lainez's opinion, the cannabis farms and nail bar raids that have been conducted across the UK in a purported endeavour to find modern slavery victims are 'highly problematic, because the vast majority of Vietnamese nationals in the UK do not consider themselves to be modern slaves, but rather undocumented migrants who do not wish to be "rescued"'.[63] Studies, including one mentioned by Lainez, have shown that migrants from

Vietnam expend a great deal of effort in financing their trip, choosing the best broker, and seeking advice from family and acquaintances. This was also the finding of a large study carried out with returnees to Vietnam, which found that much planning went into the migratory process, as opposed to kidnappings on the street.[64] Faced with such restrictions on legal work, and the pressure of making such a journey to the UK and with a substantial sum to pay back to facilitators, and no legal way to earn that money, it is unsurprising that migrants are pushed into illegal trade and choose to stay there rather than be labelled slaves and rescued by the state. One interviewee termed it a 'gambling game' for Vietnamese migrants. It is clear that while migrants may be well aware of the risks, it is still worth the gamble, as it is for many who decide to migrate irregularly, as O'Connell Davidson concedes: 'research on debt-financed migration shows migrants are often well aware of the risks with which it is associated, but choose to proceed nonetheless because the potential benefits to migration are so great'.[65]

Conclusion: Between Smuggling and Trafficking

There are many cases of 'successful' stories from irregular Vietnamese migrants in the UK who have managed to earn enough money to pay back their debts and begin earning money for their families. However, a combination of complex and intertwining factors has led to a significant number of migrants, many of whom have chosen or whose families have chosen for them to migrate to the UK, finding themselves within the criminal justice system in relation to cannabis cultivation and vulnerable to exploitation. Within the UK, the debt from being smuggled to the country—which is often so high that opportunities in the UK do not amount to an easy way of paying off that debt—creates either direct dependency or the need to enter more risky though potentially more lucrative occupations. Moreover, the lack of access to legal routes to migration or work restricts individuals such as undocumented Vietnamese migrants to certain types of precarious work, diminishing their chances of developing the means through which they can escape an exploitative situation.

In the experience of many of those carrying out interviews with Vietnamese migrants in potential trafficking cases, Vietnamese migrants generally state that they were not forced to take up certain forms of employment. However, the debt burden is what most become enslaved to, and indeed in many cases there is a sense that families back home may be under threat. Moreover, the sense of family loyalty, 'loss of face', and the issue of shame that may be accompanied by the prospect of returning home having 'failed' the migratory project—all of which have been studied in relation to Vietnamese migration—contribute to a complex picture that complicates the concepts of free choice versus coercion and trafficking versus smuggling.

The emerging dichotomy of response, which views Vietnamese migrants as either trafficked and coerced and thus in need of protection, or conscious criminals and undocumented and thus in need of deportation, leads to a simplistic narrative that obfuscates the agency, needs, and drivers that lead individuals to make these decisions in the first place and the factors that subsequently lead to their vulnerability. An understanding of these complexities may lead to more effective and intelligent responses to this issue in the UK.

7

ERITREA

FLEEING CONSCRIPTION, RISKING EXPLOITATION

Sasha Jesperson and Michael Jones

This chapter focuses on the movement of Eritreans. Movement from
Eritrea begins as people smuggling, as individuals fleeing political
violence seek out assistance to cross the border into Sudan and on to
Libya or Egypt. In some cases, Eritreans are able to travel all the way
to Europe with the assistance of smugglers. As irregular migrants in
transit, however, Eritreans are vulnerable to exploitation, and there is
an increasing risk that their journey will shift from people smuggling
to human trafficking, particularly once they have entered Sudan, where
they have few rights if they do not register as refugees.

This chapter examines the movement of Eritreans through Sudan,
but it also picks up on other nationalities moving through the country,
including Ethiopians, Somalis, and Sudanese, who are travelling towards
Egypt or Libya. Sudan has long served as a hub for individuals travelling
north from East and Central Africa, with the country's eastern periphery
serving as a particularly popular avenue for migratory streams from
Eritrea, Ethiopia, and Somalia. Transnational smuggling networks
are essential to the viability of these routes, facilitating the logistics,
accommodation, and coordination to successfully transport customers

to their destination. Unfortunately, use of this criminal infrastructure is risky, with a 2014 Human Rights Watch report claiming that thousands of refugees have been kidnapped since mid-2010 and either ransomed or sold into trafficking markets across Libya, Sudan, and the Sinai Peninsula.[1] The prevalence of domestic servitude, forced labour, and sexual exploitation led the United States to successively grade Sudan as 'Tier 3' since 2016 in its Trafficking in Persons Report as a country that is not fully meeting the minimum standards for the elimination of trafficking and making significant efforts to do so.[2]

However, these broad quantitative metrics often fail to reflect the complex and evolving dynamics of trafficking in Sudan and East Africa more widely. While human smuggling and trafficking are conceptually discrete phenomena, in practice they often intersect and conflate with one another. This fluidity is even more acute in a Sudanese context. Bonded employment and forced prostitution are usually adopted as indicators of exploitation, but they do not reflect the nature of Sudan's labour markets, where exploitative conditions are relatively normal. Nor does it account for agency: how far an individual chooses to engage in a particular activity and how far they are compelled by circumstance, or other external variables, remains ambiguous and often fluctuates over time. Importantly, the line between those actors providing a service to consumers, and traffickers exploiting victims, is blurred, and many play both roles, often during a single journey. This not only makes it difficult for migrants to identify whom to trust but complicates any determination of where smuggling ends and trafficking begins in East Africa.

Most migrants travelling into Sudan are understood to be Eritrean, followed by South Sudanese, Ethiopians, and Somalis, with UNHCR documenting more than 103,200 Eritreans alone in 2016.[3] The relatively high number can be partially attributed to the 'shoot-to-kill' policy adopted by the Eritrean Defence Forces (EDF) along the Eritrean–Ethiopian border, making Sudan a more preferable option. However, the refugee sample is unlikely to accurately reflect the composition of Sudan's aggregate migratory intake, as Ethiopians are not normally eligible for asylum and have been known to disguise themselves as Eritreans or other nationalities.[4]

A lack of trust in local authorities and the desire to transit through Sudan also tend to dissuade many from applying for refugee status in the first place, as standard protocol necessitates the accommodation of all applicants in Shagarab, a refugee camp in Kassala State.[5] Only one-third of the Eritreans whom UNHCR records crossing into Sudan register as refugees, as UN personnel do not have unlimited access to border crossings and local referral systems are inconsistent.[6] The purported drop in refugee figures after 2010 is similarly problematic for the same reasons.[7] Perhaps most importantly, irregular migrants, by definition, would not receive any formal processing. Given the paucity of mechanisms and resources for monitoring both the refugee and migrant populations in Sudan, the total number remains an open question.

Routes

From the available data, initially movement is largely consensual. From departure sites in Eritrea, aspiring migrants usually recruit smugglers to expedite their journey and cross Sudan's porous 660-kilometre border through various access points including Gergef, Kassala, and Hamdayet (see Map 3).[8] Groups would be guided through the mountains by a local *gawad* (guide) and a *shkrangi* (translator) before being passed over to Sudanese smugglers at the border, often nomadic tribal groups like the Rashaida or Hidarib.[9] Some migrants, particularly those living in the lowlands, may opt to independently trek 'the whole distance' until they reach Sudanese territory, or, if they have a permit, travel by bus to staging areas like Tesseney or Golluj.[10]

The crossing, and its immediate aftermath, are when smuggling tends to lapse into trafficking, and the propensity for migrants to experience exploitation and abuse exponentially increases. Sudan's border forces and local police are usually underpaid and ill trained, meaning they frequently fail to discriminate between irregular migrants and refugees, or follow legal procedures for screening and detention.[11] Often this involves extortion, sexual assault, or extrajudicial killings, particularly in remote security stations beyond the scope of international monitors. Migrant safe houses regularly accommodate rape-victims, a large proportion of whom were attacked during the border crossing, and many Eritrean and Ethiopian women reportedly attain a long-term contraceptive implant due to the prevalence of sexual violence en route.[12]

101

Once in Sudan, there are discrepancies in the type and risk of exploitation migrants are likely to experience depending on their profile and route. A loose typology breaks this down into three categories:

1. Migrants who can afford to pay upfront usually have the most protected journey, especially if they purchase 'full-package' solutions

With enough financial and social capital, migrants can access a range of services with various specialisations including a comfortable car-ride, pre-booked flights, and hired muscle to ensure security.[13] Rich or well-connected Eritreans opt for this method to 'avoid kidnapping and other problems', essentially renting the logistics, authority, and protection of the Eritrean army.[14] Research by the Sahan Foundation and IGAD Security Sector Programme corroborates these conclusions, describing how migrants with 'sufficient money and connections' can purchase a four-wheel drive vehicle to take them to Khartoum and arrange flights to various international destinations.[15] They are not immune from risk, and their wealth does raise their profile as lucrative kidnap targets, but their contacts are normally able to quickly pay to secure their release, and the ransom is often negotiable.

Transactions and ransom payments are usually processed through a formal exchange bureau, a hawala-affiliated money services outlet, or a designated third party, but there are occasionally deviations.[16] Somalis, for example, tend to use a specialised facilitator at the Africa International University rather than involve Sudanese interlocutors.[17] However, even if these demands are met, further exploitation is possible as they remain at the whim of smugglers seeking to profit. Examples include clients being sold on to Rashaida by their Eritrean agents once they have reached the Sudanese border, leaving them to be beaten until a ransom was extracted.[18]

2. Migrants who can cover a proportion of costs upfront but need to supplement this with work en route to finance each leg of their journey

They tend to retain a certain level of agency and have some discretion over the duration and type of labour in which they engage. Nevertheless, the boundary between this cohort and those who cannot pay at all is fluid, and both are susceptible to exploitation as they rely on profit-oriented criminal networks for transportation. For instance, despite agreeing to an initial price before their departure, many Ethiopians smuggled to Khartoum were extorted by secondary brokers once across the border.[19] This transitions into trafficking as customers were deceived about the conditions of their travel and subjected to revised arrangements or significant price-hikes when they were most vulnerable. Those able to pay continued their journey, and those migrants who could not were either sold to other trafficking groups or held in debt bondage until they had 'worked off' an inflated fine.[20]

3. Those that cannot pay at all.

This cohort has no agency or financial leverage and is typically forced into illicit work gangs without any indication of how much debt they need to repay or what other obligations they are required to fulfil. Anecdotal reports describe the confinement of victims in isolated plantations or townships in Kassala and Khartoum State, where they toil for as long as traffickers deem necessary to pay for the next leg of their journey.[21] Once their tenure is complete, migrants are often sold to other criminal outfits and repeat the cycle again, leaving many in a perpetual state of bonded-labour.[22]

This disaggregation primarily applies to Eritreans as they attempt to transit through on the way to Israel, the Gulf, or Europe. In contrast, South Sudanese and Ethiopians typically view Sudan as an endpoint, or a temporary destination to take advantage of economic and financial opportunities before returning home. These trends are not fixed—brokers in Khartoum, for example, often try to entice Ethiopian clients into travelling onwards to Libya—but they usually condition the modalities of exploitation and trafficking experienced by various migrant categories.[23]

The primary difference occurs if these flows are intercepted by the authorities. While Ethiopians illegally entering Sudan are detained and deported, security services are obligated to accommodate Eritreans in Shagarab camp to be processed by UNHCR and the Commission for Refugees (COR).

National service is compulsory in Eritrea, and anyone of 'draft age' leaving the country without permission is perceived to be a deserter, leaving them susceptible to forced labour, torture, or imprisonment under often inhumane conditions if they are returned.[24] The UN interprets the disproportionality of these sentences as persecution and has therefore enfranchised Eritrean migrants to claim refugee status. As such, border guards and police in Sudan are entitled to arrest and question unregistered foreign nationals, but they must accept and 'fairly review' asylum claims at any time.[25]

Provisions in Sudanese law also require a referral system to delineate between refugees, irregular migrants, and trafficking victims, as each category should be handled differently. In reality, the limited capacity of judicial institutions and weak regulatory mechanisms means these procedures are not always enforced, and there is a tendency to criminalise all detainees as 'smuggled migrants'.[26] This conflation led officials to deport at least 104 Eritreans in May and June 2014 without first giving UNHCR access to the group; a further 442, including six registered refugees, in May 2016,[27] and sixty-six in September 2017.[28]

Legal contradictions also sow confusion: the 2014 National Asylum Act imposes a thirty-day window for migrants in Sudan to apply for refugee status, contravening the indefinite time-frame sanctioned under international humanitarian law. Collectively, the lack of technical and procedural rigor in managing illicit migration, and the limited appetite of the Sudanese government to carry the costs for accommodating refugees, leaves Eritreans vulnerable to negligence, abuse, or extradition by local authorities.[29]

This includes the treatment of eligible refugees that are properly screened and either temporarily housed in reception centres if they are relevant to ongoing legal cases, or transferred to Shagarab, an accommodation complex made up of three contiguous camps. While its official population is 40,500, with an average of 919 referrals inducted each month from affiliated sites in Hawadayet, Gergef, and Wad Sharifey, estimates suggest the total may be as high as 90,000.[30] Funding shortfalls and neglect continue to compromise its security, with a porous compound-perimeter and inadequate manpower allowing for the abduction of residents from within the facility[31] and the interception of COR transport convoys ferrying migrants on-site.[32]

Victims have also been 'kidnapped' from the agricultural fields surrounding the complex, which are often tilled to supplement 'poor food rations'.[33] Government agencies in Kassala were supplied with new vehicles to protect refugees in transit, but additional defences for Shagarab, including fencing and barriers, contravene the modalities of UNHCR funding.[34] As such, aside from the token presence of ten police officers in Shagarab III, and a single National Intelligence and Security Service (NISS) representative, the camp remains under-resourced and exposed.[35] Allegations have also been made concerning the complicity of the camp's administrative staff, with guards, in certain instances, facilitating trafficking operations.[36]

However, it is unclear whether most of the incursions involve the forcible extraction of victims by traffickers, or whether residents voluntarily escape with the help of smugglers. Since its construction in 1985, Shagarab has gradually matured into a small economic hub, supporting micro-crediting schemes, vocational training, and commercial linkages with local satellite communities.[37] Nevertheless, the livelihoods and social prospects of residents continue to be relatively circumscribed: the camp is segregated from major towns and cities, and designated refugees are expected to remain in perpetuity. Around 65 per cent leave within two months in an attempt to reach more amenable urban centres like Khartoum or external destinations such as Egypt, Israel, and Europe.[38] Anecdotal accounts even describe former victims of trafficking escaping to try to resume their journey. In one case, several residents were removed from Wad Sharifa camp in mid-2017 before they could be transported to Shagarab. Police officers guarding the camp were found tied up, giving the incident the appearance of a kidnapping, but the refugees were later located in the desert waiting for smugglers.[39] As with the proclivities of Sudanese smuggling more broadly, it is difficult to accurately gauge the scope of individual agency and the fluid boundaries between consensual and coerced migration.

Kassala

For migrants who successfully cross the border into Sudan, the route divides into three branches: those heading towards Port Sudan,

Khartoum, and those seeking commercial opportunities in Kassala and Gedaref. In Sudan's rural periphery or along the Nile, labour-intensive agricultural industries, including gum-Arabic production and sesame cultivation, rely on workers from Ethiopia to offset seasonal demand and high turnover. While salaries and conditions are often poor and exploitation is fairly typical, migrants freely choose to apply for work permits or are voluntarily employed illegally. Many also take advantage of the weak regulatory systems to abscond to local gold mines, which are perceived as far more lucrative.[40]

As the largest city in eastern Sudan, Kassala is the first major collection point for migrants transiting through, acting either as a 'storage point' before the next leg of the journey, or as a platform for local smuggling 'companies' to compete for customers, leveraging trust, reputation, or kinship affiliations to entice consumer interest.[41] Migrants would usually be clustered in Mastora, a suburban, Rashaida-dominated district of west Kassala[42] or in a series of safe-houses along the main highway to Khartoum until a sufficient 'carton' of migrants was collected.[43] In the interim, which can often last several weeks,[44] urban youth and local facilitators would assist in sourcing accommodation, recruiting new clients from within Kassala, and performing guard duties.[45]

Egypt and Sinai

Those travelling north would then be trucked over desert pathways to the Sudan–Egypt border where their handlers would often transfer them to Sinai Bedouins.[46] This detours from the intended destination most migrants were expecting, and the route has long entailed 'abduction, displacement, captivity, extortion, torture, sexual violence and humiliation, serial selling and killing'.[47] An estimated fifty trafficking gangs operate across the Sinai Peninsula,[48] extorting migrants for up to USD 40,000 each, emboldened by their 'apparent impunity'[49] given the propensity of local police forces to accept bribes or ignore vehicles transporting human chattel across Ministry of Interior-controlled bridges. Similarly, the National Council for Childhood and Motherhood, a government entity providing assistance and protection to trafficking victims, fails to recognise survivors from the Sinai, and the shoot-to-kill policy employed by Egyptian border guards to deter illegal entry into Israel ensures migrants essentially remain trapped.[50] Reports suggest over 5,000 African migrants may have died at the hands of their captors between 2009 and 2013.[51]

There are also widespread allusions to organ harvesting by both smuggling and trafficking networks, although it is difficult to obtain reliable data and diagnose the degree of agency subjects have going into these procedures. Reports describe the kidnap and sale of victims in both Sudan and Sinai, with prices reaching USD 20,000 for their kidneys, corneas, and blood.[52]

Arguably, these concerns stem from the prohibition of organ sales in Egypt under the 2010 'Transplantation of Human Organs and Tissues Act', which pushed the trade 'underground', increased the role of informal brokers, and reduced the bargaining position of organ-sellers—thereby exposing them to greater risk of exploitation.[53] Significant cultural resistance to donations, accentuated by limitations in national healthcare, has perpetuated the reliance of Egyptians on 'live donors', raising demand and creating a thriving criminal market.[54] However, these conclusions are contested.

While 'the threat of organ extraction' is a popular trope across migrant testimonies, there is no substantive evidence of a commercial organ trade run by Sudanese trafficking networks.[55] In reality, it seems subjects initially volunteer to sell their organs. For example, the Organised Crime Unit (OCU), a specialist branch of Sudan's National Police, has investigated the movement of both foreign and local donors on buses to Cairo, where they are paid USD 8,000 to 15,000 for a kidney.[56] But these arrangements can quickly transition into trafficking if sellers reconsider after they arrive in Egypt. Conducting research into the organ trade, Sean Columb found that 'while the majority of respondents did not experience any overt violence compelling them to donate, it was clear ... they had little choice but to proceed with the operation'.[57] Others re-accounted 'an entourage of threats and warnings over the consequences' if they reneged on the agreement.[58]

Migrant flows north have diminished following punitive restrictions on non-Israeli workers adopted by the Knesset in 2012, and have been further assuaged by Egyptian counter-insurgency operations launched in 2014 against jihadist groups such as Sinai Wilayat, a local

Islamic State franchise.[59] As a result, transit into Libya has become an increasingly prominent alternative, with the route passing through Khartoum and Dongola.[60]

Khartoum

All major roadways and financial networks converge in Khartoum, a city often described as a 'city-state', thus making it an ideal hub for internal and transnational movement.[61] Temporary waiting posts for new arrivals are organised by Eritrean and Sudanese middlemen in houses clustered across Khartoum North and Omdurman[62] or surrounding villages including Abu Delieg, Um Dawan Ban, and Idd Babiker.[63] Migrants are then loaded on to four-wheel drive vehicles or trucking containers and ferried north to Dongola in preparation for the border crossing into Libya. There have been anecdotal reports of labour exploitation among male migrants, especially in the rural peripheries of Khartoum State, where in one case victims were deposited at an isolated farm and left to work for seventeen months.[64] In such situations, language barriers serve as mechanisms of control, especially for non-Arabic speakers, exacerbating their social marginalisation and dependency on their employers.[65] Children are also victimised, with Nigerian and Ethiopian gangs coercing youths into begging, street vending, or servicing affiliated teashops.[66]

However, trafficking in urban centres is far more prevalent among migrant women, particularly those travelling alone. Interviews reveal a widespread preference held by both smugglers and traffickers for female clients, who are seen as easier to control and usually embark with the consent of relatives, meaning ransoms are more likely to be delivered.[67] As ; Hassan A. Abdel Ati describes it: 'during the period of waiting in Khartoum, smuggled individuals are completely under the control of smugglers ... because of their deprivation of liberty and exploitation, these smuggled women in essence become victims of human trafficking'.[68] They tend to be separated into discrete but overlapping labour streams that include working in teashops, restaurants, cafes, brothels, or domestic work loosely based on their perceived age, beauty, and intelligence.[69] Each role involves different dynamics and varying degrees of autonomy, but in most cases any external contact is closely monitored, and the women often have their documents confiscated.[70]

Domestic work is usually conducted by female migrants, particularly Ethiopians, and organised through a matrix of coordinated networks affiliated with specific smuggling groups. Ethiopian and Eritrean brokers market these services, circulating employees across consumer households in what has become a relatively mainstream commercial practice. While women, working as maids, cooks, or nannies, receive a direct salary averaging between USD 150 to 200 a month, their agents claim a share, which fluctuates depending on their individual circumstances.[71] For example, migrants engaged in debt-bondage typically have higher deductions extracted than those employed voluntarily.[72]

Domestic workers tend to be rotated every two or three months so brokers can maximise their commissions, disrupt any relationships between the women and their clients, and avoid detection by local authorities.[73] The boundary with trafficking and labour exploitation is therefore relatively fluid: poor conditions, diminished agency, and high transaction costs are widespread norms in Sudanese industries, and many migrants consensually opt to work as household staff to receive a stable income, however low. Nevertheless, there are clear instances of domestic servitude tipping into de facto slavery: women who cannot pay the necessary broker fees have sometimes been sold on to traffickers, or detained and forced into work until their debts are paid. In some instances, this has taken over eighteen months.[74] Similarly, the regulatory safeguards mandated under the national 'Domestic Workers Act' only apply to Sudanese nationals, leaving migrants without any legal recourse for abuse or exploitation.[75]

Sex work is also a common occupation for migrant women, and many describe a high frequency of prostitution in Khartoum, Kassala, and other Sudanese cities. The 2016 and 2017 Trafficking in Persons reports highlight cases of women being forced into repurposed flats or cafes and teahouses operating as front-companies for Ethiopian-controlled brothels after being lured by promises of high-paying domestic work.[76] Given the social and political sensitivities of sex work in Sudan, reliable data is difficult to collect, but there are anecdotal references to a spectrum of activities: from specialised prostitution services for a well-connected clientele, including parties hosted by the Sudanese elite in clandestine nightclubs and hotels, to low-level, individual, ad hoc transactions by impoverished women trying to make ends meet. As with domestic work, the distinction between illicit and coerced labour is blurred: there are accounts of migrant women, refugees, and poor or displaced Sudanese engaging in sex work out of economic necessity, but they remain vulnerable to abuse and exploitation.

Slavery and captivity are more prevalent in systematised prostitution rings, which usually operate as commercial extensions of wider trafficking networks, paying off or co-opting local authorities and sourcing victims from both regional and international migratory flows, including women from Bangladesh and the Philippines.[77]

Northern State

Those transiting through Khartoum typically continue on to Northern State, congregating around the provincial capital, Dongola, or Al Dabba, in preparation for the crossing into Libya. This opens new economic opportunities for both migrants and smugglers, particularly given the concentration of artisanal gold mines in northern Darfur, areas around Dongola,[78] and the desert along the Libyan border. As a result, many Eritreans, Ethiopians, and Sudanese voluntarily enrol, irrespective of the poor work conditions.

These industries depend on cheap migrants to supply the mining complex itself and a cluster of satellite services including restaurants, ancillary vendors, and prefab accommodation. An estimated 83 per cent of mines are artisanal, small-scale enterprises run by private stakeholders and tribal powerbrokers, relegating the state to a marginal role in the continent's third largest gold market after Ghana and South Africa.[79] Such high proliferation of domestic prospecting leaves a significant proportion of mines outside any formal regulatory system, with Sudanese firms suffering from a lack of expertise, infrastructure, and mechanisation.[80] Physical risk and fatality rates are correspondingly high, especially in towns or villages experiencing huge population booms where rapid demographic swells are unaccompanied by any expansion in the capacity or availability of public utilities.[81] There are indications that local companies also leverage criminal networks to satisfy their labour demands.[82] The terms of employment are often agreed between traffickers and mine-owners rather than the migrants themselves, and, much like other forms of exploitation, victims are often left in extended bondage. Unfortunately, given the vested interests of both state and private actors in harvesting gold revenues, there is little incentive to improve this socioeconomic situation.

Exploitation is far more prominent in Northern State primarily due to the siloed distribution of, and long distances between towns; the limited financial resources of state and municipal agencies; low donor interest; and the nascent presence of local NGOs without any international support.[83] Many extraction sites also operate in the 'ungoverned' space near the Sudan–Libyan border: a 300-kilometre 'forbidden zone' saturated with gold deposits that national authorities and international monitors struggle to access. This segregation likely encourages abusive practices, and a much more explicit synergy between Sudanese mining corporations and trafficking networks, but data remain scarce.[84]

The final stage of the journey out of Sudan is the most dangerous. Migrants are smuggled from staging posts in Al Dabba and Dongola through an 850-kilometre expanse of desert to Kufra in southern Libya, with a 2013 Regional Mixed Migration Secretariat report describing an influx of between 1,000 and 3,000 people entering the district a month.[85] These risks not only include thirst, exposure, and injury from high-speed, off-road travel but also the threat of trafficking. Smuggling caravans are often intercepted by bandits or roaming armed groups, and given the complete dependence of migrants on their smugglers, many are exploited or extorted when they literally have nowhere to run.[86]

Sudanese authorities offer little recourse. In 2014, border protection and migration management was partially delegated to the 'Rapid Support Forces' (RSF), a formalised iteration of the pro-government militias previously mobilised for counter-insurgency operations in Darfur.[87] Branded as a 'janjawid reincarnate' by critics, this 'new' paramilitary force has been fully integrated into the state's security apparatus, receiving sophisticated equipment, salaries, and full legal immunity under national law.[88] In contrast to other militant groups, the RSF is recognised as an official arm of the Sudanese state and has developed an unusual 'semi-autonomous status' under the control of the presidency, 'mushrooming' its roles and responsibilities.[89] Crucially, provisions authorised in the 2017 national budget also insulate its funding streams from those allocated to NISS or the Sudanese Armed Forces (SAF), creating a frenetic, incoherent framework for oversight, accountability, and financial regulation.

This is problematic, as international observers, including the UN, argue the RSF is culpable for numerous war crimes and human rights abuses in conflict areas of Darfur, Blue Nile, and South Kordofan, including the killing, raping, and torturing of civilians in an 'organised, deliberate and systematic way'.[90] To make bilateral cooperation more palatable for external audiences, political discourse in Khartoum tends to frame the RSF as a professional security service, ignoring its genealogy and emphasising its role in migration management and counterterrorism.[91]

Despite receiving training from SAF supervisors to improve the group's conduct, critics claim the government is once again 'deputising local proxies who operate with impunity and end up being impossible to rein in'.[92] The RSF continues to act fairly synonymously with other Sudanese militias, adhering to the same proclivities but with greater capacity, resources, and political authority.

Discrepancies between the success rate touted by its commander General Mohamed Hamdan Dagolo Hemeti, who described the interception of over '20,000' irregular migrants in 2016, and the official figure of 816 documented by the Sudanese Ministry of Defence, allude to a systemic lack of transparency and institutional accountability.[93] There is no international verification, standardised operating procedures, or mechanisms for monitoring detention suspects by RSF, leaving scope for abuse and alleged collaboration between security patrols and traffickers.[94] The group's control over border security also allows local commanders to tap into a smuggling nexus stretching between Sudan, Chad and Libya. Confiscating or levying fines on illegal vehicles, extorting illicit arms flows, and extorting toll fees through official and improvised checkpoints all supplement the RSF's public funding and feeds a growing patronage network.[95]

Trafficking operations usually map on to these existing circuitries, and reports describe RSF members regularly accepting bribes, using forced labour in RSF-affiliated gold mines, or, more rarely, capturing and ransoming the victims themselves.[96] Elements of both the RSF and NISS have been accused of collusion, with officials 'receiving part of the smuggling profits on most trips to southern Libya', and accounts describe the RSF as often being the 'main organiser of the trips', supplying camouflaged vehicles to ferry migrants across the border, and ensuring the routes are open by talking with 'whoever's commanding the next area'.[97] However, concrete data is scarce, and the Sudanese government denies these accusations, arguing the 'problem did not extend beyond a few bad apples'.[98] Nevertheless, there are concerns that similar dynamics may surface in Kassala after the RSF was deployed in January 2018 following a declared state of emergency.[99]

In summary, throughout the journey across Sudan there are frequent instances of smuggling lapsing into human trafficking, activities perpetrated by hired criminals, opportunists, and the authorities themselves.

Drivers

Human smuggling, trafficking, and labour exploitation are all intrinsically linked to the prevailing political and socioeconomic conditions in East Africa, with a diverse but overlapping set of national circumstances precipitating migratory flows into and across Sudan. In this sense, the character and functionality of local trafficking networks cannot be understood without appreciating the regional 'push and pull' factors driving migration in the first place.

Push factors

Military conscription and bonded labour operating under the rubric of 'national service' are largely responsible for creating a 'generation of Eritrean refugees'[100] amounting to around 475,000 or 12 per cent of the population as of 2015.[101] An existential fear of Ethiopia, ideological atrophy, and a militarised political culture have collectively manufactured a 'garrison state' in Eritrea, entailing the maintenance of a 200,000-strong army.[102] The 'Proclamation of National Service' introduced by the Isaias Afewerki regime in 1995 was designed to support this leviathan, declaring recruitment mandatory for citizens between the ages of eighteen and fifty, and creating a centralised system of 'forced labour on a national scale'.[103] Ostensibly lasting eighteen months, a supplementary programme, the 'Warsai-Yikealo Development Campaign', was launched in 2002 to stretch statutory deployments indefinitely and integrate new civilian beneficiaries including municipal authorities, the civil service, and state-owned corporations.[104]

Although it is too early to predict, these high demands may start to dissipate with the easing of tensions between Ethiopia and Eritrea. The appointment of Prime Minister Abiy Ahmed in April 2018 and his commitment to the Algiers Peace Agreement (2000), involving the withdrawal of Ethiopian troops from Badwe without economic preconditions, may lead to diplomatic normalisation. Whether these aspirations will succeed, and subsequently encourage any reduction in Eritrea's military strength, remains open to speculation.

Eritrean society is entirely configured to this collectivist model, regulated by a police state that eliminates any individual or civic agency, and exercises a 'monopoly over opinion' that essentially abolishes 'the free communication of fact and interpretation'.[105] National education has been similarly revamped as a mechanism for surveillance and indoctrination, securing the universal entry of young people into the army.[106] Any deviation or dissent is quickly stifled through what Kjetil Tronvoll refers to as a 'Gulag archipelago'[107] composed of 'political prisons, detention centres and labour camps that stretch across the country like a chain of islands'.[108] While serving in the military, Eritreans are barred from any formal employment, vocational training, or additional educational opportunities, and exist on a salary of less than USD 30 a month.[109] As Martin Plaut argues, this translates into a form of perpetual limbo, with some conscripts serving for twenty years or more without the ability to support their families.[110] The UN has similarly called the system 'an institution where slavery-like practices are routine',[111] characterised by physical abuse, domestic servitude, and rape, particularly among young women.

There are also serious economic ramifications—harvests are routinely neglected, traditional pastures have been appropriated, and labour shortages increase the price of manufactured goods. The crop and livestock sectors together employ the vast majority of the population, but domestic food production, even in good years, remains 'well below' requirements, leaving Eritrea reliant on commercial imports and food aid.[112]

Despite spiralling poverty levels, the nucleus of Afewerki's state, the EDF, consumes more than 20 per cent of GDP and is supported by a subsidiary command economy that allows the government to co-opt private enterprise and remittance payments.[113] Supplemented with an opaque and largely illicit matrix of front companies and 'unaffiliated' multinational conglomerates in the UAE and Qatar, the ruling People's Front for Democracy and Justice (PFDJ) party has created a closed circuit for funnelling cash to its leadership, leaving the vast majority of those in and outside national service with an 'impoverished, desolate life, bereft of hope'.[114] This blend of economic and political repression has fostered an intolerable environment, with estimates in 2016 that 5,000 Eritreans were fleeing the country each month.[115] Following the rapprochement between Ethiopia and Eritrea, there are signs this trend may change—although the immediate opening of the border resulted in thousands crossing into Ethiopia.[116]

In contrast, Ethiopia's underlying migratory dynamics are far more varied. In more recent years, climate change, ecological degradation, and drought associated with El Niño have exacerbated pre-existing human insecurities, with more than 10 million people requiring food assistance.[117] The government continues to struggle with youth unemployment, increasing public debt, inflation, and a shortage of foreign currency, all of which contribute to socioeconomic pressures. Political pressures, particularly in the aftermath of the Oromo and Amhara protests in 2016, have also accelerated departures from specific ethnic groups and political activists.[118] For all its economic dividends and accelerated industrialisation, Ethiopia's patrimonial model of state-led development and ethno-federalism has been divisive, with high growth rates failing to translate into better living standards for many people.[119]

However, this is very different to the situation in Eritrea – as most departing Ethiopian migrants are seeking short term opportunities, but plan to eventually return home.

Ironically, there are also concurrent problems with labour shortages hindering local industries. The stigma attached to menial or low-quality occupations tends to incentivise migration so workers can pursue the same jobs elsewhere, without experiencing the congruent social costs.[120] These normative considerations are acute in, but not exclusive to, Ethiopia, with similar concerns emerging elsewhere in the region, including Sudan.[121] They also tend to precipitate transnational migratory chains, with foreign works over-saturating local job markets, depressing salaries, and encouraging the migration of native populations to find alternative opportunities elsewhere.[122] However, this is very different from the situation in Eritrea–as most departing migrants are seeking short-term opportunities but plan to return home eventually.

Understanding the cultural and societal nuance of employment is essential in East Africa, as doing so underlines why many of the recommendations prescribed by Western donors and national governments fail to generate substantive returns.[123] The programmatic logic of investing in industrial parks or accelerating job creation schemes is inherently flawed if recipients are not willing to do those jobs in the first place.

Pull Factors

In both Eritrea and Ethiopia, these political, social, and economic 'push' factors are compounded by the shared attraction of a 'better life' in Europe and the Global North, although this is more pertinent for Eritreans who have no desire to return home. Western states are usually considered the ideal destination for those seeking financial opportunities or fleeing political persecution, perceptions often accentuated by sensationalist online content. Narratives shared virtually via Facebook, WhatsApp, and Telegram, or through peer and familial networks, have a tendency to exaggerate the economic and social prospects for migrants entering Europe.[124] While this can be malicious, deriving from falsified messages deliberately disseminated by traffickers, a large proportion is spread by those in the diaspora 'who have already made it' promoting their own success and social stature. The dangerous realities of illicit migration are well known and frequently broadcast on media outlets including Radio Erena,[125] but cultural pressures often conflate migration with personal, social, and material success, and 'staying at home with failure'.[126] Despite the risks, many feel that leaving is the 'only feasible way to improve their lives'.[127]

Sudan is also becoming attractive as both a conduit and destination state for migratory streams due, primarily, to its economic fertility and the closure or dilapidation of more traditional hubs like Israel and Libya.

There has always been a demand for seasonal labour in Sudanese agriculture, particularly for the cultivation and harvesting of national staples like sesame, sorghum, sugar, and gum Arabic. Historically, truckloads of Ethiopian workers would be smuggled over the border, with authorities deliberately looking the other way. However, these trends have become more pronounced following structural transformations in Sudan's economy. Reductions in petroleum production following the secession of South Sudan in 2011 severely compromised its performance, accelerating a largely unorganised and retrospective process of diversification to find and expand substitute sectors including farming and mineral extraction.

State-led and artisanal mining is particularly popular among Sudanese workers, creating a domestic 'gold rush' and subsequent shortages in labour-intensive agrarian industries.[128] In this context, rural smallholders all the way up to corporate plantations increasingly rely on smuggling and trafficking networks to satisfy their labour requirements, generating a ready infrastructure capable of absorbing both legal and illicit migration. Irrigated production, sharecropping, mechanised rain-fed farming schemes, and livestock herding all depend on cheap, unregulated labour, incentivising a variety of political and commercial measures to mobilise the necessary workforce for low-status, low-wage jobs.[129] Migrants are used partially out of convenience, but the practice also derives from popular perceptions of 'foreigners' as 'hardworking' and their willingness to do jobs culturally antithetical to the sensibilities and societal norms of the Sudanese.[130]

Perhaps most importantly, preferable alternatives to Sudan are disappearing. In 2012, Israel tightened its migratory and labour laws, restricting the eligibility of foreigners for asylum and introducing stricter requirements for work permits.[131] Libya, a traditional hub for East Africans, has become similarly unpalatable. As discussed in Chapter 4, the rule of law vacuum in Libya means migrants are extremely vulnerable to exploitation and violence, but this was not always the case.

During forty-two years of dictatorship, Muammar Gaddafi not only relied on violence and coercion to secure his regime but allocated rents, resources, and political power to a constellation of subnational stakeholders, creating a clientelist system to cultivate 'support from a highly fragmented tribal society'.[132] The imposition of international sanctions in the late 1980s precipitated a black market in basic commodities, incentivising the proliferation of transnational smuggling as a staple livelihood for otherwise 'under-served border communities'.[133] The regime deliberately weakened state institutions and leased control of such activities to local clients as a mechanism for purchasing loyalty and satiating grievances. As many beneficiaries were constituents of wider cross-border social networks, these illicit trades not only profited Libyan nationals but also produced commercial opportunities for migrants who could embed themselves into recipient tribal communities on the basis of kinship or familial ties.

Similarly, rising oil prices and a centralised hydrocarbon industry insulated Libya from much of the fallout from the Financial Crisis in 2008, facilitating a lucrative market for foreign investment and tourism. The country's official and criminal economies flourished, generating new revenues that were partially re-invested in labour-intensive construction projects and 'white elephants', fostering ample capacity to absorb foreign workers and creating vocational opportunities for migrants.

State dispensation under Gaddafi also proffered considerable welfare services and public benefits: citizens enjoyed Africa's highest GDP per capita and life expectancy, and petro-dollars were redistributed back to the population through a panoply of subsidies.[134] Finally, the Rome–Tripoli Accord ratified in 2009 closed sea routes across the Mediterranean, with the Libyan coastguard detaining illegal migrants before they reached international waters, which reduced migratory rates by 75 per cent.[135] Libya therefore became an attractive end-destination in and of itself, rather than just a transit state for accessing Europe, and actively raised barriers to further travel.

The 17 February Revolution in 2011 changed these arrangements completely. Gaddafi's 'controlled system of favoured contractors' in the licit and illicit economy collapsed into a factionalised free for all.[136] Oil production shrank, welfare services collapsed, and the migrant-smuggling economy became both commoditised and exponentially more abusive, with revolutionary brigades and local militias contracting migrants out as 'informal work gangs' with no compensation.[137] Without the security and regularity provided by Gaddafi's patronage machine, Libya's smuggling infrastructure was easily co-opted by human-trafficking networks that 'specialise in the exploitation, extortion and enslavement of sub-Saharan Africans', with Eritreans, Sudanese, and Somalis being disproportionately targeted for detention in centres more akin to 'torture chambers'.[138] Importantly, any coordinated management of the coastline was also suspended under a dysfunctional transitional government, leaving the country's 'maritime surveillance and rescue capacities non-existent'.[139] In this context, the choices available to aspiring migrants shifted: either they attempt a dangerous journey to Europe or search for substitute opportunities in other African transit states like Sudan.[140]

Permissive Environment

In addition to these 'push and pull' factors, there is a permissive environment for migration within Sudan. Although not officially condoned, authorities generally look the other way as migrant labour is essential to the functioning of the economy, and authorities can extract rents from migrants for allowing them to stay.

Political

While authority nominally revolves around a political–military elite in Khartoum, any state-centric analysis of Sudanese institutions risks ignoring the currency of 'personal affinity, loyalty and reward'.[141] As described by Alex de Waal, patronage is often the circulatory system of real politics, functioning as a salient source of security in lieu of strong state infrastructure. The distribution of power at every institutional level across Sudan generally derives from the logic of a

119

'political marketplace', where corruption is not symptomatic of system failure—'it is the system'.[142] Political rulers levy wealth and resources to bargain for loyalty with intermediate elites who control the means of violence, using political capital to purchase the provisional allegiance of governmental and non-governmental actors. Sudanese 'retail politics' has therefore led to a commercialisation of violence, meaning state-legitimacy and institutional activity is transactional, transient, and conditional.

The governing coalition operating under President Omar al-Bashir pursues separate political, military, and commercial policies, with coordination limited to ensuring they do not threaten the regime itself.[143] The Sudanese Armed Forces, national security apparatus, RSF, and strands of civil government, including the Ministry of Interior, all entertain competing and often contradictory agendas, leading to systemic corruption, dilapidated welfare provision, and dysfunctional state services.[144]

These dynamics have severely weakened the legitimacy, efficiency, and capacity of national institutions, with chunks of the public and security sectors being captured, cannibalised, and converted to vehicles for dispensing patronage. This has not only precipitated the systemic decay of state institutions but also entrenched a culture of impunity and corruption now integral to the functionality of contemporary Sudanese governance.[145] In outlying areas, including Darfur, formal processes of budgeting are inoperable, and municipal authorities are often starved of funds, contributing to the aversion of paramilitaries looting.[146] Civil servants similarly moonlight to supplement their basic salaries or leverage their positions to extract additional funds from their constituents.[147]

As such, there is an absence of robust accountability and oversight across federal government, and the state lacks both the capacity and inclination to comprehensively enforce its labour regulations, the rule of law, or monitor the conduct of its security forces.[148] Consequentially, it is clear police, military, and administrative personnel are profiting from opportunistic transactions and kickbacks from traffickers along specific junctures of the migration route.[149]

This operates on two levels. Petty corruption often allows traffickers to 'buy the road', bribing border guards, local commissioners, and army personnel, and appropriating police vehicles to transport migrants.[150] Human Rights Watch has similarly collated evidence of officers arresting and ransoming victims before selling them to local trafficking rings.[151] Other examples include police in Khartoum ripping up the work permits of Ethiopian migrants so they could arbitrarily impose fines and make some cash on the side.[152] This 'improvised' criminality is not confined to frontline personnel: senior SAF personnel have been prosecuted for running extortion rackets, although it is often unclear whether these arrests were indicative of genuine law enforcement or the fallout from Sudan's precarious politicking.[153]

The second, more pernicious level involves 'high positioned' bureaucrats in Kassala, Khartoum, and other urban hubs like Gedaref sponsoring smuggling operations as an extension of their personal patronage network.[154] Crucially, however, this is often context-specific, orchestrated by senior and middle managers rather than entire strands of government, and there does not appear to be any evidence of systematic collusion at the national level.[155] The state as a whole remains ambivalent to, rather than complicit with, human trafficking.

As smuggling and trafficking activities are not considered existential threats to the regime, they are not prioritised by the Sudanese intelligence services or in the allocation of federal funding.[156] This financial bottleneck often leaves criminal outfits better armed and resourced than local police forces or SAF contingents, providing scope for the co-optation, circumvention, or mitigation of law enforcement. Nevertheless, such negligence can at least be partially explained by the history and cultural realities defining Sudan. The country has always had porous borders given the population's supranational kinship networks. These historic linkages are far more resilient than the boundaries established under British colonialism and remain embedded in the social fabric of East Africa. Nor is there any incentive to stem the mobility of Sudanese wanting to work abroad and send remittances back home, which helps fund Sudan's formal and grey economies. While Khartoum is currently aligning itself with the priorities of Western donors, focusing, at least rhetorically, on counterterrorism and counter-trafficking, this does not necessarily translate into real or sustainable action. Sudan's primary concern is diplomatic normalisation, and programming is frequently used as leverage for reducing international sanctions.[157]

But there are some success stories. Incremental progress is being made as a result of autonomous, municipally led programming. The regional administration in Kassala has become increasingly aware of associations between border guards and smuggling networks and has increased the rotation of security personnel to stop collusion.[158] This only temporarily mitigates the problem and cannot substitute for interventions tackling the underlying causal factors of human trafficking.[159]

A Migration Committee established in Northern State points to other, more institutionalised efforts to grapple with smuggling and human trafficking at a local level. Comprising delegates from the NISS, the police, the Sudanese Red Cross, and a constellation of government ministries, the committee creates a platform for cross-department collaboration.[160] Irrespective of funding shortages, it could represent a credible model for addressing irregular migration and has already improved inter-governmental cooperation in Dongola, where the Wali and his security service counterpart are now sharing intelligence on trafficking networks operating in the area.[161]

The problems typically stem from the national level. For example, the OCU has improved its investigative capacity and efficiency in data collection, rolling out a new set of standard operating procedures as a template for partner agencies. The conviction of eighteen Eritrean and Sudanese traffickers in 2017 was partly attributed to these measures, and the reforms have received both input and appraisal from independent evaluators. Unfortunately, there appears to be little appetite for upscaling this progress, and the OCU lacks the budget, mobility, and manpower to tackle trafficking in a comprehensive or durable way.

These issues have also beset the creation of the National Committee for Combating Human Trafficking (NCCT) and its cross-government action plan. Designed in collaboration with IOM Sudan, the plan is one of Khartoum's 'forward-looking' concessions to external donors, representing a 'basis for effective action in the future'.[162] Its main features focus on reducing populations vulnerable to trafficking by raising public awareness and improving community engagement, alongside structural reforms to strengthen referral mechanisms, enforce legal guarantees for victim protection, and ensure a more erudite delivery of welfare services.[163] However, Sudan's commitment has been nominal at best, stripping the NCCT of clout, resources, and political capital.[164] It does not have a natural home among participating ministries, and rather than becoming a hub for coordinating state activity, it has been largely frozen out of the decision-making process.

There are concerns the committee may, in reality, be the latest iteration in a long-held Sudanese tradition of 'isomorphic mimicry', where Khartoum parrots international donors to receive their funding by disingenuously subscribing to humanitarian and developmental norms.[165] Crucially, the NCCT also carries practical and programmatic risks. The Plan of Action relies on a cascading model: establishing a string of sub-committees across the country to manage the demands of each region. Without rigorous institutional mapping and contextual sensitivity, both of which consume time and money, there is a risk that organic, locally led innovations like the Migration Committee in Northern State will either be duplicated or replaced all together, setting counter-trafficking efforts back further.[166]

Conflict

Conflict, and newly emerging 'post-conflict' landscapes, also provide permissive spaces for irregular migration, labour exploitation, and human trafficking, although the mechanics of these relationships are gradually starting to shift. The country's intersecting conflict systems are complex and variable, affecting vast stretches of Sudan's periphery, including Northern Darfur, and Southern Kordofan and Blue Nile following the secession of South Sudan in 2011. While the causal factors remain diverse in each case, particularly at the local level, broad patterns can be identified: the political and socioeconomic exclusion of various communities; the militarisation of identity politics; competition over land, water, and other natural resources, usually amplified by ecological pressures; and a weak, relatively ambivalent central state.

These dynamics have precipitated waves of refugees and internal displacement, turning Sudan into both a transit and departure country. In December 2016, there were up to 3.2 million internally displaced persons nationally, including 2.6 million in Darfur, and over 355,000 refugees scattered across the region.[167] As of November 2018, there were over 1 million refugees—851,313 from South Sudan and 153,620 others, mostly Eritreans.[168]

Fluctuating levels of violence have also disrupted historical socioeconomic and political configurations, creating new local and transnational networks operating outside the parameters of the state.[169] This milieu is often best described as a 'militia-state', referring to areas experiencing systemic 'de-institutionalisation' where violence is sub-contracted to non-state armed groups.[170] Such actors typically owe their loyalty 'to the barrels of their guns', invoking various forms of predation and, in the case of Darfur, the violent expropriation of farmlands, pasturage, and mineral concessions.[171] As in South Sudan[172] and Côte d'Ivoire, conflict created space for political entrepreneurs to divvy up the Sudanese countryside, capture various facets of economic activity, and 'extract personal wealth from both legitimate and criminal activities' in territory under their control.[173] In doing so, they disrupted existing societal hierarchies by exploiting violence and looting. While most of these experiments were short lived, warlords like Musa Hilal, leader of the Border Guards and the Sudanese Revolutionary Council, nevertheless carved space for trafficking without state interference, and created new opportunities for profit that were not available during peace.[174]

However, more durable centres of political and economic authority have started to consolidate.[175] This has significant implications for smuggling and trafficking, as criminal syndicates are no longer operating in 'ungoverned' spaces contested by resource-strapped tribal militias or makeshift community defence forces. Instead, they must negotiate with new, increasingly assertive parastatal structures operating under the security umbrella provided by the RSF.

In other post-conflict contexts, non-state actors including the Rashaida in eastern Sudan were tacitly allowed to continue their smuggling and trafficking activities without state interference on the basis that they refrained from directly confronting government forces. A nominal peace agreement was signed in 2006 between Khartoum and the 'Eastern Front', an umbrella insurgent movement incorporating the Beja Congress, Rashaida Free Lions, the Sudanese People's Liberation Army (SPLA), and the Justice and Equality

Movement (JEM), but many of its underlying provisions were never implemented. Fundamentally, the pact was a deal between Sudan and the Front's Eritrean sponsors, who acted like any other 'rent-seeking actor' on the periphery of Sudan's political marketplace by using violence to elicit a 'mixture of direct payoff in the form of cheap fuel and commercial opportunities' for stakeholders in Asmara.[176] The economic deprivation and underlying grievances precipitating conflict in the early 1990s were largely paved over. Instead, under the pretext of peacebuilding, the government co-opted local elites and tacitly preserved space for armed groups to continue their smuggling activities in return for regional stability.[177]

In contrast, rather than a covert agreement or non-interference arrangement, the RSF enjoys a formalisation of its power as a branch of the Sudanese state while simultaneously capturing federal resources and wielding influence vis-à-vis national powerbrokers. Khartoum relies on the group's manpower to maintain its authority, and this leverage has given Hemeti free rein to systematically exploit conflict economies and congruent commercial opportunities in Darfur, mimicking the practice of local warlords but on an industrial scale. Security provision for Darfur's interior has been almost entirely delegated to the RSF. Local police and administrative services are largely defunct, with no authority over the group's activities. Given the impunity it now receives from representing the Sudanese government, the RSF has gradually accumulated monopolies over local markets, protection rackets, and commodity chains, feeding a patronage system to service Hemeti's personal interests.

In many respects, the RSF has therefore imposed a new model of 'institutionalised criminality' in the areas it governs, introducing a degree of predictability, and marking a change from Darfur's intractable lawlessness. This is not a complete departure: the group does not hold a monopoly over the use of violence, and the region still experiences low-intensity conflict. However, if these trends persist, the RSF as a *de jure* state body may represent a more resilient, long-term, and predictable version of local authority.

This is crucial as war zones are unstable environments, generating lucrative new opportunities, but also eroding trust, increasing protection payments and transaction costs, limiting market access, and undercutting available economies of scale.[178] A strong and expanding RSF could instead help lower these security costs, improving security and predictability in the local economy. Trafficking and smuggling networks can pull out of expensive and cumbersome relations with local warlords, and instead pay off a single patron backed by the Bashir regime.

This obviously remains problematic, as the RSF is not necessarily a coherent group. Its loyalty with the central government is similarly precarious: Hemeti, for example, instigated a mutiny in 2007 over salary and property distributions.[179] RSF loyalty, like that of other militia outfits, remains conditional. Nevertheless, the group's control and co-optation of elites in Darfur streamlines the costs otherwise facing criminal syndicates and could reduce the risk and provide incentives for trafficking networks to expand.

Economic

The need for cheap labour has not only attracted migrant workers to Sudan but discouraged authorities from intercepting or disrupting smuggling routes on any major scale. As Ati summarises: 'high unemployment, high poverty rates and rising costs of living, the impact of refugees on services, housing, the job market, together with social tolerance of smuggling and trafficking, and loose security controls, have motivated many youth to engage in such activities as a means of making quick money'.[180]

Sudanese society has largely normalised these arrangements. The exploitation of foreign workers has become convention and is now intrinsic to the commercial logic, and profit, of national and local industries, alongside an easy, quick, and accessible revenue course of traffickers, smugglers, and host populations. Sudan's eastern provinces are particularly susceptible to these practices. Immiseration, nascent development, and weak institutions create incentives for deprived communities along the border to collaborate with, and protect, smugglers and traffickers who offer scarce financial opportunities.[181] In this context, the lines between cheap, bonded, and slave labour can often start to blur as migrants have become an accessible commodity that various actors along the migration corridor seek to benefit from, with the risks borne out by the migrants themselves.

Similarly, the ubiquity of these illicit practices lends itself to a degree of opportunism along the migrant chain, especially in hubs such as Kassala, Khartoum, Al Fashar, and Dongola. Victims describe how local residents profit from occasionally informing traffickers where migrants live, particularly if they are in need of quick cash.[182]

Regional Dynamics

As with other East African countries, kinship, linguistic, cultural, and tribal linkages are critical in facilitating the transit of irregular migrants into and through Sudan. Smuggling circuitries tend to map on to ethnic, social, and familial networks, particularly across the Sudanese–Eritrean border, allowing for more efficient cooperation. In lieu of any formal regulatory mechanisms, illicit markets typically rely on personal affinities and, when necessary, coercive enforcement. This strengthens connections between various nodes to ensure a cohesive transit network that stretches across the country. The predominance of tribal and identity politics similarly tends to cut across state institutions and the civil service, allowing for 'ethnic-based social protection for perpetrators and even a condoning of the practice'.[183]

This social capital is also helpful in the upstream marketing of services in departure states. To build trust and strengthen consumer confidence, migration is typically framed in the same terms as legal travel, with a single 'company'—often those embedded in Eritrean communities—casting itself as responsible for the organisation and management of the journey. These outlets exploit clan affiliations to placate customers and advertise the experience as 'low risk' by emphasising the degree of support they will receive from diaspora populations.[184] Many migrants therefore sign up with distorted expectations, assuming brokers will provide an informal 'safety net' and assist them in finding employment at their destination. Brokers can also transmit information downstream, identifying lucrative clients to be kidnapped and ransomed by partner groups once they are in Sudan.[185]

127

Identity-based bonds are therefore crucial for facilitating both the supply and demand dimensions of human trafficking. The Rashaida, a sub-group of ethnic Bedouin Arabs, are key actors in the trade and appear to be ubiquitous in accounts of human trafficking and abuse.[186] This is logical given their particular history, skills, and the lack of other economic opportunities in the region, but these narratives tend to homogenise the community as a monolith, branding all Rashaida as complicit when in reality only a small contingent is actively involved.[187]

Emigrating from the Arabian Peninsula in the mid-nineteenth century, these predominately nomadic pastoralists were concentrated in the arid interior of eastern Sudan before diffusing up along the coast, and establishing connections with Egypt and rump communities in Saudi Arabia.[188] Strands of Rashaida embedded themselves in transnational smuggling networks from the 1960s, supplementing camel farming with transit fees from importing illicit Gulf commodities into Sudanese markets. They have also been responsive to broader shifts in the national economy: exploiting agricultural mechanisation and the expansion of rural irrigations systems by transporting migrant workers to isolated plantations. Over time, elements of this practice transitioned into human trafficking, generating concurrent revenue streams that allow the Rashaida to preserve their independence and self-sufficiency.

The Rashaida remain insular, heavily armed, and eschew any form of social assimilation or political affiliation.[189] As the services they provide are integral to labour-intensive industries stretching across Kassala, Gedaref, and Red Sea States, and renewed conflict could disrupt output from oil concessions clustered along Sudan's eastern periphery, there is little appetite at the federal level to directly intervene.[190] Thus Rashaida smugglers operate more efficiently, securely, and confidently than their competitors.[191] However, their opacity and social segregation also inevitably accentuate the scale of their involvement. The 'Rashaida' label has gradually become a pejorative term for trafficking more generally, making it difficult to accurately delineate between genuine Rashaida syndicates and those of other ethnic groups including the Beni Amir, Hadandawa, and Shukriya.[192] These distinctions are further convoluted by the gradual conflation of different networks. Whereas previously each border tribe functioned in discrete areas, the geographic and commercial expansion of the trade has necessitated cross-tribal cooperation to exploit available economies of scale and expand local operations. The ethno-centric disposition of human traffickers remains important but is increasingly difficult to map.[193]

The collusion of neighbouring states in facilitating, or actively encouraging, illicit migration, is also essential for trafficking activities. This can be traced back to shifts in Eritrea's political economy. Corruption in the army and a concurrent expansion of Eritrea's domestic extraction industries created new opportunities for strategic rents, moving the country towards a more 'conventional rentier political market-place system'.[194] As a result, President Isaias was compelled to start a new strategy of 'marketisation' in the 2000s, licensing EDF officials to exploit illicit commercial activities in return for their loyalty, and blurring the lines between state and criminal enterprises. As the US embassy describes it:

> the schemes and scams of individual military officers clearly occur with the full knowledge and support of the Office of the President in order to buy the military's loyalty ... while the PFDJ controls many of the industries, the EDF generals have managed to get their individual fingers in the pie as well, especially in trade, smuggling and foreign exchange.[195]

The haemorrhaging of Eritrean refugees offered state officials a particularly lucrative revenue stream to tap, encouraging the evolution from a 'shoot to kill policy' into an improvised 'pay to leave' trade.[196] Since 2011, UN monitors have identified Brigadier General Taklai Kifle Manjus, commander of the Eritrean Defence Forces western region, and moonlighting arms dealer, as an important interlocutor primarily because he was able to recycle the same networks, mechanisms, and criminal infrastructure for smuggling guns.[197] For an initial down payment of USD 3,000 each, agents of the Border Surveillance Unit will drive customers through military checkpoints and across the border into Sudan, sometimes travelling as far as Khartoum. A second tranche of USD 5,000 to USD 7,000 would then be transferred on arrival, with the money usually being sent by relatives in the diaspora or third-party stakeholders.[198]

The cheaper alternative involved Manjus, and other senior members of the EDF, coordinating with ex-paramilitaries and criminal networks to ferry migrants through Sudan once they have made it over the border. Asmara's sponsorship of the Sudanese Eastern Front insurgency in the 1990s created a latent client-base that state officials could reactivate, allowing them to outsource smuggling to local proxies such as residual elements of the Beja Congress and the Rashaida Free Lions. This is where smuggling is most likely to lapse into trafficking. Rashaida and Hidarib truckers sell seats for an average fee of USD 3,000 but will often demand an additional ransom payment of up to USD 20,000 per head to release their charges, with EDF partners receiving a cut.[199]

Concomitantly, the unreliability of Eritrean conscripts and their reluctance to shoot their peers has also compelled strands of the Eritrean Border Surveillance Unit to subcontract border-security to nomadic militiamen. These groups were originally deployed on both sides of the Eritrean–Sudanese border to 'fire at deserters', but they quickly started to detain and ransom victims, with families paying EDF members affiliated with Manjus as interlocutors to secure their release.[200] In this context, leveraging the threat of tribal surrogates and Rashaida ex-paramilitaries was 'crucial to generating revenues'. Rented criminal networks also enabled Eritrean officials to link up with Sudanese and sub-Saharan gangs, creating an entry point for embedding into pre-existing transnational smuggling systems.[201]

Dynamics

The volume of migrant trafficking flowing across East Africa has led observers, including the EU border agency Frontex, to describe these smuggling circuitries as 'sophisticated, well-organised networks stretching from Eritrea through to Libya'.[202] The Sahan Foundation, the Intergovernmental Authority on Development (IGAD), and various UN reports similarly point to profligate 'king-pins' orchestrating the trade, identifying: Manjus, Colonel Fitsum Yishak of the Eritrean Army,[203] Sudanese businessmen such as Mabrouk Mubarak Salim and Hamid Abdallah,[204] and Eritrean nationals operating in the diaspora like Maesho Tesfamariam and Medhanie Yehdego Mered.[205] However, this tends to give an impression of a hierarchical framework that may not reflect the spectrum of relationships forming, dissipating, and re-forming along specific routes, flows, and opportunities.[206]

The East African smuggling industry integrates high-profile stakeholders and is often assumed to be 'the most professional, organised and profitable' due to its long exploitation of the Somali conflict, but it is not a homogenous entity.[207] Nor are there any mafia-type corporate outfits controlling the entire migratory corridor. Instead, the market is saturated with competing cells facilitating movement across contiguous sub-regions, transporting migrants for a certain stretch before passing them on to the next group.[208] Figureheads with particular political or social connections may emerge in restrictive areas such as the Eritrean border, but this monopoly immediately dissipates in a relatively open and unregulated context like eastern Sudan, where barriers to entry are far lower.

These secondary configurations reflect the 'supermarket principle' outlined by Peter Tinti and Tuesday Reitano: high volume with low costs, high turnover, and mass movement.[209] Nomadic and urban-based Sudanese gangs typically rely on their territorial knowledge and are fairly localised, exploiting buy-in from their communities and building on longstanding relationships with the relevant authorities. Smugglers venturing farther afield can hire young men with the necessary language skills to navigate extra-local social dynamics, but it is more common to adopt a 'pay as you go' methodology, ferrying migrants between groups.[210] Any coordination usually derives from ethnic, financial, or personal linkages, with loose 'working relationships' based on 'transactional rather than collaborative enterprises'.[211] The Rashaida, Bedouins, and Hidarib, for example, are all related in terms of dialect and ethnography, creating linguistic and kinship bonds to facilitate smuggling across the Sahara.[212] These relationships are often ad hoc, dispersing and coalescing in different combinations depending on the particular transaction,[213] and there have been cases of groups stealing 'cartons' of migrants from their rivals to increase their profits.[214] Crucially, the polycentric disposition of Sudanese smuggling also means these low-level networks are extremely versatile, adapting to the closure of routes and re-forming to manage fluctuations in demand.

Conclusion

Sudan has a dynamic criminal ecosystem, supported in part by the normalisation of exploitative labour practices, deficient state institutions, weak rule of law, and near-universal complicity from a spectrum of actors en route. The boundaries between people smuggling and human trafficking often conflate, making it difficult to intervene and adequately support victims. Many migrants voluntarily use this infrastructure despite the risks, complicating assessments of agency and intent.

There have been some attentive moves to improve the response at the national and international level. However, these need to be more targeted and coordinated in order to maximise benefits, and the implementation of durable solutions remains difficult. Migration flows show no signs of slowing, which makes any prescriptions responsive. While there is scope to provide better protection and support to victims of trafficking, it is clear that any action needs to be part of a regional approach.

8

PEOPLE SMUGGLING VERSUS HUMAN TRAFFICKING
A QUESTION OF AGENCY?

Anne-Marie Barry and *Sasha Jesperson*

Human trafficking has become a priority for governments worldwide, with victim-centred responses being strengthened. While this constitutes a major step forward in protecting the human rights of trafficking victims, it often embeds a well-established dichotomy of helpless victim/barbaric exploiter. Although there are many cases that firmly fit the definition of human trafficking—where an individual is coerced into exploitation—the four case studies reveal that human trafficking and people smuggling are not as distinct as the UN Protocols suggest. With many countries tightening migration controls, the market for and role of people smugglers and irregular migration channels have increased. Lacking eligibility for entrance status in transit and destination countries, migrants become vulnerable to a form of exploitation that fits the definition of human trafficking, even though they have chosen to travel. In these cases, though, the victim-centred response to human trafficking is not wholly appropriate and may undermine the agency of migrants as well as skewing overall numbers of trafficking victims. Even for those with less agency, there is still a risk that anti-trafficking measure could undermine opportunity.

In these cases, the support commonly provided to returnees through small-scale livelihoods programmes is redundant.

David Gadd and Rose Broad point out that 'political claims-making about modern slavery tends to rely on a portfolio of racialised binaries Anglophone governments have long deployed to justify greater immigration control'.[1] In the process of tightening border controls, governments effectively create a role for criminal groups to facilitate migration. This establishes a binary between 'deserving victims and non-deserving illegal immigrant'.[2] Kiril Sharapov argues that this is evident in the UK government's policies towards trafficking and smuggling. The result is a vacuum where exploitation can persist unchecked. The cases explored in this book, however, have highlighted that this binary is imagined—people on the move are rarely one or the other, but move up and down the spectrum between these categories throughout their journey.

This chapter draws out how categories shift. It sets out two examples where defining a practice as people smuggling or human trafficking is not straightforward even when it is assumed to be. The first is the exploitation of migrants—those who choose to move but are vulnerable because of their irregular status, as discussed in the cases of Vietnam and Eritrea. The second example is the smuggling of people into exploitative labour. In both instances, individuals have chosen to travel but end up in exploitative situations that fit the definition of human trafficking. The complexity of these cases requires a more nuanced response that respects the agency of the individual rather than treating them solely as victims.

Identifying Victims

In the UK, a 'victim-centred approach' to addressing human trafficking cases has been rightly championed, driving positive practices such as a law enforcement response that questions, for example, whether an individual may be committing crimes as a result of force and coercion, and thus treated as a victim before they are a criminal. This has been seen in cases of cannabis cultivation or county-lines criminality. However, rhetoric surrounding the 'anti-slavery' drive of recent years, particularly in the public arena and policy response, often falls into an already well-established dichotomy of helpless victim/barbaric exploiter, which, when applied too liberally to cases involving poor working conditions, dependency, child labour, or criminality, is insufficient to describe what is often a complexity of circumstances, denying individuals (usually migrants) their agency and thus any responsibility, and creating both simplistic and ineffective responses and indeed confusion for those tasked with responding.

The difficulty in applying the victim/criminal binary has been highlighted in interviews with members of UK law enforcement, who frequently encounter this schism between the label and the reality in their front-line work. As one detective inspector told us: 'we don't go from zero to modern slavery on every single case, but that's the way it's been dealt with over the last few years.'[3] An inability to fit referrals of people into categories that appear to be either 'slave' or 'free' creates frustration and an inability to respond to the complexity of situations and contexts in which people are found in-between these two categories.

This chapter does not address the cases that would fall under the strict legal category of human trafficking, of which there are many in every country, including the UK. It instead seeks to highlight the grey area—where the individuals in question who are deemed to be victims of modern slavery in the UK not only refuse the protection that the state makes it its mission to provide but also do not recognise the label with which they are provided.

One senior member of a police force's human trafficking unit spoke of the difficulty in getting disclosures for human trafficking: 'we're coming across lots of locations where you'd anticipate we would find victims and for any number of reasons victims are not presenting as victims of trafficking'.[4] This particular officer described how clear cases of trafficking occur, but does 'equally wonder if there's people who we would look at and say surely you've been exploited, but the reality is they're going to be saying, for cultural reasons, I'm sorry I haven't been exploited, I'm here earning this amount of money'.[5]

Another interviewee from a different force described an unsuccessful attempt at persuading a female working in the sex industry to enter the National Referral Mechanism (NRM) for potential victims of modern slavery, asserting that 'the biggest problem mainly is convincing a victim that they are a victim because they don't see it that way, they are still better off very often than they would be if they went back home'.[6]

Sharapov argues that 'victims['] naivety and powerlessness must be manifest to meet the government set benchmark of "genuine" and "deserving" victimhood'.[7] But even in clear cases of trafficking, victims will at times reject that status. Belgian Federal Police, for example, picked up a young Nigerian prostitute in Brussels with the intention of transferring her to an NGO that could provide support and education. She demanded to be let out of the vehicle because she was earning EUR 3,000 per week, much of which was being sent to her single mother and four siblings back home in Nigeria, a sum outlandishly out of reach for her even if she could transition through education into a regular job.[8]

Perhaps the issue is not that these individuals need to be convinced of their victim status, but that the 'victim' status is wholly inadequate, denying them both freedom and responsibility and thus simplifying the response of 'rescue' (and often return to home country) in a way that ignores the structural and policy factors that have led them to choose this precarious path, and into conditions that many would deem exploitative.

Nicola Mai has long questioned the adequacy of the term 'trafficked' to describe the experience of women, men, and transgender people working in the sex industry, and after interviewing a number of workers concluded that 'the current emphasis on trafficking and exploitation to explain the variety of the trajectories of migrants into the UK sex industry risks concealing their individual and shared vulnerabilities and strengths, the understanding of which could form the basis of more effective social interventions'.[9]

This is not to overlook the fact that there are extremely vulnerable people who are severely exploited and subject to heinous crimes. And it is also not to dismiss the essential work taking place in the UK to improve the labour inspection regime to better address issues of low pay and poor working conditions, creating UK standards to define and address labour exploitation. But when those people that the authorities deem to be slaves do not see themselves as such, then there is a clear need to re-evaluate what it is we are looking at. This is particularly important as 'victims are idealised, with those not according to this ideal being criminalised', and likely punished despite their vulnerability.[10]

Definitional Challenges

The grey area this chapter focuses on is the increasingly blurred line between people smuggling and human trafficking. As highlighted in Chapter 1, the legal definition of people smuggling and human trafficking set out in the two protocols to the UN Convention against Transnational Organised Crime are substantially different. People smuggling is 'the procurement, in order to obtain, directly or indirectly, a financial or other material benefit, of the illegal entry of a person into a state party of which the person is not a national'.[11] For the destination state, people smuggling is a circumvention of the border, a crime against the state. For migrants, smugglers are providing a service, getting them across borders that have become harder to cross through legitimate means.

In contrast, the definition of human trafficking focuses on the exploitation of the individual being trafficked. Rather than being a service provider, the trafficker is committing a crime against the individual being trafficked. Human trafficking refers to

> the recruitment, transportation, transfer, harbouring or receipt of persons, by means of the threat or use of force or other forms of coercion, of abduction, of fraud, of deception, of the abuse of power or of a position of vulnerability or of the giving or receiving of payments or benefits to achieve the consent of a person having control over another person, for the purpose of exploitation. Exploitation shall include, at a minimum, the exploitation of the prostitution of others or other forms of sexual exploitation, forced labour or services, slavery or practices similar to slavery, servitude or the removal of organs.[12]

The role of consent is the key difference between people smuggling and human trafficking. For people who seek to leave their homes, whether they are fleeing conflict or persecution, or seeking better opportunities, official means of migration have become increasingly difficult as many countries have tightened their migration regimes and border controls. As a result, they often rely on irregular migration routes and actively seek out smugglers to facilitate their journey.

In contrast, human trafficking is done without the consent of those being trafficked, either through the use of force or other forms of coercion as outlined in the Palermo Protocol above. This includes deception, such as false promises of employment as a nanny or domestic worker, when in reality the individual will be working as a prostitute. Furthermore, if any coercive measures are used, such as deceit, fraud, or abuse of power, the Palermo Protocol states that consent is irrelevant. In Nigeria, even if girls are aware that they will be working as prostitutes, pressure from families, and even the use of *juju* to control them, undermines any consent. For individuals under eighteen years of age, none of these factors need to be employed for it to be considered trafficking. Their age defines the practice as human trafficking regardless, as they are deemed unable to give informed consent.

In reality, however, the distinction between people smuggling and human trafficking is not clearly defined, as even those who choose to move are vulnerable to a form of exploitation that meets the definition of human trafficking, particularly when they have clearly been deceived. The case study chapters have highlighted the fluidity of the movement between categories of people smuggling and human trafficking within each journey. Two examples stand out as particularly difficult to define whether a practice is people smuggling or human trafficking. First is the exploitation of migrants—those who choose to move but are vulnerable because of their irregular status and reliance on smugglers, who are still driven by a profit motive. Second is the deliberate smuggling of people into exploitative labour. In both instances, individuals have chosen to travel but end up in exploitative situations. The complexity of these cases requires a more nuanced response that respects the agency of the individual rather than treating them merely as victims.

Exploitation of Migrants

As many countries have tightened their migration controls, it has become much harder for migrants to access visas and board a plane to their intended destination. This is particularly true for those fleeing conflict or persecution, as there is a need to leave quickly and via the path of least resistance. As a result, many people on the move rely on irregular migration channels, usually paying smugglers to get them through border crossings and ultimately to their intended destination.

Irregular migration is defined by Albert Kraler and Dita Vogel as when a migrant 'at some point in his migration, has contravened the rules of entry or residence'.[13] This may involve illegal entry into a country, or overstaying a visa. Once the rules of migration have been contravened, the migrant does not have legitimate status, which makes them vulnerable to exploitation, particularly as they are reliant on smugglers to facilitate their journey. Their lack of status may mean they are unable to exercise their rights or seek redress because of fear of arrest or deportation. They may also be unaware of what recourse is available to them if they are exploited.

The potential for exploitation increases as the means to pay for the journey decrease. Migrants who are able to pay for their journey, whether upfront or in segments as they travel, are the most protected. They are in a position to negotiate with their smugglers, and these journeys usually end up being 'express'. Many migrants have ceased travelling with cash because of the risk it poses, instead having required amounts transferred along the journey. However, along many migration routes, the risk of kidnapping for ransom has increased as host communities seek to benefit from the transit of migrants, where the families of migrants are contacted and urged to send money or their family member will be tortured or killed. This occurs across North Africa, including Sudan, Niger, and Libya. The perceived wealth of migrants makes them a target for kidnapping, with various tactics for extracting ransoms. A number of cases in Libya have revealed the regularity with which migrants are beaten while family members are on the phone to coerce them into sending money. In some instances, this has resulted in family members selling property to pay ransoms.

Even for those who are not held to ransom, there is a reliance on their smugglers and a need to trust that they will hold up their end of the deal, often in countries with inadequate rule of law to protect migrants, or as mentioned above, when any form of redress is inaccessible because of the irregular status of migrants, or because authorities are complicit with smugglers. In many countries, the barriers to becoming a smuggler have decreased, particularly in countries bordering Libya.[14] As such, smuggling has become less organised and more ad hoc. Rather than an organised network that can support each node, the criminal network is now often formed of independent actors that pass migrants on to the next node along the route, being paid for their segment of the journey.[15] Many of these smugglers are inexperienced, and some cases have been reported of the smugglers fleeing danger, taking migrants' possessions and leaving them in the desert.[16] In some instances, each node will seek to extract as much as they can from the migrant.

Some migrants are able to pay for some of their journey, often the initial leg, and have the intention of working along the way to pay for each leg. This has become increasingly dangerous as growing numbers of people seek to profit from migration. Because they have some resources, they still tend to have a certain level of control over the work they do and for how long. As a result, they are less likely to be forced to work, or be held in debt bondage. But because of their irregular status, any work is likely to be below the standards available to local workers. They may be paid less, work longer hours, and risk wages being withheld, or fines being levied, and as in the scenario above, they have few options to hold employers to account. They also face similar risks in needing to trust their smugglers.

A third scenario emerges from migrants who are unable to pay for their journey. They are often talked into travelling by brokers who convince them that they can pay for their journey as they travel. These migrants have much less agency than the previous two scenarios, and may end up in debt bondage. Although they have chosen this path, they may have no control over the type of work they do, or for how long. In some instances, smugglers will arrange to be paid directly by employers, removing the migrant from the transaction altogether.[17] There have also been cases of smugglers selling migrants to other smugglers or traffickers to recoup their expenses.[18]

Although all of these cases concern consensual migration, each scenario has the potential to shift from people smuggling to human trafficking. In all cases, there is a high risk of abuse of power arising from the migrant's vulnerability and the potential for forced or exploitative labour. Deception also plays a role, particularly with brokers that persuade people to travel even when they lack the means to pay.

Many Ethiopians travel to Sudan to work. They are often approached by brokers who offer transportation in exchange for payment. Migrants agree a price, which many pay upfront, and commence their journey. The broker transports them towards the border, and at night they walk the last section until they find a second broker on the other side of the border, with a truck that will transport them the remainder of the journey. At this point, however, there is a second fee. Usually, several members of the group are raped or killed to 'encourage' the others to pay. Those who are still unable to generate the money may be sold on to traffickers, or forced into debt bondage in Khartoum. Even those who are able to pay are vulnerable in Khartoum. Work permits are no deterrent for police, who regularly round up migrant workers and tear up their papers, demanding bribes to release them.[19]

Even though these cases clearly become exploitative, those travelling have chosen to do so and would do so again if faced with the same choice. This is evident among many migrant groups who are well aware of the risks of their journey. For example, many Eritrean women who travel through Sudan in an attempt to reach Europe— aware of the potential for rape—use a long-term contraceptive to avoid getting pregnant. There is an argument to be made here about limited choice—particularly for those fleeing conscription in Eritrea. However, any response that treats individuals only as victims undermines their agency in choosing to migrate using the only means available.

Categorisation also becomes a question of resources at destination countries. It is reminiscent in many ways of the differentiation between refugees and migrants. If a large number of migrants are categorised as victims, this relativises the victim status of those who are genuinely and wholly trafficked and draws focus and resources away from the latter group. Migrants driven by a desire to improve their lives, and who undergo a journey with large risks of being exploited and who choose to work as prostitutes, are in a different category from those who are forced through violence and threats of violence against them and their families to serve as forced prostitutes, and enduring abuse, threats, and continued violence with no opportunity to escape.

Smuggling into Exploitation

The helpless victim/barbaric exploiter paradigm is no more clearly challenged than in the cases of Vietnamese and Albanian migration to the UK. Both nationalities have seen some of the largest numbers of 'potential victims of modern slavery' identified through the UK's NRM, and both cases involve substantial numbers of seemingly unaccompanied young men (and potential minors) entering the UK through illegal means. Many of these migrants 'disappear' upon arrival, having integrated into their national communities. For minors who are identified, there is also a pattern with both nationalities absconding from foster care and safe housing for victims of modern slavery. The circumstances under which these young men and minors abscond, and whether traffickers are involved in forcing or coercing them, are not known, but to present these individuals simply as 'slaves' ignores the process and agency through which they may have taken the decision to migrate in the first instance, and the reasons why they may be refusing protection, and thus in effect upholding their desire to continue what they are doing, despite difficult conditions.

Vietnamese migration to the UK has taken place in phases since the 1970s, with irregular migration occurring from the late 1980s.[20] Research into migratory movement from Vietnam to the UK overwhelmingly shows that the main drivers for migration are economic, with migrants working illegally upon arrival, usually within Vietnamese businesses.

The UK's response to illegal migration from Vietnam has been framed by the modern slavery agenda. The primary focus has been on cannabis farms, where previously Vietnamese minors were arrested for their involvement in illegal activity but are now treated as victims. Concerns have also been raised around unsafe migration and the risks posed to Vietnamese migrants and the element of debt bondage and exploitation of minors in nail bars and farms. These are all valid concerns, but the impression from both media sources and NRM statistics that depict hundreds of Vietnamese slaves and slave-drivers in the UK is complicated by research showing that the trafficking victim label does not fit so easily with many of these cases.

While the conditions in which many Vietnamese migrants work are clearly exploitative, the realities of restricted choice resulting from irregular migration status, the pressure to both provide for and not disappoint family back home, and the belief that anything here is better than back home leads to decisions that are forced not necessarily by a criminal but by a multitude of conditions. Contradicting the image many may have of people being forced from Vietnam to the UK, migration to the UK (which is often long, difficult, and risky) is carefully considered—families are consulted, factors weighed up, including which smuggling ring to choose from, and as one interviewee asserted, many people still find ways to travel clandestinely to the UK regardless of financial and life-threatening risks; indeed, some may even try to re-migrate after a failed attempt.[21]

Moreover, interviews with returnees suggests that a large proportion of migrants knew they would be working in cannabis cultivation, despite the risk and horrendous conditions this entails, and have chosen to do so since the alternative opportunities as an illegal worker would never recover the debt they had incurred by travelling.[22] One interviewee linked the tightening of immigration laws to the restricted options available to Vietnamese workers, who may previously have been able to work in legal establishments such as restaurants, and have thus been pushed into illegal activity, or activities through which they could be easily exploited.[23] Where in many cases exploitation by a facilitator or 'employer' is not claimed, the exploitation was said to have manifested in different ways, that is, resulting from their undocumented status, leaving migrants reliant upon agents and intermediaries who will inevitably take a proportion of earnings.

As noted above, in many people smuggling situations, most migrants buy this service as the only one available to them, and like effective salespeople, facilitators may sell migrants a picture of wealth and opportunity at the end, omitting information of the difficult reality resulting from precarious status in a country with uncompromising immigration laws. Legally, this deception shifts migrants into the human trafficking category, but many migrants may have made the same decision even if they knew the outcome.

Despite an attractive pitch from facilitators, however, research has also shown the often rational and considered decision-making involved in migration, even for such a difficult journey as from Vietnam to the UK. Within the information-gathering stage of the decision process, the role of the family and family consultation in migration is fundamental for Vietnamese nationals, as almost all of those who choose to migrate are thought to consult family members beforehand.[24]

Similar to those who migrate from Vietnam, the role of the family is extremely important in the decision for teenagers and young males to migrate to the UK from Albania. In this particular case, parents may actively facilitate part of the movement, with the intention of the minor remaining in Europe for asylum, where prospects—though precarious—are certainly viewed as better than those within the area from which they have come. These decisions to migrate are celebrated within towns in Albania, just as they are in Vietnam. A side effect of this celebration is the pressure for the young migrating male to pay back the money owed for the journey and earn sufficient money to send back to their home country to support their family. Perhaps it is unsurprising, then, that it is within these two nationalities that the UK sees a high amount of absconding from foster parents or safe houses for trafficked victims. Residing in foster care does not create income for these young men, which is the main preoccupation because of the burden of debt and fulfilling the intention of migrating, which was to earn money.

The issue of child migration is a larger and separate discussion, but of relevance here are the differing perceptions of the appropriate age for a child or young person to leave their country and earn money for the family. For Albanian families, for example, that may be from the age of fifteen.[25] In the UK, this may be viewed as abandonment, coercion, or even trafficking, and as Samantha Punch asserts, instead of recognising a conscious strategy aimed at reducing the economic vulnerability of both the migrant and the family in the future, 'children's migration experiences have usually been assumed to be negative'.[26] Punch speaks of the 'need to move away from minority world assumptions that independent child migration is a necessarily exploitative or damaging experience for children'.[27] Of course, in the case of Albanian and Vietnamese migration, the dangers throughout the journey arise from using 'illegal' means and under the auspices of people committing criminal acts (i.e. smuggling). In some cases, that may mean being exploited along the journey for labour and sex, but in others just by the nature of these migrants being reliant upon smugglers, their ability for freedom is restricted.

Similarly, the illegal status of both Albanian and Vietnamese migrants when attempting to earn money in the UK leads them to illegal trades and thus criminal groups. Criminal groups are of course taking advantage of this supply of illegal minors and young people who are ready to work, but the idea that these migrants are passive is problematic. Faced with such restrictions on legal work, and the pressure of making such a journey to the UK and with a substantial sum to pay back to facilitators, and no legal way to earn that money, it is unsurprising that migrants are pushed into illegal trade and choose to stay there rather than be labelled slaves and rescued by the state. One interviewee termed it a 'gambling game' for Vietnamese migrants. For both Vietnam and Albania, it is clear that while migrants may be well aware of the risks, it is still worth the gamble, as it is for many who decide to migrate irregularly, as Julia O'Connell Davidson concedes: 'research on debt-financed migration shows migrants are often well aware of the risks with which it is associated, but choose to proceed nonetheless because the potential benefits to migration are so great'.[28]

Individuals are exploited when they have limited choices, and others will be ready to take advantage of that lack of choice, exploiting these individuals to make a profit. Often, those who choose to leave the situation they are in do so determinedly, and while it is of course dangerous to ignore the risks that then come upon them, it can be equally dangerous to take away these people's agency and merely call them victims who have been naively trusting of a ruthless criminal. O'Connell Davidson points out that many of those who are considered trafficking victims 'invariably want to move, and generally have excellent reasons for wishing to do so'.[29]

Those who take advantage of young people for criminal gain, using them as pawns, clearly need to be prevented from doing so. But viewing these dynamics solely through the prism of young passive actors who have been coerced and duped by exploitative criminals and thus requiring an aggressive crime control response is inadequate to describe and thus address the active choices that adults, minors, and their families may make—in many instances as a result precisely of the lack of choice for economic advancement in their own national contexts, and the driver of their position in dangerous, underpaid work, which is often their position as illegal persons. Protection and

145

safeguarding of the most vulnerable is rightly the priority when it comes to addressing situations of potential danger and exploitation.

Beyond that, understanding debt-financed migration through the binaries of forced/voluntary, trafficked victims/illegal criminal is not sufficient to describe most of these situations and undermines the self-determination of these people, which thereby removes the need to look further into the complexities of why people choose to put themselves into a path they know can be dangerous. Seeing them as subjugated and lacking in self-determination strips them of agency, which further undermines efforts to understand what it is that really pushes people into acceptance of anything from low pay to relations with an exploitative agent. Understanding the drivers as well as the situations that create demand for criminal enterprises is the only way to effectively address exploitation.

What This Means for Responses

The division between people smuggling and human trafficking has consequences for the response. In most cases, the response tends to engage with one or the other rather than the blurred line in-between.

As a crime against the state, people smuggling justifies activities that strengthen borders and makes migration more difficult. This has the potential to increase the risk of exploitation. As migration becomes more difficult, migrants—including asylum seekers—need to rely on criminal actors to bypass borders and border officials to ensure access to the desired destination country. Yet at the same time, opening up borders is not an alternative for states that have made political decisions to restrict certain types of migration. But for the individual migrants there is a risk transfer taking place when there is a crackdown on people smuggling. As people smuggling is a crime against the state, the countermeasures place the individuals who are smuggled at more risk. The question of agency is important here, because the responsibility does lie exclusively with the facilitators, as it does in the case of trafficking. The migrants are undergoing the journey in large measure of their own volition and decision-making. In many cases, this happens even if there is knowledge of the risks it entails, for example after a border crossing has become even more restrictive and rerouting is more expensive and dangerous the migrants may still decide to continue on their original route. In contrast, responses to human trafficking are victim-centred and seek to repair the damage done by traffickers. This is the aim of the UK NRM—providing support for exploited individuals. Trafficking cases are more straightforward in this context, as the people involved are easier to categorise as victims.

In the UK, the victim-centred response does not always meet the needs or desires of those it targets. It may be an actively unwanted intervention. Instead, migrants may be angry at the loss of their livelihood or the prospect of being sent back home. They may also be upset by the perceived waste of the resources that were invested in their travel by their families and/or communities. The result is a disjuncture between a human rights-based approach and what migrants actually want. For example, Tuesday Reitano argues that 'often what the international community labels as human trafficking are in fact locally acceptable labour practices that offer the only meaningful employment available'.[30] The challenge, then, is to prioritise between what are harmful cases in both trafficking crimes against victims, and illegal border crossing crimes against the state. And further to prioritise between types of situation and intervene in the worst cases. Such priorities clearly must make the balancing act between the use of resources, the consequences of inaction, and reducing suffering in a crime type where the product is human beings.

Along irregular migration routes, donors and NGOs are beginning to engage with the blurred line between people smuggling and human trafficking. Safe houses and referral mechanisms are being developed in primary transit hubs. In Sudan, for example, the EU-funded Better Migration Management programme is supporting the National Action Plan to Combat Human Trafficking with safe houses and referral mechanisms, which respond to exploitation that has occurred to migrants along their journey. However, attempts to prevent exploitation shift back to a people smuggling response—seeking to arrest and prosecute the smugglers.

This chapter does not seek to downplay the importance of protecting and supporting victims of exploitation and abuse. But there is space for a more nuanced approach that engages with the needs of migrants who have chosen to travel in order to improve their circumstances.

The binary and persistent terms that produce a helpless victim and a barbaric perpetrator need to be constantly interrogated so that a complicated reality is not met with a simplistic response.

In many cases, what is needed are initiatives that make migration safer, and thus less exploitative. However, this contravenes the current approaches to migration taken by many of the destination countries for migrants. In order to address the nuances of exploitation and agency effectively, human trafficking and people smuggling would be better viewed through a migration lens, as different variants of a similar phenomenon. This would open the door to mapping the role of agency, the groups facilitating migration, and the desires of those on the move, to identify better solutions.

9

A CRIMINAL PYRAMID SCHEME

Sasha Jesperson

The system thrives on the fact that recruits for the sex industry are not actually trafficked—meaning taken against their will—but are socially obligated to take part in a very exploitative business.

—Stephen Ellis[1]

Regardless of the level of agency of victims, the movement of people through illegal border crossings and their exploitation remains a criminal endeavour, whether the crime is perpetrated against the individual in cases of human trafficking, or against the state, in cases of people smuggling. The level of organisation of this criminal enterprise differs from case to case. It ranges from a highly organised hierarchy to a cell-based model or even an ad hoc model that draws on social networks. As with other forms of organised crime, the facilitators of smuggling and trafficking are seeking to minimise the risk of their activities and to maximise their profit.

Chapter 1 outlined some of the key differences in human trafficking compared with other forms of organised crime, in particular the impact of a human commodity in transportation and control. However, the human commodity also presents an opportunity for criminal actors— they can be manipulated to support the criminal endeavour. All of the case studies highlighted that human trafficking has shifted away from common perceptions of kidnapping and coercion, with victims instead being controlled in other ways. Sometimes this is coercive, such as the use of *juju* rituals in Nigeria, but increasingly it is by instilling a belief that victims or their families have something to gain.

Because of the different factors that push people into human trafficking or people smuggling, the industry constitutes a pyramid scheme of criminals, families and communities, and victims, where everyone is trying to maximise their own gains. The result is that there is too much to lose by turning in perpetrators, which would undermine the potential for victims and their families to benefit. However, this challenges a response that seeks to undermine the criminality. This chapter explores how organised crime more broadly has evolved to minimise risk before focusing specifically on human trafficking, drawing on the four case studies to highlight the emergence of a criminal pyramid scheme.

Minimising Risk

Organised crime is renowned for its agile and dynamic nature and ability to remain two steps ahead of law enforcement. This adaptability was cited by Marc Goodman in the *Harvard Business Review* in a think piece discussing what business can learn from organised crime. Goodman was referring to the use of technology by the attackers of the Taj Mahal Palace Hotel in Mumbai in 2008, which resulted in 'one of the best orchestrated, most technologically advanced terrorist strikes in history'.[2] One of the lessons was to outsource to specialists, highlighting how the hierarchical structures of mafia-type organisations have long been abandoned for more agile networks that bring in individuals with specific expertise. This has been increasingly important with the rise of credit card fraud and other online criminal activity. Europol's 2017 Serious and Organised Crime Threat Assessment (SOCTA) recognised this as an emerging feature of criminal markets, where organised crime groups openly advertised ad hoc opportunities, and particularly with online crime, the true identity of these individuals may never be known.

This is just one example of how organised crime has evolved to avoid detection and disruption. The 'balloon effect'—where effective

150

law enforcement activity pushes crime in new directions—has been well documented, particularly in relation to the drugs trade. Heavy-handed American responses to the cocaine trade stemming from Colombia, Bolivia, and Peru to the United States via the Caribbean or Central America, for example, led cartels to open up supply to European markets, sending container loads across the Atlantic from ports in Venezuela or Brazil. But a series of large interdictions called for intermediaries, and Colombian cartels in particular sought transit hubs in West Africa as a decoy, resulting in the restoration of 'Highway 10' and the transformation of Guinea Bissau into a narco-state.[3]

However, a shift in route has not been the only way organised crime has evolved. The primary focus has been removing risk to evade arrest even if some of the product is lost in the process. For example, many high-value commodities, such as drugs and weapons, have traditionally relied on high-volume transfers. Drug trafficking originally relied on multi-tonne shipments, which are easier to detect and constitute a larger blow to the drug trafficking organisation when seized.

Organised crime networks are increasingly shifting to low-volume, high-frequency activity. As Charlie Edwards and Calum Jeffray point out in their report on the illicit trade in tobacco, alcohol, and pharmaceuticals in the UK, 'organised crime groups have begun to realise that law enforcement agencies find it much more difficult to respond to illicit trade when goods are broken down and transported in smaller consignments'.[4] These strategies have made the illicit trade in tobacco, alcohol, and pharmaceuticals particularly lucrative because there is a 'lower risk of detection, and sanctions for offences are typically less severe'.[5] As a result, it has become a key strategy for minimising the risk associated with criminality.

However, an important feature in the illicit trade in tobacco, alcohol, and pharmaceuticals is the difficulty involved in distinguishing it from the trade in legitimate commodities. In many instances, organised crime networks are merely engaging in tax evasion but with genuine products. This does not mean it does not do serious damage—between 1994 and 2002, the Montenegrin economy was kept afloat through cigarette smuggling.[6] Once passed on to the end market, these goods cannot be separated from those imported officially.

When high-value commodities are too lucrative for organised crime networks to ignore, the networks that facilitate trafficking seek to distance themselves from the actual transaction. For decades, the higher-level members of drug trafficking organisations have been far removed from the actual production and distribution of drugs, making them difficult to target in law enforcement operations. The use of drug mules, for example, was adopted to move drugs because, if they are arrested, there is no direct link between them and the organised crime network that employed them, and only a small amount of product is seized. When cocaine trafficking was at its peak in West Africa, flights would have scores of mules on the same plane because law enforcement could not arrest them all. In one operation, every passenger on a flight from Nigeria was searched, and as more than 100 were found to be carrying cocaine, there was no more capacity to keep searching.[7]

Other methods have also been adopted. Rather than using light aircraft and yachts to move cocaine across the Atlantic, the tactic of rip-on/rip-off was used. This tactic involves a smaller quantity of drugs being placed inside a container just before it is sealed, and removed as soon as it arrives, before customs search the full container. Such a strategy relies on bribing the appropriate people, but it results in high-frequency, low-volume shipments that displace the risk to lower levels of the criminal network.

For people smuggling, criminal networks have developed strategies to remove their presence altogether. At the beginning of the 'migrant crisis' in 2014 and 2015, two ships were intercepted en route from Turkey to Italy. The *Blue Sky M*, with nearly 1,000 passengers aboard, was intercepted on 31 December 2014 in Greek waters,[8] and the *Ezadeen*, with over 350 passengers on board, was brought into an Italian port on 2 January 2015.[9] Both of these vessels had been left without crew and were sailing on autopilot. On the *Blue Sky M*, one of the passengers, Rani Sark, was reportedly promised a payment of USD 10,000 to control the ship. People who are prepared to risk their lives to escape conflict are then left to face the consequences, while those facilitating the trade remain unidentified and continue to be able to fill boats with more willing passengers.

In line with the entrepreneurialism frequently attributed to criminal groups, this phenomenon took advantage of European policies to ensure the safety of passengers after the boats were abandoned, which promotes ongoing business. The Italian government stepped up its patrols of the Mediterranean in October 2013 after two boats carrying migrants from Libya sank off the island of Lampedusa.[10] Frontex, the EU's border agency, also launched a surveillance mission in the Mediterranean in October 2014 to control the area, monitor the border, and carry out search-and-rescue operations.[11] These operations ensured that passengers were not left to drown. But they also resulted in the prosecution of many people smugglers, requiring a new strategy from criminal groups. By leaving the boats without crew, criminal groups evade law enforcement and can continue their activities.

People smugglers use many of the existing skills of criminal groups. The boats have all been flying flags of countries with inadequate regulations for shipping companies, or that lack the capacity to monitor vessels, such as Sierra Leone, Moldova, and Tonga. This allows criminal groups to use boats that are discarded by shipping companies and sold off cheaply for scrap metal. It also makes it difficult to track the owners of the ships. These tactics are used in other forms of illicit activity such as drug trafficking and illegal fishing. Another form of illicit entrepreneurship, this approach fits with a new trend of criminal groups avoiding violence so as not to draw attention to their activities. They also provide good conditions for passengers, with reports of mattresses and other comforts on board, thereby maintaining a positive reputation and ensuring future business. Criminal groups have also managed to distance themselves from the activity, making it difficult to disrupt.

Controlling a Human Commodity

Criminal networks involved in human trafficking, however, do not have the same capacity to distance themselves from their commodity. The challenge for networks that facilitate human trafficking is that their 'commodity' can escape and tell authorities about their ordeal. This requires strategies to control the commodity.

The movement of human trafficking victims employs similar strategies to drug trafficking, using foot soldiers to recruit, transit, or control victims.[12] But because human trafficking victims are 'enduring if replaceable "commodities" that are consumed repeatedly rather than just once',[13] the potential for continued profit has resulted in more innovative control mechanisms.

The Polaris Project reports that

> traffickers employ a variety of control tactics, including physical and emotional abuse, sexual assault, confiscation of identification and money, isolation from friends and family, and even renaming victims. Often, traffickers identify and leverage their victims' vulnerabilities in order to create dependency. They make promises aimed at addressing the needs of their target in order to impose control. As a result, victims become trapped and fear leaving for a myriad of reasons, including; psychological trauma, shame, emotional attachment, or physical threats to themselves or their children's safety.[14]

More than one strategy is employed, as traffickers identify what is likely to work with a particular victim and exploit it.

Because of the need for control, human trafficking is renowned for being violent. Misha Glenny found that Bulgarian organised crime networks that became involved in sexual exploitation regularly used rape and violence to coerce their victims into submission.[15] But it is not just physical violence that is used. Elizabeth Hopper and José Hidalgo highlight how psychological abuse and coercion is easier to conceal: 'coercive systems utilize high levels of control, exposure to chronic stress and threat, isolation, provocation of fear, and the creation of a sense of helplessness in victims'.[16] Given the vulnerability of many victims when they are in a country other than their own, these tactics are extremely effective. Much more is understood about the control of victims of sexual exploitation, but Kevin Bales et al. report that psychological abuse is also applied to victims of labour exploitation: 'cut off from contact with the outside world, they can lose their sense of personal efficacy and control, attributes that mental health professionals have long considered essential to good mental and physical health'.[17]

A growing body of research has emerged on control methods linked to sexual exploitation. This can include the confiscation of travel documents, the use of violence, the threat to harm family members, and financial dependency upon the human trafficker.[18] These categories have been expanded by Donna Hughes, who explored the form of isolation and threats, as well as shame, humiliation, and culturally specific forms of control through an analysis of sex trafficking from Ukraine.[19] Based on empirical research on the sex trade in the Netherlands, Maria Ioannou and Miriam Oostinga have developed a typology—victims as objects, involving direct possession and subjugation of victims; victims as vehicles, involving emotional and psychological control through threats; and victims as persons, involving control through manipulation.[20]

What has been found across all forms of violence, whether physical or psychological, is that victims become 'increasingly dependent on the perpetrator, not only for survival and basic bodily needs, but also for information and even for emotional sustenance'.[21] This has been linked to 'Stockholm syndrome', the term developed to explain the relationship that often emerges between hostages and their hostage-takers, where they become protective of their captor. This emerges from a combination of a perceived threat to survival, perception of kindness (even if it follows severe abuse), isolation, and a perceived inability to escape.[22] The result is that victims are reluctant to testify against their traffickers, meaning that law enforcement needs to rely on other methods to build a case.[23] The knock-on effect is that authorities see victims as unreliable. The Centre for Social Justice uncovered cases where law enforcement had been working on cases for over a year before victims decided to withdraw from providing oral evidence.[24]

For traffickers, this is an ideal situation, as it has been difficult to build cases without victim testimony. As discussed in Chapter 1, many of the evidence collection techniques applied to other forms of organised crime are dangerous to victims of human trafficking. However, controlling victims is a resource-intensive activity. In some examples, trafficking networks have employed people specifically to manage the control of victims. In the same vein as the strategies above to remove risk and increase profit, human traffickers have also sought out other control mechanisms that are more cost effective.

Moving to Less Direct Forms of Control

One factor that crosses all forms of criminality is that criminal groups adapt their activity to the market dynamics that are present. Accordingly, how each type of criminality adapts will differ and thus needs careful analysis. The cases investigated in this book reveal a criminal pyramid scheme, where all layers are complicit in denying and hiding the criminality.

When presented as an organised crime problem, 'criminals are presented as the main beneficiaries of human trafficking'.[25] But the situation is more complex than this binary distinction suggests. Offenders are generally established as the polar opposite of victims, but in many cases this distinction is inappropriate as many traffickers were previously trafficked and have worked their way up to become the exploiters.[26] This is evident in the Nigerian case, where the goal of many girls travelling to Europe is to become a madam.

For the Nigerian trafficking industry, a series of control measures have been put in place to reduce the need for violence. This is not to say that violence is completely removed from the transaction—in Libya, as conditions have deteriorated, violence has become commonplace. However, to control women and girls, *juju* rituals have been used extensively. During the ritual, the girls' hair or nails are taken and they swear an oath to the deity. This process binds the girl to the contract to repay her debt for transportation. Girls are genuinely scared of the ritual and believe they will be plagued by nightmares or go crazy if they do not fulfil their obligation.

The use of *juju* manipulates culturally specific conventions to control girls in order to minimise the need for direct oversight. The girls instead self-discipline as they are indirectly controlled by their fear of *juju*. This is particularly useful when they are working on the street and not directly controlled. NGOs providing assistance to Nigerian girls state that *juju* prevents the girls from sharing their experiences. In one case, a young woman took months to reveal her story, sharing a little bit at a time to test what would happen.[27]

Other mechanisms are also used in case the power of *juju* is not enough. In some cases, a contract is signed by a lawyer and the girl's family, adding another layer of pressure to adhere to the agreement. When girls breach the contract, there are often reprisals against the family. For example, one girl went to the police in Ceuta, Spain, and her family's home was promptly burnt down.[28]

These control mechanisms have been coming under increased pressure. Counsellors have been working with trafficked women to overcome the belief in *juju*. The Oba, or monarch, of Benin City in Edo State has also placed a curse on perpetrators of human trafficking and traditional priests who conduct *juju* rituals with girls about to be trafficked, and the Edo State governor is also condemning the use of *juju*.[29]

Accordingly, a different strategy emerged in parallel. Within Nigeria, there is a powerful narrative of success linked to making it in Europe. As long as girls return with money, no questions are asked about the work they were doing. These returning girls are then powerful and can even 'buy a husband'.[30] Previously, madams would visit Benin City with their expensive clothes to appeal to girls and young women and offer them work in Europe. As awareness around the nature of the work increased, it is mostly acknowledged that they are madams that worked their way up. This creates an aspiration among girls travelling to Europe to become madams—they all think they will be one of the lucky ones, even though they have to make it through three to five years of hard work first to pay off their debt.[31] However, these aspirations prevent girls from speaking about the criminal facilitators of trafficking, as their ultimate goal is to move up in the business.

The pressure from families and the broader community creates a middle layer of pressure to maintain silence around the criminal actors involved in trafficking. As discussed in Chapter 2, the economy of Edo State in Nigeria is heavily reliant on the income from trafficking. This has resulted in civil society organisations that seek to prevent trafficking coming under attack. Families that invest in the girls want to see a return on their investment. If the girls call home to complain about the conditions, a common response is along the lines of 'so-and-so's daughter made enough to buy them a house'.

The Nigerian example highlights the emergence of a criminal pyramid scheme—the criminal facilitators, including recruiters, transporters, and madams who make the most money and have an interest in maintaining discretion are at the top of the pyramid. The middle layer includes families and communities that are eager to profit from the exploitation of young women and girls. Accordingly, they are not going to speak out about the trafficking industry. At the bottom of the pyramid are the trafficked girls themselves. Some of the girls have been silenced by *juju* or a contract demanding they repay their debts. But increasingly, these girls are driven by aspirations to become madams themselves, which helps maintain their silence.

While the presence of a criminal pyramid scheme is the most obvious in the Nigerian case, its presence is identifiable in any case where the distinction between human trafficking and people smuggling is not clear-cut, in any case where the 'victim' has something to gain. In Sudan, for instance, there have been examples of direct involvement by police or authorities in the transportation of migrants. However, there have been numerous examples where authorities are paid off by smugglers to allow passage or look the other way. There have been cases of police taking migrants out of camps and handing them over to smugglers. In one case, several refugees were removed from Wad Sharifa camp in mid-2017. Police guards were tied up, which made it appear to be a kidnapping, but the refugees were found in the desert waiting for smugglers.[32] In this example, the migrants became complicit with the smugglers, even though there was a risk that the relationship may become exploitative and shift into the category of human trafficking.

When the relationship becomes exploitative along the journey, migrants have no avenue to recourse, or do not know what avenues exist, so they are unable to report exploitation, thus contributing to the impunity of their exploiters. One entrepreneurial resident of Kassala State spent her days by the *hafir* (water pond) with a large stick. When migrants approached to drink from the *hafir*, she charged them 5 Sudanese pounds, threatening to call the police if they did not pay. Not wanting to be picked up by police, the migrants paid or refrained from drinking, but they did not seek to have the water broker arrested or removed. As such, she was able to continue collecting revenue from migrants passing by.

This is perhaps a minor example compared with the silence regarding large-scale trafficking networks, but it is indicative of a larger trend—unless the exploitation exceeds the perceived potential benefit of the migrant, they will remain silent. Some of the trafficking victims are strongly motivated, or have been so brutalised that they have a high threshold for complaining, if that is even possible. This is why part of the role of brokers and smugglers is the selling of a dream—they need the perception of benefit to be significant enough to excuse horrific practices. As seen by the Eritrean women who make use of long-term contraceptive implants because they are aware of the likelihood of rape or sexual assault along their journey, the perceived benefit of arriving in Europe has made this worth the risk.

In the case of minors from Albania and Vietnam, there are parallels to the family and community pressure placed on Nigerian girls. In Albania, minors usually come from middle-class families that may have to sell their house to send their child to Europe or the UK, and there is an expectation that this will be repaid. The process is similar in Vietnam, but it is more likely that the family will enter into debt bondage, with an implicit threat of violence. To earn enough to repay these debts and contribute to family income, these minors often end up in exploitative industries—from cannabis farms to nail bars to drug distribution—because of the earning potential. The Centre for Social Justice found that 'traffickers often do not need to resort to physical violence which would make the exploitation more visible. Trafficked children do not consider themselves to be in an exploitative situation, but rather perceive their exploitation as loyalty to their family.'[33] Accordingly, in these cases, neither the family nor the child will reveal the criminal facilitators that brought them to their destination.

Conclusion

Criminals have always had an interest in being discreet in order to avoid attracting unwanted attention from law enforcement. This was the driving force behind the reduction of violence and the increasingly business-like nature of organised crime groups. Each form of criminality has also developed tactics to strengthen the profit-making potential of their activities and minimise risk.

Traditionally, human trafficking has been violent and coercive, relying on complicity from border officials to facilitate passage to destination countries. However, the cases discussed in this book reveal new modalities. By giving communities, families, and even victims a stake in the business—an aspiration that they will benefit, even if distant—they are more likely to be complicit and protect the criminal groups that facilitate their movement. This approach builds on the methods of psychological control that traffickers have used in the past and minimises the need for more physical forms of control, leading to the emergence of criminal pyramid schemes where all parties have an interest in protecting the business.

10

CONCLUSION

A COMPLEX CRIMINAL PICTURE

Rune Henriksen and *Sasha Jesperson*

As human trafficking has been prioritised around the world, many assumptions have been made. The UK government summarises modern slavery as 'working long hours for little or no money or food, forced into a life of crime or pushed into the sex industry. Their entire life and liberty is in the hands of another, with no say and no way out.'[1] In a similar vein, the role of organised crime has been pinpointed as the crux of the problem, with increasing resources going to law enforcement agencies to address human trafficking.

These perspectives are mirrored in media portrayals. One edited collection reviewed representations of human trafficking, traffickers, and victims, finding that 'victims are idealised, with those not according to this ideal being criminalised'.[2] Gillian Wylie argues that the popular understanding of human trafficking is 'based on, unreliable statistics, maps and visual images, and selective, binary, and simplified representations'.[3]

The challenge of this simplified view is that it informs the policy response—resulting in myriad unintended consequences and a human trafficking problem that will not go away. For instance, the criminalisation of people smuggling in Europe, but also in transit hubs such as Niger, has inadvertently created a lucrative role for sophisticated criminal networks.

But perhaps most worrying is assumptions around the nature of organised criminal involvement. A nuanced understanding of the form, nature, and tactics of criminal networks involved in trafficking is sorely lacking. As a result, the response that is applied is not targeted. Rather, it draws more lessons from other forms of criminality, such as drug trafficking, which do not easily transfer across when the commodity is a human being.

This book has sought to investigate the relationship between organised crime and human trafficking, focusing on three countries that have become a primary source for trafficking to Europe, and the UK specifically—Nigeria, Albania, and Vietnam. As the blurred line between trafficking and smuggling became apparent throughout the research, a fourth case was added to understand the dynamics when movement began as consensual: the movement of Eritreans into Sudan and farther north.

Across these case studies, a complicated picture emerged of organised crime in that it rarely fits a hierarchical, mafia model, but was much more dispersed. Two trends were clear, however, in all four case studies—how frequently individuals move between the categories of human trafficking and people smuggling, and compounding this, the emergence of a criminal pyramid scheme, where victims, their families, and communities become complicit in trafficking because they believe they have something to gain.

Nigeria

Nigeria is notorious for organised crime—with regular attention focused on its 'imaginative criminals, formed into organisations with international reach'.[4] Similar attention has been paid to human trafficking, highlighting the role of university cults, including the Black Axe and Air Lords (or Supreme Eiye), which reportedly have networks across Europe to facilitate the movement and exploitation of young women and girls.[5] Whereas sex trafficking had previously relied on air transportation, the bribing of airport officials, and knowledge of immigration loopholes in Europe, the dynamics of the trade have now changed. The overland route had always functioned, mostly for the movement of economic migrants to Libya or farther afield. However, as security at MMIA airport in Lagos increased, and Libya descended into a governance vacuum, the popularity of the overland route increased exponentially. Accordingly, the barrier to entry for traffickers, at least at the recruitment and transportation level, dropped dramatically.

Madams became the controllers of the industry, and while they relied on others to transport girls to Europe, they were rarely involved directly, except for paying the way of those girls who did not pay upfront. This effectively established two parallel criminal networks—transporters and exploiters. However, neither resembled a hierarchical criminal network. Transporters tend to operate along a certain part of the journey, before passing the girls on to another transporter, resulting in a cell-based network where each node is easily replaced, and often has multiple individuals working along each stage of the journey. Once they have paid off their debts, some girls become madams, bringing additional girls to Europe to work below them. They usually rely on their social and family networks to recruit girls but in Europe work mostly independently with staff to support them. There are reports of networks of madams that agree on whether girls can become madams themselves to control the industry.

Along the route, conditions are regularly changing, with the journey becoming increasingly dangerous since 2018. In an attempt to prevent people smuggling and human trafficking, the Nigerien government introduced anti-smuggling legislation in 2015, criminalising the movement of people north of Agadez. This effectively removed regular transporters from the industry, undermining their livelihood and creating a market that only more sophisticated criminals could fill. In Libya, fighting between militias has increased the costs of transportation, with most if not all girls having to work as prostitutes as they are passed from node to node, resulting in high levels of exploitation before they reach Europe.

Albania

Albania also has a reputation for organised crime; indeed, the Albanian mafia is infamous for violence throughout Western Europe. Despite strong beliefs to the contrary, Albanian organised crime has not been heavily involved in human trafficking. Trafficking from Albania garnered widespread attention in the 1990s when the 'loverboy' tactic was widespread—men posing as lovers to young women, persuading them to travel to Europe and then telling them they had to work as prostitutes to make enough money for the couple to survive. These operations tended to be small scale, with at most a small group of men working together to pimp out the girls they had deceived.

For the Albanian mafia, human trafficking is not as lucrative as other illicit activities, particularly drug trafficking. Where the two activities do intersect is when human trafficking is used to generate the capital to become involved in more lucrative criminal activities.

As the loverboy tactic is now widely known, it has become less effective, although it is still attempted with vulnerable girls. Increasingly, however, Albanian pimps are working with Romanian prostitutes or Albanian women who have consented to travelling to Europe to work as prostitutes. Yet even when it is consensual, the relationship is usually violent and controlling.

A growing business of people smuggling has emerged in Albania. Typically, those facilitating smuggling are not the same as those who have been involved in trafficking. This usually involves the transportation of unaccompanied minors into Europe and particularly the UK. This is where the intersection with the Albanian mafia is likely to occur. Because these unaccompanied minors are undocumented, they cannot find legitimate employment on their arrival and may end up working with established criminal groups distributing drugs.

Vietnam

The movement of Vietnamese throughout South East Asia is longstanding, but movement to Europe has increasingly come under the spotlight. The UK government has identified that 'Vietnamese organised crime networks also recruit and transport Vietnamese nationals, especially children, to Europe, and particularly the UK, where victims are often subjected to forced labour on cannabis farms.'[6] This is an organised business, where families are usually involved in having their children sent to Europe. Movement either takes place through the overland route via Russia, which relies on collaboration between Russian, Chechen, and Vietnamese smugglers and is more convenient because visas are easy to obtain, or a more expensive route that involves flights to mainland Europe and then onward transportation.

Eritrea

The Eritrean case is different from the others as it begins as consensual movement, with Eritreans fleeing political conscription. They recruit smugglers to move them across the border into Sudan and farther north—either to Egypt or Libya, before continuing to Europe. However, this case highlights the difficulties in categorising irregular migrants along the smuggling/trafficking spectrum. Once in Sudan, Eritreans can register as refugees but do not have the right to work or travel without a permit. As their goal is to move out of the country, they are reliant on smugglers who are eager for profit. Accordingly, reports of exploitation are rife, particularly when migrants have to earn money along the way to pay for their journey. Bonded labour in gold mines, domestic work, tea shops, and even prostitution are common. For those able to pay, kidnap for ransom is commonplace. Even host communities seek to exploit migrants—charging for drinking water or threatening to call the police. Once migrants reach Libya, the potential for exploitation only increases.

As Liz Kelly indicates, 'the length of the journey increases the probability that a person is coerced or deceived, as well as exploited, as longer journeys increase people's vulnerability'.[7] While Eritreans start their journey being smuggled, for many it transitions into trafficking. As with Nigerians, the networks are cell-based, with smugglers fighting for business and even stealing each other's 'cartons' of victims, before selling them on to the next node who will recoup the fee and an additional profit before selling them on again. Within Sudan, there is very little recourse for exploited migrants, although this is increasing with the work of the National Committee for Combating Human Trafficking (NCCT).

The Spectrum between Smuggling and Trafficking

The prioritisation of human trafficking has portrayed the phenomenon as a violent practice with passive victims. However, all four cases have highlighted that this is not the case. Sex trafficking from Albania and Nigeria was originally coercive, with girls deceived into travelling, and control measures put in place. In Nigeria, this was commonly through *juju* rituals. For Albania, the tight-knit community made threats against the family a plausible measure.

However, there is increasing awareness of the kind of work girls are getting into, and while deception and control still play a role, there is a certain level of consent—even if it is driven by family or community pressure. Although there are limited choices for girls in Albania and Nigeria for sustainable and lucrative livelihoods, their journey into sex work does not entail an absolute lack of agency, particularly when girls aspire to become madams in order to make substantial profit.

In contrast, those who begin their journey consensually are often criminalised for seeking to breach border restrictions. Even though they have chosen to travel, they lack a legitimate status in transit and destination countries, which means they are vulnerable to the type of exploitation that fits the definition of human trafficking. This is evident in the case of Eritrea, as well as unaccompanied minors smuggled from Albania and Vietnam, who end up in industries classified as modern slavery, even when they, or their families, consented to their movement. It is also the case with Nigerian women as they enter Libya and lose all control over their onward journey. Their choice comes down to prostitution or being abused or killed without protection from smugglers.

Individuals are exploited when they have limited choices, and others will be ready to take advantage of that lack of choice, exploiting these individuals to make a profit. Often, those who choose to leave the situation that they are in do so determinedly. While it is dangerous to ignore the risks to which they are exposed, by labelling them all as victims who have naively trusted ruthless criminals is not adequate as it takes away their agency in the process.

A Criminal Pyramid

Organised crime has always evolved to avoid detection by law enforcement. Examples of this evolution were discussed in Chapter 9. As potential trafficking victims gain more freedom, responsibility, and awareness, traffickers in turn lose control over them. To combat this, traffickers have adapted by switching to a more consensual business model, where they give victims the perception of future ownership in the business. In the case of both Nigerian girls and Vietnamese migrants, traffickers can successfully exploit an existing narrative of success and harness existing pull factors, rather than simply relying on brute force and threats to ensure compliance. Nigerian girls who have been trafficked into prostitution aspire to be madams as a means to increase their wealth. This goal means that they have an interest in obeying their madam in order to move up in the business and also means that they are less likely to run away and point the finger at their madam or traffickers. Traffickers also have other ways of ensuring compliance, as in the case highlighted where a Nigerian girl went to police in Ceuta, Spain, and her family home was subsequently burnt down. In an age of social media and increasing communication between potential and actual victims, controlling behaviour through examples like this is particularly effective.

Another layer of control also exists—families and communities. In Nigeria, families support sending their daughters to Europe as they expect to profit from them having done so at some stage in the future. Similar cases were seen in Albania and Vietnam, where families got into debt to cover the expenses for their child's travel, believing that the child would earn enough money to repay the debt and then profit from their work. Families will also pressure the victims to stay in situations of exploitation, as they will still be benefiting from the situation and there are no other options for the family.

Increasing the interest for victims, their families, and communities in human trafficking further complicates the difference between human trafficking and people smuggling because the victims are more likely to go along with their exploitation, feeding an abusive industry in the hope that they will benefit in the future, even if that means exploiting others. For criminal groups, this complicity has substantial benefits. Their human cargo is much easier to disguise when passing through borders, as they are less likely to display the signs that safeguarding officers are trained to spot. If they are questioned, they are also more likely to deny their exploitation, as this would prevent them from any future benefits. Pressure from their family to succeed and send money home also adds another layer to the complicity, resulting in a criminal pyramid scheme.

Implications

The research discussed in this book unpacks the nuances of human trafficking, focusing on four commonly discussed cases. This detailed analysis makes it clear that the common representations of human trafficking, usually simplified by the media, and even by governments and INGOs seeking to stop slavery, are inadequate. The picture is much more complicated—with victims moving through multiple categories along their journey and once they reach their destination, shifting from smuggled migrant to trafficking victim and back again multiple times. The emergence of the criminal pyramid scheme also makes many victims complicit in their own exploitation because they perceive they have something to gain—this alone challenges many strategies to identify potential trafficking victims and remove them from abusive situations.

This book discusses the state of human trafficking from Nigeria, Albania, Vietnam, and Eritrea at the time of writing, but the situation is dynamic and constantly changing. In tracking some of the changes over time, this book shows that a detailed picture of the human trafficking/ people smuggling industry is essential in order to develop targeted responses. Otherwise recommendations will be rudimentary, focused on arrested transporters that are rapidly replaced, or creating jobs in industries that are not appealing, such as agriculture.

NOTES

1. THE HUMAN TRAFFICKING INDUSTRY: AN ORGANISED CRIME?

1. For commentary on this, see Rutvica Andrijasevic and Nicola Mai, 'Trafficking (in) Representations: Understanding the Recurring Appeal of Victimhood and Slavery in Neoliberal Times', *Anti-Trafficking Review*, 7 (2016), pp. 1–10.
2. Alliance 8.7, *Global Estimates of Modern Slavery: Forced Labour and Forced Marriage*. Geneva: ILO, 2017.
3. Home Office, *Draft Modern Slavery Bill*, Norwich: H.M. Stationery Office, 2013.
4. Anti-Trafficking Monitoring Group, 'All Change: Preventing Trafficking in the UK', London: Anti-Slavery International, 2012.
5. See, e.g., IASC, 'Independent Anti-Slavery Commissioner's Annual Report 2015–16', 2016, available at: http://www. antislaverycommissioner.co.uk/media/1097/annual-report-2016.pdf
6. US State Department, 'Trafficking in Persons Report 2017', Washington, DC: Department of State, 2017.
7. National Crime Agency (NCA), 'National Referral Mechanism Statistics: End of Year Summary 2017', 2018, available at http://www. nationalcrimeagency.gov.uk/publications/national-referral-mechanism-statistics/2017-nrm-statistics/884-nrm-annual-report-2017
8. Because of restrictions on access and security concerns, research was not conducted in Eritrea. Research has been conducted in Sudan, Nigeria, Niger, Libya, Albania, Vietnam, Italy, France, Belgium, the Netherlands, Germany, and the UK.

9. UN News, 'Human Trafficking Fastest Growing Form of Organized Crime: UN Anti-Crime Chief', 2001, available at: https://news. un.org/en/story/2001/11/19272-human-trafficking-fastest-growing-form-organized-crime-un-anti-crime-chief

10. Anti-Trafficking Monitoring Group, 'All Change'.

11. UNODC, 'Organised Crime Involvement in Trafficking in Persons and Smuggling of Migrants', Vienna: UNODC, 2010.

12. ILO, 'Profits and Poverty: The Economics of Forced Labour', 2014, available at: http://www.ilo.org/wcmsp5/groups/public/---ed_norm/---declaration/documents/publication/wcms_243391.pdf

13. Human Rights First, 'Human Trafficking by the Numbers', 2017, available at: https://www.humanrightsfirst.org/resource/human-trafficking-numbers

14. Gary Craig et al., 'Editorial Introduction', in Craig et al. (eds), *The Modern Slavery Agenda: Policy, Politics and Practice in the UK*, London: Policy Press, 2018.

15. UNODC, 'Human Trafficking: Organized Crime and the Multibillion Dollar Sale of People', 2012, available at: http://www.unodc.org/unodc/en/frontpage/2012/July/human-trafficking_-organized-crime-and-the-multibillion-dollar-sale-of-people.html

16. Louise Shelley, 'International Trafficking: An Important Component of Transnational Crime', in Shiro Okubo and Louise Shelley (eds), *Human Security, Transnational Crime and Human Trafficking: Asian and Western Perspectives*, London: Routledge, 2011.

17. Julia O'Connell Davidson, 'The Right to Locomotion? Trafficking, Slavery and the State', in Prabha Kotiswaran (ed.) *Revisiting the Law and Governance of Trafficking, Forced Labor and Modern Slavery*, Cambridge: Cambridge University Press, 2017.

18. Craig et al., 'Editorial Introduction'.

19. Cited in Jean Allain et al., 'REPORT: Forced Labour's Business Models and Supply Chains', London: Joseph Rowntree Foundation, 2013.

20. Shelley, 'International Trafficking'.

21. James Cockayne, *State Fragility, Organised Crime and Peacebuilding: Towards a More Strategic Approach*, Oslo: NOREF, 2011.

22. 'Full Circle: An Old Route Regains Popularity with Drugs Gangs', *The Economist*, 24 May 2014, available at: https://www.economist.com/the-americas/2014/05/24/full-circle

23. Thorsten Sellin, 'Organised Crime: A Business Enterprise', *The Annals of the American Academy of Political and Social Science*, 347 (1963), pp. 12–19.

24. Marc Goodman, 'What Business Can Learn from Organised Crime', *Harvard Business Review* (2011), available at: https://hbr.org/2011/11/what-business-can-learn-from-organized-crime

25. Phil Williams, 'Trafficking in Women: The Role of Transnational Organised Crime', in Sally Cameron and Edward Newman (eds), *Trafficking in Humans: Social, Cultural and Political Dimensions*, New York: United Nations University Press, 2007.

26. Centre for Social Justice, *A Modern Response to Modern Slavery*. London: CSJ, 2015.

27. Louise Shelley, *Human Trafficking: A Global Perspective*, Cambridge: Cambridge University Press, 2010.

28. *Juju* is a spiritual belief in parts of Nigeria. Traffickers have recruited priests to bind victims to an oath as a method of controlling them.

29. Louise Shelley, *Human Trafficking: A Global Perspective*.

30. Ibid.

31. Ibid.

32. Klaus von Lampe, 'Definitions of Organized Crime', 2012, available at: http://www.organized-crime.de/organizedcrimedefinitions.htm

33. Vanda Felbab Brown, 'The Hellish Road to Good Intentions: How to Break Political–Criminal Alliances in Contexts of Transition', United Nations University Centre for Policy Research Crime–Conflict Nexus Series, no 7, 2017, available at: https://i.unu.edu/media/cpr.unu.edu/attachment/2453/The-Hellish-Road-to-Good-Intentions-How-to-Break-Political-Criminal-Alliances-in-Contexts-of-Transition.pdf

34. Ibid.

35. 'R v. James John Connors and Josie Connors Sentencing Remarks of HHJ Michael Kay QC', Luton Crown Court, available at: https://www.judiciary.gov.uk/wp-content/uploads/JCO/Documents/Judgments/james-connors-josie-sentencing-remarks-12072012.pdf

36. The Passage, 'Understanding and Responding to Modern Slavery within the Homelessness Sector', 2017, available at: http://passage.org.uk/540927-2/the-passage-anti-slavery-document-for-web-24-01-17/

37. UNSC Resolution 1820 S/RES/1820, 2008.

38. UN Human Rights Council, '"They Came to Destroy": ISIS Crimes against the Yazidis', Report to the Human Rights Council, Thirty-Second Session, 2016, A/HRC/32/CRP.2.

39. UN University, 'Human Trafficking in Conflict: 10 Ideas for Action by the United Nations Security Council', Workshop Report, 2016, available at: http://collections.unu.edu/eserv/UNU:5780/UNUReport_Pages.pdf?utm_source=UNU%20Campaign%20page&utm_medium=Web&utm_campaign=Human%20Trafficking

40. Nicola Harley, 'We're Not Slaves, More Than 100 Migrant Workers Say as They Launch Protest at Arrest of Farm Bosses', *The Telegraph*, 9 February

2018, available at: https://www.telegraph.co.uk/news/2018/02/09/not-slaves-100-migrant-workers-say-launch-protest-arrest-farm/

41. 'Bedfordshire "Slaves" Case: Nine Refuse to Help Police', BBC News, 12 September 2011, available at: http://www.bbc.co.uk/news/uk-england-beds-bucks-herts-14878624

42. Interview, UK law enforcement, January 2018.

43. Interview, Belgian Federal Police, November 2017.

44. Williams, 'Trafficking in Women'.

45. Ibid.

46. Misha Glenny, *McMafia: Crime without Frontiers*, London: Bodley Head, 2008.

47. UN General Assembly, 'Protocol against the Smuggling of Migrants by Land, Sea and Air, Supplementing the United Nations Convention against Transnational Organised Crime', 12 December 2000.

48. UN General Assembly, 'Protocol to Prevent, Suppress and Punish Trafficking in Persons, Especially Women and Children, Supplementing the United Nations Convention against Transnational Organised Crime', 15 November 2000.

49. Tuesday Reitano, 'Human Trafficking in Africa: Do We Need a New Definition?', Global Initiative, 2017, available at: http://globalinitiative.net/does-human-trafficking-need-a-new-definition/

50. Stephen Ellis, *This Present Darkness: A History of Nigerian Organized Crime*, London: Hurst, 2016.

2. NIGERIA

1. May Ikeora, *Bilateral Cooperation and Human Trafficking: Eradicating Modern Slavery between the United Kingdom and Nigeria,* New York: Springer, 2017.

2. Interview, Sabha, Libya, January 2018.

3. Interview, Abuja, September 2017.

4. Jørgen Carling, 'Fra Nigeria til Europa: Innvandring, menneskesmugling og menneskehandel', International Peace Research Institute, Oslo (PRIO), 2005.

5. Interview, Benin City, Nigeria, September 2017.

6. Cited in Ikeora, *Bilateral Cooperation and Human Trafficking*.

7. Interview Lagos, Nigeria, September 2017.

8. Interview, Abuja, Nigeria, September 2017, and Ikeora, *Bilateral Cooperation and Human Trafficking*.

9. Interview, Benin City, Nigeria, September 2017.

10. Interview, Benin City, Nigeria, September 2017.

11. 'Doctor and Husband Jailed for Appalling Exploitation of "Slave" Nanny', Court News UK, 20 June 2017, available at: http://courtnewsuk. co.uk/doctor-husband-jailed-appalling-exploitation-slave-nanny/

12. Press Association, 'Civil Servant Kept Woman from Nigeria in "Domestic Servitude"', *The Guardian*, 2017.

13. Interview, Lagos, Nigeria, September 2017.

14. Interview Lagos, Nigeria, September 2017.

15. Interview, Benin City, Nigeria, September 2017.

16. Interview, Sabha, Libya, February 2018.

17. Tuesday Reitano, 'Human Trafficking in Africa: Do We Need a New Definition?', Global Initiative against Organised Crime, 2017.

18. Odita Sunday, 'Police Uncover Another "Oluwole" in Lagos', *The Guardian Nigeria*, 14 March 2016.

19. Interview, Abuja, Nigeria, September 2017.

20. Interview, Benin City, Nigeria, September 2017.

21. Carling, 'Fra Nigeria til Europa'.

22. Stephen Ellis, *This Present Darkness: A History of Nigerian Organized Crime*, New York: Oxford University Press, 2016.

23. Carling, 'Fra Nigeria til Europa'.

24. Ibid.

25. Ibid.

26. Ellis, *This Present Darkness*.

27. Interview, Benin City, Nigeria, September 2017.

28. Interview, Benin City, Nigeria, September 2017.

29. Interview, Lagos, Nigeria, September 2017.

30. Ellis, *This Present Darkness*.

31. Interview, Abuja, Nigeria, September 2017.

32. Interview, Lagos, Nigeria, September 2017.

33. Interview, Benin, Nigeria, September 2017.

34. Interview, Benin City, Nigeria, September 2017.

35. Ellis, *This Present Darkness*.

36. Interview, Catania, Italy, December 2017.

37. Interview, Benin City, Nigeria, September 2017.

38. Interview, Benin City, Nigeria, September 2017.

39. Interview, Benin City, Nigeria, September 2017.

40. Interview, Benin City, Nigeria, September 2017.

41. Ellis, *This Present Darkness*.

42. Interview, Lagos, Nigeria, September 2017.

43. Ellis, *This Present Darkness*.

44. Carling, 'Fra Nigeria til Europa'.

45. Ellis, *This Present Darkness*.

46. Carling, 'Fra Nigeria til Europa'.
47. Interview, Benin City, Nigeria, September 2017.
48. Ellis, *This Present Darkness*.
49. Interview, Lagos, Nigeria, September 2017.
50. Interview, Lagos, Nigeria, September 2017.
51. Interview, Benin City, Nigeria, September 2017.
52. Interview, Benin City, Nigeria, September 2017.
53. Interview, Benin City, Nigeria, September 2017.
54. Interview, Benin City, Nigeria, September 2017.
55. Ikeora, *Bilateral Cooperation and Human Trafficking*.
56. NAPTIP, 'Oba of Benin Revokes Oaths on Victims of Human Trafficking … Places Curses on Perpetrators and Unrepentant Juju Priests', 2018, available at: https://www.naptip.gov.ng/?p=1683, and Adaobi Tricia Nwaubani, 'A Voodoo Curse on Human Traffickers', *The New York Times*, 24 March 2018.
57. Interview, Benin City, Nigeria, September 2017.
58. Ikeora, *Bilateral Cooperation and Human Trafficking*.
59. Interview, Benin City, Nigeria, September 2017.
60. Interview, Benin City, Nigeria, September 2017.
61. Interview, Abuja, Nigeria, September 2017.
62. Carling, 'Fra Nigeria til Europa'.
63. Ibid.
64. Ibid.
65. Interview, Lagos, Nigeria, September 2017.
66. Ellis, *This Present Darkness*.
67. Interview, Abuja, Nigeria, September 2017.
68. Interview, Lagos, Nigeria, September 2017.
69. Interview, Lagos, Nigeria, September 2017.
70. This route became increasingly dangerous and violent in 2018.
71. Interview, Abuja, Nigeria, September 2017.
72. A journey is limited to ninety days, which is established from the entry stamp on the migrants' travel documents.
73. Interview, Abuja, Nigeria, September 2017.
74. Interview, Lagos, Nigeria, September 2017.
75. Interview, Abuja, Nigeria, September 2017.
76. Interview, Benin City, Nigeria, September 2017.
77. Interview, Abuja, Nigeria, September 2017.
78. Interview, Abuja, Nigeria, September 2017.
79. Interview, Benin City, Nigeria, September 2017.
80. Ellis, *This Present Darkness*.
81. Franco Prini cited in Ellis, *This Present Darkness*.

82. Carling, 'Fra Nigeria til Europa'.
83. Interview, Benin City, Nigeria, September 2017.
84. Interview, Catania, Italy, December 2017.
85. Interview, Abuja, Nigeria, September 2017.
86. Interview, Abuja, Nigeria, September 2017.
87. Interview, Abuja, Nigeria, September 2017.
88. Interview, Abuja, Nigeria, September 2017.
89. Carling, 'Fra Nigeria til Europa'.
90. Abdoulaye Massalaki, 'Niger Passes Law to Tackle Migrant Smuggling, First in West Africa', Reuters, 2015.

3. NIGER

1. Interview, Niamey, Niger, January 2018.
2. Interview, Niamey, January 2018.
3. Fransje Molenaar, 'Irregular Migration and Human Smuggling Networks in Niger', CRU Report, The Hague: Clingendael and Netherlands Institute of International Relations, 2017.
4. Interview, Niamey, Niger, January 2018.
5. Molenaar, 'Irregular Migration and Human Smuggling Networks'.
6. IOM, 'Niger: Flow Monitoring Report (December 2016)', DTM Understanding Displacement, 2017.
7. Unit RA, 'Risk Analysis for 2018', Warsaw: Frontex, 2018.
8. IOM, 'Population Flow Monitoring: Niger IOM', 2018.
9. Molenaar, 'Irregular Migration and Human Smuggling Networks'.
10. IOM, 'Statistical Report Overview: Niger Flow Monitoring (FMP)', 2016.
11. Interview, Niamey, Niger, January 2018.
12. Laura Smith-Spark and Arwa Damon, 'Sahara Desert Deaths: 92 Migrants Perish in Niger after Vehicle Breakdowns', CNN, 31 October 2013.
13. Interview, Niamey, Niger, January 2018.
14. Interview, Niamey, Niger, January 2018.
15. Interview, Niamey, Niger, January 2018.
16. Interview, Niamey, Niger, January 2018.
17. Reuters, 'Dozens of Migrants Dying in Sahara Desert Trying to Reach Europe', The Guardian, 17 June 2015.
18. Agence France-Presse, '34 Migrants, Including 20 Children, Found Dead in Niger Desert', The Telegraph, 16 June 2016.
19. 'Niger Migrants: 52 Die during Desert Crossing', BBC News, 26 June 2017, available at: https://www.bbc.co.uk/news/world-africa-40408599

20. Joe Penney, 'Why More Migrants Are Dying in the Sahara', *New York Times*, 22 August 2017.

21. Moustapha Diallo, 'Niger: Thousands of Migrants Trapped in Agadez Face a Bleak Future', IFRC News, 26 February 2018, available at: https://media.ifrc.org/ifrc/2018/02/26/niger-thousands-migrants-trapped-agadez-face-bleak-future/

22. Interview, Niamey, Niger, January 2018.

23. Molenaar, 'Irregular Migration and Human Smuggling Networks'.

24. Ibid.

25. Ibid.; interview, Niamey, Niger, January 2018.

26. Ibid.

27. Ibid.

28. Luca Raineri and Neil Howard, 'Human Smuggling: The Pride of Niger's Economy', OpenDemocracy, 30 August 2017, available at: https://www.opendemocracy.net/en/beyond-trafficking-and-slavery/human-smuggling-pride-of-nigers-economy/

29. Molenaar, 'Irregular Migration and Human Smuggling Networks'.

30. Interview, Niamey, Niger, January 2018.

31. Molenaar, 'Irregular Migration and Human Smuggling Networks'.

32. Interview, Niamey, Niger, January 2018.

33. Molenaar, 'Irregular Migration and Human Smuggling Networks'.

34. Interviews, Niamey, Niger, January 2018.

35. Interview, Niamey, Niger, January 2018.

36. Molenaar, 'Irregular Migration and Human Smuggling Networks'.

37. Interview, Niamey, Niger, January 2018.

38. Interview, Niamey, Niger, January 2018.

39. Interview, Niamey, Niger, January 2018.

40. Molenaar, 'Irregular Migration and Human Smuggling Networks'.

41. Ibid.

42. Ibid.

43. Interview, Niamey, Niger, January 2018.

44. Interview, Niamey, Niger, January 2018.

45. Interview, Niamey, Niger, January 2018.

46. Molenaar, 'Irregular Migration and Human Smuggling Networks'.

47. Ibid.

48. Ibid.

49. Ibid.

50. Ibid.

4. LIBYA

1. RHIPTO, 'Libyan Militias Agents of Permanent Instability', Threat Network Assessment, 16 September 2016, Norwegian Center for Global Analyses (RHIPTO).
2. Ibid.
3. Ibid.
4. Ibid.
5. Ibid.
6. Ibid.
7. Ibid.
8. Ibid.
9. Ibid.
10. RHIPTO, 'Strategic Value, Routes and Incomes to Armed Groups in Libya from 143,000–343,000 Migrants', 18 January 2018.
11. Ibid.
12. Ibid.
13. Ibid.
14. Interview, Sabha, Libya, January 2018.
15. Interview, Sabha, Libya, January 2018.
16. Interview, Sabha, Libya, January 2018.
17. Interview, Tripoli, Libya, February 2018.
18. Interview, Sabha, Libya, February 2018.
19. Interview in Catania, Italy, December 2017.
20. Interview, Tripoli, Libya, December 2017.
21. Interview, Tripoli, Libya, February 2018.
22. Interview, Sabha, Libya, February 2018.
23. Interview, Sabha, Libya, January 2018.
24. Interview, Tripoli, Libya, December 2017.
25. Interview, Tripoli, Libya, December 2017.
26. Interview, Tripoli, Libya, February 2018.
27. Interview, Tripoli, Libya, February 2018.
28. Interview, Tripoli, Libya, February 2018.
29. Interview, Sabha, Libya, January 2018.
30. Interview, Tripoli, Libya, February 2018.
31. Interview, Tripoli, Libya, February 2018.
32. Interview, Tripoli, Libya, February 2018.
33. Interview, Sabha, Libya, January 2018.
34. Interview in Catania, December 2017.
35. Interview, Sabha, Libya, January 2018.
36. Interview, Sabha, Libya, January 2018.

37. Interview, Tripoli, Libya, December 2017.
38. Interview, Tripoli, Libya, February 2018.
39. Interview, Tripoli, Libya, February 2018.
40. Interview, Tripoli, Libya, February 2018.
41. Interviews, Sabha, Libya, January 2018 and February 2018.
42. Interviews, Tripoli, Libya, February 2018.

5. ALBANIA

1. National Crime Agency (NCA), 'National Referral Mechanism Statistics: End of Year Summary 2017', London: NCA, 2017.
2. Ibid.
3. NCA, 'Strategic Assessment of Serious and Organised Crime', London: NCA, 2017.
4. Interviews, UK, July 2017, and Albania, September 2017.
5. Interview, UK, July 2017.
6. Interview, UK, July 2017.
7. Vasilika Hysi, 'Human Trafficking and Democratic Transition in Albania', in Richard Friman and Simon Reich (eds), *Human Trafficking, Human Security and the Balkans*, Pittsburgh: University of Pittsburgh Press, 2007.
8. Nick Mai, 'The Psycho-Social Trajectories of Albanian and Romanian "Traffickers"', ISET Working Paper 17, 2010.
9. Interview, Albania, September 2017.
10. Global Initiative against Transnational Organised Crime, 'Crooked Kaleidoscope: Organised Crime in the Balkans', Geneva: Global Initiative against Transnational Organised Crime, 2017.
11. Interview, Albania, September 2017.
12. Interview, Frankfurt, June 2018.
13. Nick Mai, 'Albanian Migration to Italy: Towards Differential Circulations?', Metoikos Project: European University Institute, 2010, available at: https://www.eui.eu/Projects/METOIKOS/Documents/CaseStudies/METOIKOSItaloAlbaniancasestudyreport.pdf
14. 'The Albanian Community: Annual Report on the Presence of Migrants in Italy', Ministerio de Lavoro e de Politiche Sociale, 2016, available at: http://www.integrazionemigranti.gov.it/Areetematiche/PaesiComunitari-e-associazioniMigranti/Documents/ES_ALBANIA_en.pdf
15. Ibid.
16. 'Consolidated Act of Provisions concerning Immigration and the Condition of Third Country Nationals', Legislative Decree no. 286,

1998, available at: https://ec.europa.eu/migrant-integration/librarydoc/legislative-decree-2571998-no-286-on-consolidated-act-of-provisions-concerning-immigration-and-the-condition-of-third-country-nationals

17. Interview, Turin, March 2018.

18. Interview, Turin, March 2018.

19. Interview, Turin, March 2018.

20. 'National Anti-Mafia and Anti-Terrorism Directorate Annual Report 2016', Direzione nazionale antimafia e antiterrorismo, 2017.

21. Julie Vullnetari, 'Women and Migration in Albania: A View from the Village', *International Migration*, 50, 5 (2009), pp. 169–88.

22. Interview, law enforcement, Albania, September 2017.

23. John Davies, *'My Name Is Not Natasha': How Albanian Women in France Use Trafficking to Overcome Social Exclusion*, Amsterdam: Amsterdam University Press, 2009.

24. Ibid.

25. Interview, law enforcement, Tirana, Albania, September 2017.

26. Interview, law enforcement, Belgium, February 2018.

27. Interview, law enforcement, Belgium, February 2018.

28. UK Home Office, 'Report of a Home Office Fact-Finding Mission: Albania', 2018, available at: https://assets.publishing.service.gov.uk/government/uploads/system/uploads/attachment_data/file/681071/Home_Office_FFM_Report_-_Albania.pdf

29. Davies, *'My Name Is Not Natasha'*.

30. NCA, 'Strategic Assessment of Serious and Organised Crime 2017', London: NCA, 2017.

31. Interview, prosecutor, Tirana, Albania, November 2017.

32. Johan Leman and Stef Janssens, 'Albanian Entrepreneurial Practices in Human Smuggling and Trafficking: On the Road to the United Kingdom via Brussels 1995–2005', *International Migration*, 50, 6 (2011), pp. 166–79.

33. Interview, the Netherlands, December 2017.

34. Enzo Ciconte, *Mafie Straniere in Italia: Storia ed evoluzione* (Foreign mafia in Italy: History and evolution), Soveria Mannelli: Rubbettino, 2003.

35. Interview, Belgium, February 2018.

36. Refugee Council, 'Children in the Asylum System', 2018, available at: https://www.refugeecouncil.org.uk/assets/0004/2701/Children_in_the_Asylum_System_Feb_2018.pdf

37. Interview, Tirana, November 2017.

38. Aleksandra Bogdani and Bashkim Shala, 'Interrupted Childhoods: The Exodus of Albanian Adolescents to the UK', 24 February 2017, available

at: http://prishtinainsight.com/interrupted-childhoods-the-exodus-of-albanian-adolescents-to-the-uk-mag/

39. Russell King, 'Albania as a Laboratory for the Study of Migration and Development', *Journal of Southern Europe and the Balkans*, 7, 2 (2005), pp. 133–55.

40. Government of Albania, 'National Strategy on Migration 2005', drafted in cooperation with the IOM, 2005.

41. Republic of Albania, Minister of State on Diaspora, 'National Strategy on Diaspora and Migration 2018–2024', 2017, available at: http://www.diaspora.gov.al/wp-content/uploads/2017/12/Strategy-English.pdf

42. INSTAT, 'Migration in Albania', 2014, available at: https://unstats.un.org/unsd/demographic/sources/census/wphc/Albania/04-analysis.pdf

43. Interview, Tirana, November 2017.

44. The survey, which was carried out by GALLUP, interviewed 587,000 people over the age of fifteen in 156 countries between 2013 and 2016. GALLUP, 'Number of Potential Migrants Worldwide Tops 700 Million', 2017, available at: https://news.gallup.com/poll/211883/number-potential-migrants-worldwide-tops-700-million.aspx

45. Calogero Carletto et al., 'Internal Mobility and International Migration in Albania', ESA Working Paper no. 04-13, 2004, available at: https://ageconsearch.umn.edu/bitstream/23797/1/wp040013.pdf

46. Gero Carletto, Benjamin Davis, and Marco Stampini, 'Familiar Faces, Familiar Places: The Role of Family Networks and Previous Experience for Albanian Migrants', ESA Working Paper no. 05-03, 2005, available at: http://www.fao.org/3/a-ae592t.pdf

47. INSTAT, 'Migration in Albania', 2014, available at: https://unstats.un.org/unsd/demographic/sources/census/wphc/Albania/04-analysis.pdf

48. Zana Vathi and Iva Zajmi, 'Children and Migration in Albania: Latest Trends and Protection Measures Available', Terre des hommes, 2017, available at: http://tdh-europe.org/upload/document/7270/MIGRATION%20REPORT%20ALBANIA%20(eng)_web.pdf

49. Carletto, Davis, and Stampini, 'Familiar Faces, Familiar Places'.

50. Luljeta Ikonomi and Nikolle Ndoci, 'The Impact of Visa Liberalization for the Western Balkans: The Case of Albania', 2012, available at: http://dspace.epoka.edu.al/handle/1/334

51. Europol, 'Serious and Organised Crime Threat Assessment 2017', The Hague: Europol, 2017.

52. Europol, 'Criminal Network Involved in Migrant Smuggling and Document Fraud Dismantled', 2017, available at: https://www.

europol.europa.eu/newsroom/news/criminal-network-involved-in-migrant-smuggling-and-document-fraud-dismantled

53. NCA, 'Operation Brings Down Athens-Based People Smuggling Gang Targeting the UK', 2017, available at: http://www.nationalcrimeagency. gov.uk/news/1236-operation-brings-down-athens-based-people-smuggling-gang-targeting-the-uk

54. Tom Kelly, 'Sophisticated Fake Passport Laboratory Helping Hundreds of Migrants Sneak into Britain Is Smashed by Police in Albania', *Daily Mail*, 18 May 2018, available at: http://www.dailymail.co.uk/news/ article-5746395/Sophisticated-fake-passport-laboratory-smashed-police-Albania.html

55. Interviews, law enforcement, Tirana, Albania, November 2017.

56. Interview, Europol, the Netherlands, December 2017.

57. Interview, the Netherlands, December 2017.

58. Interview, Belgium, February 2018.

59. Leman and Janssens, 'Albanian Entrepreneurial Practices in Human Smuggling', pp. 166–79.

60. Interview, Belgium, February 2018.

61. Interview, Europol, the Netherlands, December 2017.

62. Jana Arsovska, *Decoding Albanian Organized Crime: Culture, Politics and Globalization*, Berkeley: University of California Press, 2015.

63. 'National Anti-Mafia and Anti-Terrorism Directorate Annual Report 2016', Direzione nazionale antimafia e antiterrorismo, 2017.

64. Ibid.

65. Russell King, 'Albania as a Laboratory for the Study of Migration and Development', *Journal of Southern Europe and the Balkans*, 7, 2 (2005), pp. 133–55.

66. Ewelina U. Ochab, 'The World's Fastest Growing Crime', Forbes, 2017, available at: https://www.forbes.com/sites/ewelinaochab/ 2017/07/29/the-worlds-fastest-growing-crime/#60bf9fe63aae

67. Minna Viuhko, 'Hardened Professional Criminals, or Just Friends and Relatives? The Diversity of Offenders in Human Trafficking', *International Journal of Comparative and Applied Criminal Justice*, 42, 2–3 (2017), pp. 177–93.

6. VIETNAM

1. ECPAT, 'The Sexual Exploitation of Children in South East Asia', Bangkok: ECPAT International, 2017.

2. US Department of State, 'Trafficking in Persons Report 2017', Washington, DC: US Department of State, 2017.

3.   Alison Holt, 'Victims Trafficked from Vietnam to Work on Illegal UK Cannabis Farms', BBC News, 4 May 2014, available at: https://www. bbc.co.uk/news/av/26443575/victims-trafficked-from-vietnam-to-work-on-illegal-uk-cannabis-farms

4.   Home Office, 'Country Policy and Information Note: Vietnam; Victims of Trafficking', Version 2.0, 2016.

5.   NCA, 'National Referral Mechanism Statistics: End of Year Summary 2017', 2017, available at: http://www.nationalcrimeagency.gov. uk/publications/national-referral-mechanism-statistics/2017-nrm-statistics/884-nrm-annual-report-2017/file

6.   Andy Shipley, 'Teenage "Slaves" Trafficked to Work in Capital', *The Scotsman*, 18 September 2017, available at: https://www. edinburghnews.scotsman.com/news/teenage-slaves-trafficked-to-work-in-capital-1-4562979

7.   Karl Miller, 'From Humanitarian to Economic: The Changing Face of Vietnamese Migration', Migration Policy, 2015, available at: https:// www.migrationpolicy.org/article/humanitarian-economic-changing-face-vietnamese-migration

8.   Ibid.

9.   World Bank Group, 'Migration and Remittances', Migration and Development Brief, no. 28, October 2017.

10.   Interview, Hanoi, October 2017.

11.   Rebecca Ratcliffe, 'Vietnam Braced for Second Storm after Devastating Impact of Typhoon Damrey', *The Guardian*, 11 November 2017, available at: https://www.theguardian.com/global-development/2017/ nov/11/vietnam-braced-for-second-storm-after-devastating-impact-of-typhoon-damrey-kaikui

12.   Interview, Hanoi, October 2017.

13.   Daniel Silverstone and Stephen Savage, 'Farmers, Factories and Funds: Organised Crime and Illicit Drugs Cultivation within the British Vietnamese Community', *Global Crime*, 11, 1 (February 2010), pp. 16–33.

14.   IRASEC and France terre d'asile, 'En Route to the United Kingdom: A Field Study of Vietnamese Migrants', 2017.

15.   Tamsin Barber, 'The Integration of Vietnamese Refugees in London and the UK: Fragmentation, Complexity and "In/Visibility"', Working Paper 2018/2: UNU-WIDER, Helsinki, 2018.

16.   Interview, Hanoi, October 2017.

17.   Tamsin Barber and Hai Nguyen, 'Becoming Adult by Remaining a Minor: Reconfigurations of Adulthood and Well Being by Young Vietnamese Migrants in the UK', Working Paper, Oxford Brookes University, 2017.

18. IRASEC and France terre d'asile, 'En Route to the United Kingdom'.

19. UNICEF UK, 'Victim, Not Criminal: Trafficked Children and the Non-Punishment Principle in the UK', 2017.

20. NCA, 'National Referral Mechanism Statistics: End of Year Summary 2017'.

21. Anti-Slavery International, 'Trafficking for Forced Criminal Activities and Begging in Europe: Exploratory Study and Good Practice Examples', September 2014.

22. Interview, UK, July 2017.

23. CEOP, 'The Trafficking of Women and Children from Vietnam', Child Exploitation and Online Protection Centre in Association with the British Embassy, Hanoi, 2011.

24. Barber and Nguyen, 'Becoming Adult by Remaining a Minor'.

25. Annie Kelly and Mei-Ling McNamara, '3,000 Children Enslaved in Britain after Being Trafficked from Vietnam', *The Guardian*, 23 May 2015, available at: https://www.theguardian.com/global-development/2015/may/23/vietnam-children-trafficking-nail-bar-cannabis

26. Amelia Gentleman, 'Home Office Accused of Cruelty for Ordering Cannabis Slave Back to Vietnam', *The Guardian*, 12 January 2018, available at: https://www.theguardian.com/world/2018/jan/12/child-trafficking-cruel-home-office-orders-cannabis-slave-back-to-vietnam

27. ECPAT UK and Missing People, 'Heading Back to Harm: A Study on Trafficked and Unaccompanied Going Missing from Care in the UK', London, November 2016.

28. Interview, UK, July 2017.

29. International Organization for Migration, 'Viet-Nam Migration Profile 2016', Hanoi, Vietnam, 2017.

30. Ibid.

31. Interviews, various countries, 2018.

32. Interview, UK, May 2018.

33. Interview, UK, July 2017.

34. Nicolas Lainez, 'Informal Credit in Vietnam: A Necessity Rather Than an Evil', *Research Note: Journal of Southeast Asian Economies*, 31, 1 (2014), pp. 147–54.

35. Julia O'Connell Davidson, 'Troubling Freedom: Migration, Debt and Modern Slavery', *Migration Studies*, 1, 2 (2013), pp. 176–95.

36. Interview, UK, 2018.

37. Interview, UK, 2018.

38. Interview, UK, 2018.

39. Danièle Bélanger, 'Labor Migration and Trafficking among Vietnamese Migrants in Asia', *The Annals of the American Academy of Political and Social Science*, 653 (May 2014), pp. 87–106, here p. 88.
40. Ibid., p. 92.
41. Interviews, various countries, 2017/18.
42. Interview, the Netherlands, December 2017.
43. Silverstone and Savage, 'Farmers, Factories and Funds', pp. 16–33.
44. Daniel Silverstone and Claire Brickell, 'Combating Modern Slavery Experienced by Vietnamese Nationals En Route to, and within, the UK', London: UK Anti-Slavery Commissioner, 2017.
45. Interviews, Hanoi, October 2017.
46. Interview, UK, June 2018.
47. Interview, Hanoi, October 2017.
48. Interview, Hanoi, October 2017.
49. Interview, Hanoi, October 2017.
50. Amelia Gentleman, 'Inside Vietnam City, the French Holding Camp for Vulnerable UK-Bound Migrants', *The Guardian*, 10 September 2017, available at: https://www.theguardian.com/law/2017/sep/10/vietnam-city-french-holding-camp-uk-migrants
51. Interviews, various countries, 2017/18.
52. Europol, 'Early Warning Notification: Re-emergence of Vietnamese OCGs', 2013, available at: https://www.europol.europa.eu/publications-documents/re-emergence-of-vietnamese-organised-crime-groups-ocgs
53. Interview, the Netherlands, July 2018.
54. IRASEC and France terre d'asile, 'En Route to the United Kingdom'.
55. Interview, Hanoi, October 2017.
56. Interview, UK, July 2017.
57. Interview, Hanoi, October 2017.
58. Interview, Hanoi, October 2017.
59. Interview, Hanoi, October 2017.
60. Interview, UK, May 2018.
61. Interview, Hanoi, October 2017.
62. Yvette M. M. Schoenmakers, Edward Kleemans, and Bo Bremmers, 'Strategic versus Emergent Crime Groups: The Case of Vietnamese Cannabis Cultivation in the Netherlands', *Global Crime*, 14, 4 (2013), pp. 321–40.
63. Nicolas Lainez, 'Modern Vietnamese Slaves in the UK: Are Raid and Rescue Operations Appropriate?', OpenDemocracy, 29 November 2017, available at: https://www.opendemocracy.net/beyondslavery/

nicolas-lainez/modern-vietnamese-slaves-in-uk-are-raid-and-rescue-operations-appropria

64. Interview, Hanoi, October 2017.
65. Julia O'Connell Davidson, 'The Right to Locomotion?', in Prabha Kotiswaran (ed.), *Revisiting the Law and Governance of Trafficking, Forced Labour and Modern Slavery*, Cambridge: Cambridge University Press, 2017, p. 159.

7. ERITREA

1. Human Rights Watch, '"I Wanted to Lie Down and Die": Trafficking and Torture of Eritreans in Sudan and Egypt', 11 February 2014, available at: www.hrw.org/report/2014/02/11/i-wanted-lie-down-and-die/trafficking-and-torture-eritreans-sudan-and-egypt
2. US State Department, 'Trafficking in Persons Report', Washington, DC: US State Department, 2016; US State Department, 'Trafficking in Persons Report', Washington, DC: US State Department 2017.
3. UNHCR, 'Global Focus Sudan', 2017, available at: http://reporting.unhcr.org/node/2535; International Refugee Rights Initiative, 'Tackling the Root Causes of Human Trafficking and Smuggling from Eritrea: The Need for an Empirically Grounded EU Policy on Mixed Migration in the Horn of Africa', London: IRRI, 2017.
4. Interview, Kassala, November 2017.
5. Miriam van Reisen, Meron Estefanos, and Conny Rijken, *The Human Trafficking Cycle: Sinai and Beyond*, Oisterwijk, the Netherlands: Wolf Publications, 2014.
6. 'The Road Less Taken: Migration from Eritrea Slows', *The Economist*, 25 May 2017, available at: https://www.economist.com/middle-east-and-africa/2017/05/25/migration-from-eritrea-slows
7. UNHCR, 'Smuggling and Trafficking from the East and Horn of Africa: Progress Report', UNHCR Strategy and Regional Plan of Action, 2016, available at: www.unodc.org/documents/congress/workshops/UNHCR-Smuggling_and_Trafficking-Progress_Report-screen-final.pdf
8. Interviews, Kassala, November 2017; Hassan A. Abdel Ati, 'Human Smuggling and Trafficking in Eastern Sudan', Sudan Report no. 2, September 2017.
9. Ati, 'Human Smuggling and Trafficking'.
10. Rachel Humphris, 'Refugees and the Rashaida: Human Smuggling and Trafficking from Eritrea to Sudan and Egypt', New Issues in Refugee Research, Research Paper no. 254, Geneva: UNHCR, 2013.
11. Interview, Kassala, November 2017.

12. Interview, Kassala, November 2017; interview, Khartoum, November 2017.

13. Martin Plaut, *Understanding Eritrea: Inside Africa's Most Repressive State*, London: Hurst, 2016.

14. Ibid.

15. SAHAN and IGAD, 'Human Trafficking and Smuggling on the Horn of Africa–Central Mediterranean Route', 2016, available at: http://www.igad.int/attachments/1284_ISSP%20Sahan%20HST%20Report%20%2018ii2016%20FINAL%20FINAL.pdf

16. Ati, 'Human Smuggling and Trafficking'.

17. Interview, Khartoum, October 2016; Ati, 'Human Smuggling and Trafficking'.

18. IFRC, 'Stories from the Field: Inside Kassala Safe House', Kassala: IFRC, 2017.

19. Interview, Khartoum, November 2017.

20. Interview, Khartoum, November 2017.

21. Interview, Khartoum, October 2017.

22. Interview, Khartoum, October 2017.

23. Interview, Khartoum, November 2017.

24. Human Rights Watch, 'Service for Life: State Repression and Indefinite Conscription in Eritrea', New York: Human Rights Watch, 2009; Amnesty International, 'Eritrea: Refugees Fleeing Indefinite Conscription Must Be Given Safe Haven', London: Amnesty International, 2015.

25. Human Rights Watch, 'Sudan: Hundreds Deported to Likely Abuse', 2016, available at: https://www.hrw.org/news/2016/05/30/sudan-hundreds-deported-likely-abuse

26. Interview, Kassala, November 2017; interview, Khartoum, November 2017.

27. Human Rights Watch, 'Sudan: Hundreds Deported to Likely Abuse'.

28. Jehanne Henry, 'EU Must Put Sudan under Microscope at Africa Summit', EUObserver, November 2017, available at: www.euobserver.com/opinion/139980

29. Interview, Kassala, November 2017.

30. Sally Hayden, 'Captured, Raped, Ransomed: The Kidnappers Preying on Eritrean Refugees', *The Guardian*, 18 January 2018, available at: www.theguardian.com/global-development/2018/jan/19/everyday-thing-kidnappers-preying-on-eritrean-refugees

31. Joe DeCapua, 'Kidnappers Target Refugees in Sudan', Voice of America, 2013, available at: www.voanews.com/a/sudan-egypt-kidnapping-3apr13/1633774.html; Hayden, 'Captured, Raped, Ransomed'.

32. UNHCR, 'UNHCR Deeply Concerned about Abduction of Asylum-Seekers in Eastern Sudan', UNHCR Press Release, 5 June 2015, available at: www.unhcr.org/uk/news/press/2015/6/5571bce09/unhcr-deeply-concerned-abduction-asylum-seekers-eastern-sudan.html

33. Ati, 'Human Smuggling and Trafficking'.

34. Interview, Kassala, November 2017.

35. Van Reisen, Estefanos, and Rijken, *Human Trafficking Cycle*; interview, Kassala, November 2017.

36. Interview, Kassala, November 2017.

37. Interview, Kassala, November 2017.

38. UNHCR, 'New Arrivals Fact Sheet', August 2017.

39. Interview, Kassala, November 2017.

40. Interview, Kassala, November 2017.

41. Interview, Kassala, November 2017.

42. Humphris, 'Refugees and the Rashaida'.

43. Migrants awaiting transportation are referred to as 'cartons' or 'boxes', highlighting how they are viewed as commodities. In some cases, brokers will take migrants from others by force in order to increase their own profits.

44. Van Reisen, Estefanos, and Rijken, *Human Trafficking Cycle*.

45. Ati, 'Human Smuggling and Trafficking'.

46. Van Reisen, Estefanos, and Rijken, *Human Trafficking Cycle*.

47. Mirjam van Reisen and Conny Rijken, 'Sinai Trafficking: Origin and Definition of a New Form of Human Trafficking', *Social Inclusion*, 3, 1 (2015), pp. 113–24.

48. Van Reisen, Estefanos, and Rijken, *Human Trafficking Cycle*.

49. Phoebe Greenwood, 'Egyptian Authorities Look the Other Way as Bedouin Kidnap Refugees', *The Guardian*, 14 February 2012.

50. Van Reisen, Estefanos, and Rijken, *Human Trafficking Cycle*.

51. 'Houses of Torture: Human Trafficking in the Sinai', *The Economist*, 5 December 2013, available at: https://www.economist.com/blogs/pomegranate/2013/12/human-trafficking-sinai

52. Ati, 'Human Smuggling and Trafficking'.

53. Sean Columb, 'Excavating the Organ Choice: An Empirical Study of Organ Trading Networks in Cairo, Egypt', *The British Journal of Criminology*, 57, 6 (2017), pp. 1301–21.

54. Ibid.

55. Van Reisen, Estefanos, and Rijken, *Human Trafficking Cycle*.

56. Interview, Khartoum, November 2017.

57. Columb, 'Excavating the Organ Choice'.

58. Ibid.

59. 'Houses of Torture: Human Trafficking in the Sinai'. Van Reisen, Estefanos, and Rijken, *Human Trafficking Cycle*; Mokhtar Awad and Mostafa Hashem, *Egypt's Escalating Islamist Insurgency*, 2015. Washington DC: Carnegie Middle East Centre.

60. SAHAN and IGAD, 'Human Trafficking and Smuggling'.

61. Richard Cockett, *Sudan: The Failure and Division of an African State*, New Haven: Yale University Press, 2010.

62. Interview, Khartoum, November 2017; interview, Khartoum, October 2017.

63. Ati, 'Human Smuggling and Trafficking'.

64. Interview, Khartoum, October 2017.

65. Interview, Khartoum, November 2017.

66. Interview, Khartoum, October 2017.

67. Interview, Khartoum, October 2017.

68. Ati, 'Human Smuggling and Trafficking'.

69. Interview, Khartoum, October 2017.

70. Interview, Khartoum, October 2017; Ati, 'Human Smuggling and Trafficking'.

71. Interview, Khartoum, October 2017 and November 2017.

72. Interview, Khartoum, October 2017 and November 2017.

73. Interview, Khartoum, October 2017.

74. Interview, Khartoum, November 2017.

75. Interview, Khartoum, October 2017.

76. US State Department, 'Trafficking in Persons Report', Washington, DC: US State Department, 2017.

77. Interview, Kassala, November 2017.

78. Ati, 'Human Smuggling and Trafficking'.

79. Suwareh Darbo, 'Sudan 2015', African Economic Outlook, Abidjan: AfDB, 2015, available at: www.africaneconomicoutlook.org/en/country-notes/east-africa/sudan/

80. Peter Schwartzstein and Leyland Cecco, 'Sudan's New Gold Rush: Miners Risk Their Lives in Search of Riches', *The Guardian*, 27 December 2015, available at: https://www.theguardian.com/world/2015/dec/27/sudan-gold-rush-artisanal-miners

81. Interview, Dongola, November 2017.

82. Interview, Dongola, November 2017.

83. Interview, Khartoum, October 2017.

84. Interview, Khartoum, October 2017.

85. Regional Mixed Migration Secretariat, 'Going West: Contemporary Mixed Migration Trends from the Horn of Africa to Libya and Europe', Nairobi: RMMS, 2014; Altai Consulting, 'Mixed Migration: Libya at

the Crossroads: Mapping Migration Routes and Drivers of Migration in Post-Revolution Libya', Tripoli: Altai Consulting, 2013.

86. Ati, 'Human Smuggling and Trafficking'.

87. Suliman Baldo, 'Border Control from Hell: How the EU's Migration Partnership Legitimizes Sudan's Militia State', Enough Project, 2017, available at: https://enoughproject.org/reports/border-control-hell-how-eus-migration-partnership-legitimizes-sudans-militia-state

88. Akshaya Kumar and Omer Ismail, 'Janjaweed Reincarnate: Sudan's New Army of War Criminals', Enough Project, June 2014, available at: https://enoughproject.org/files/JanjaweedReincarnate_June2014.pdf

89. Baldo, 'Border Control from Hell'.

90. Human Rights Watch, 'Men with No Mercy: Rapid Support Forces Attacks against Civilians in Darfur, Sudan', New York: Human Rights Watch, 2015.

91. Baldo, 'Border Control from Hell'.

92. Jeffrey Gettleman, 'Sudan Said to Revive Notorious Militias', *New York Times*, 24 June 2014, available at: https://www.nytimes.com/2014/06/25/world/africa/sudan-darfur-janjaweed-militia-khartoum.html

93. Interview, Khartoum, October and November 2017; Baldo, 'Border Control from Hell'; Government of Sudan Defense Ministry, 'Ministry of Defense Discusses Anti-Human Trafficking Efforts of Regular Forces in a Press Conference Yesterday', 31 August 2016, available at: www.mod.gov.sd

94. Caitlin Chandler, 'Inside the EU's Flawed $200 Million Migration Deal with Sudan', Special Report, IRIN News, 30 January 2018, available at: https://www.irinnews.org/special-report/2018/01/30/inside-eu-s-flawed-200-million-migration-deal-sudan

95. Baldo, 'Border Control from Hell'.

96. Ibid.; Hiba Morgan, 'Sudan's RSF Unit Accused of Abuses against Migrants', Al Jazeera, 17 November 2017, available at: https://www.aljazeera.com/blogs/africa/2017/11/sudan-rsf-unit-accused-abuses-migrants-171117133237654.html

97. Patrick Kingsley, 'By Stifling Migration, Sudan's Feared Secret Police Aid Europe', *New York Times*, 22 April 2018, available at: https://www.nytimes.com/2018/04/22/world/africa/migration-european-union-sudan.html

98. Ibid.

99. 'Man Killed by RSF Militiamen in Eastern Sudan', Dabanga, 9 April 2018, available at: https://www.dabangasudan.org/en/all-news/article/man-killed-by-rsf-militiamen-in-eastern-sudan; 'Civilians: RSF

Out of Sudan's Kassala', Dabanga, 23 March 2018, available at: https://www.dabangasudan.org/en/all-news/article/civilians-rsf-out-of-sudan-s-kassala

100. Amnesty International, 'Just Deserters: Why Indefinite National Service in Eritrea Has Created a Generation of Refugees', London: Amnesty International, 2015.

101. 'Eritrea: Events of 2016', Human Rights Watch, 2017, available at: www.hrw.org/world-report/2017/country-chapters/eritrea; UNHCR, 'New Arrivals Fact Sheet', August 2017.

102. Alex de Waal, *The Real Politics of the Horn of Africa: Money, War and the Business of Power*, Cambridge: Polity Press, 2015.

103. Amnesty International, 'Eritrea'.

104. Plaut, *Understanding Eritrea*.

105. Kjetil Tronvoll and Daniel Mekonnen, *The African Garrison State: Human Rights and Political Development in Eritrea*, Woodbridge: Boydell & Brewer, 2014.

106. De Waal, *Real Politics of the Horn of Africa*.

107. Tronvoll and Mekonnen, *African Garrison State*.

108. Plaut, *Understanding Eritrea*.

109. 'Miserable and Useless: National Service in Eritrea', *The Economist*, 10 March 2014, available at: https://www.economist.com/baobab/2014/03/10/miserable-and-useless

110. Plaut, *Understanding Eritrea*.

111. Zachary Laub, 'Authoritarianism in Eritrea and the Migrant Crisis', Council on Foreign Relations, 2016, available at: https://www.cfr.org/backgrounder/authoritarianism-eritrea-and-migrant-crisis

112. 'Miserable and Useless'.

113. De Waal, *Real Politics of the Horn of Africa*.

114. Plaut, *Understanding Eritrea*.

115. Mark Anderson, 'Trapped and Bereft in the World's Fastest Emptying Country', *The Guardian*, 28 September 2016, available at: https://www.theguardian.com/world/2016/sep/28/eritrea-military-service-life-people-left-behind

116. 'For the First Time in Years, Eritreans Can Leave Their Country Freely', *The Economist*, 11 October 2018, available at: https://www.economist.com/middle-east-and-africa/2018/10/11/for-the-first-time-in-years-eritreans-can-leave-their-country-freely

117. Interview, Khartoum, October 2017.

118. Interview, Khartoum, October 2017.

119. Harry Verhoeven, 'Behind Violence in Ethiopia: Will Its Experiment in Ethnic Federalism Work?', *Foreign Affairs*, 29 June 2016, available

at: https://www.foreignaffairs.com/articles/ethiopia/2016-08-29/
behind-violence-ethiopia

120. Interview, Khartoum, October 2017.

121. Interview, Khartoum, October and November 2017.

122. Interview, Khartoum, 2017.

123. Interview, Khartoum, 2017.

124. Interview, Khartoum, November 2017.

125. Humphris, 'Refugees and the Rashaida'.

126. Becky Carter and Brigitte Rohwerder, 'Rapid Fragility and Migration
Assessment for Ethiopia: Rapid Literature Review', GSDRC, 2016,
available at: http://gsdrc.org/publications/rapid-fragility-and-
migration-assessment-for-ethiopia/

127. Anna Louise Strachan, 'Rapid Fragility and Migration Assessment for
Sudan: Rapid Literature Review', GSDRC, February 2016, available
at: http://www.gsdrc.org/wp-content/uploads/2016/02/Fragility_
Migration_Sudan.pdf

128. Schwartzstein and Cecco, 'Sudan's New Gold Rush'.

129. Jok Madut Jok, *War and Slavery in Sudan*, Philadelphia: University of
Pennsylvania Press, 2001.

130. Interview, Khartoum, October and November 2017.

131. 'Israel Coercing Eritreans and Sudanese to Leave', BBC News, 9
September 2014, available at: https://www.bbc.co.uk/news/world-
middle-east-29122352; '"MakeTheir Lives Miserable": Israel's Coercion
of Eritreans and Sudanese Asylum Seekers to Leave Israel', Human
Rights Watch, 9 September 2014, available at: https://www.hrw.org/
report/2014/09/09/make-their-lives-miserable/israels-coercion-
eritrean-and-sudanese-asylum-seekers

132. Peter Tinti and Tuesday Reitano, *Migrant Refugee, Smuggler Saviour*,
London: Hurst, 2016.

133. Tuesday Reitano and Mark Shaw, 'The Politics of Power, Protection,
Identity and Illicit Trade', Crime–Conflict Nexus Series no. 3, United
Nations University Centre for Policy Research and UKAID, 2017.

134. Ibid.

135. Tinti and Reitano, *Migrant Refugee, Smuggler Saviour*

136. Ibid.

137. Ibid.

138. Ibid.; 'Libya: Widespread Torture in Detention', Human Rights Watch,
17 June 2017, available at: https://www.hrw.org/news/2015/06/17/
libya-widespread-torture-detention

139. Tinti and Reitano, *Migrant Refugee, Smuggler Saviour*.

140. Interview, Khartoum, November 2017.

141. Alex de Waal, 'Dollarised', *London Review of Books*, 32, 12 (2010), pp. 38–41.

142. De Waal, *Real Politics of the Horn of Africa*.

143. 'Sudan's Deep State: How Insiders Violently Privatized Sudan's Wealth, and How to Respond', Enough Project, Violent Kleptocracy Series: East and Central Africa, 2017, available at: https://enoughproject.org/reports/sudans-deep-state-how-insiders-violently-privatized-sudans-wealth-and-how-respond

144. 'Sudan's Islamists: From Salvation to Survival', Brussels: International Crisis Group, 2016.

145. Interview, Khartoum, October 2017.

146. De Waal, *Real Politics in the Horn of Africa*; Alex de Waal and Julie Flint, *Darfur: A New History of a Long War*, London: African Arguments, 2008.

147. Ibid.

148. Interview, Khartoum, October and November 2017.

149. Interview, Kassala, November 2017; interview, Khartoum, November 2017.

150. Interviews, Khartoum and Kassala, 2017.

151. Human Rights Watch, '"I Wanted to Lie Down and Die"'.

152. Interview, Khartoum, November 2017.

153. Interview, Khartoum, October 2017.

154. Interview, Khartoum, November 2017.

155. Interview, Khartoum, November 2017.

156. Interview, Khartoum, October 2017.

157. Interview, Khartoum, October and November 2017.

158. Interview, Khartoum, October and November 2017.

159. Interview, Kassala, November 2017.

160. Interview, Khartoum, October and November 2017.

161. Interview, Khartoum, November 2017.

162. 'The Government of Sudan Launches Its First National Action Plan to Combat Human Trafficking', International Organization for Migration, 2017, available at: www.sudan.iom.int/news/press-releases/government-sudan-launches-its-first-national-action-plan-combat-human

163. Ibid.

164. Interview, Khartoum, November 2017.

165. Interview, Khartoum, November 2017.

166. Interview, Khartoum, November 2017.

167. UN OCHA, 'Humanitarian Bulletin Sudan', 11 (2016), pp. 7–13.

168. 'Sudan: Population Dashboard; Refugees from South Sudan', UNHCR, 2018, available at: http://reporting.unhcr.org/sites/default/files/

UNHCR%20Sudan%20-%20Population%20Dashboard%20-%20
Refugees%20from%20South%20Sudan%20-%2030NOV18.pdf;   UN
OCHA, *Humanitarian Bulletin: Sudan*, 6 (2018), available at: https://www.
unocha.org/sites/unocha/files/dms/OCHA_Sudan_Humanitarian_
Bulletin_Issue_06_%2819_March_-_1_April_2018%29.pdf

169. De Waal, *Real Politics in the Horn of Africa*; De Waal and Flint, *Darfur*.
170. Baldo, 'Border Control from Hell'.
171. Eric Reeves, 'Darfur, the Most Successful Genocide in a Century', The World Post, Huffington Post, 21 April 2017, available at: www.huffingtonpost.com/entry/darfur-the-most-successful-genocide-in-a-century_us_58fa0eb9e4b086ce58980fe3
172. Clemence Pinaud, 'South Sudan: Civil War, Predation and the Making of a Military Aristocracy', *African Affairs*, 113, 451 (2014), pp. 192–211.
173. Baldo, 'Border Control from Hell'.
174. Paul Collier, 'Doing Well Out of War: An Economic Perspective', in Karen Ballentine and Jake Sherman (eds), *The Political Economy of Armed Conflict: Beyond Greed and Grievance*, Boulder, CO: Lynne Rienner, 2003.
175. Interview, Khartoum, October 2017.
176. De Waal, *Real Politics in the Horn of Africa*.
177. Interview, Khartoum, November 2017; Small Arms Survey, 'Eastern Sudan', Human Security Baseline Assessment for Sudan and South Sudan, 2013, available at: http://www.smallarmssurvey.org/focus-projects/human-security-baseline-assessment-for-sudan-and-south-sudan.html
178. Aisha Ahmad, *Jihad & CO: Black Markets and Islamist Power*, Oxford: Oxford University Press, 2017.
179. Andrew McGregor, 'Why the Janjaweed Legacy Prevents Khartoum from Disarming Darfur', Special Report, Aberfoyle International Security, 2017, available at: https://www.aberfoylesecurity.com/?p=4027
180. Ati, 'Human Smuggling and Trafficking'.
181. Interview, Khartoum, November 2017.
182. Interview, Khartoum, November 2017.
183. Ati, 'Human Smuggling and Trafficking'.
184. Interview, Kassala, November 2017.
185. Interview, Kassala, November 2017.
186. Human Rights Watch, '"I Wanted to Lie Down and Die"'.
187. Humphris, 'Refugees and the Rashaida'.
188. Ibid.
189. Interview, Khartoum, November 2017.
190. Interview, Khartoum, November 2017; Interview, Kassala, November 2017.

191. Humphris, 'Refugees and the Rashaida'.
192. Ati, 'Human Smuggling and Trafficking'.
193. Ibid.
194. De Waal, *Real Politics of the Horn of Africa*.
195. US Embassy, Asmara, 2007; De Waal, *Real Politics of the Horn of Africa*.
196. 'Eritrea: Ending the Exodus', Update Briefing, Africa Briefing, Brussels: International Crisis Group, 2014.
197. De Waal, *Real Politics of the Horn of Africa*.
198. Plaut, *Understanding Eritrea*.
199. Van Reisen, Estefanos, and Rijken, *Human Trafficking Cycle*.
200. International Crisis Group, 'Eritrea: Ending the Exodus'.
201. Ibid.
202. 'Press Pack on the General Migratory Situation at the External Borders of the EU', Frontex, 2015, available at: www.fullfact.org/wp-content/uploads/2015/09/general-press-pack-september-2015.pdf
203. UN Monitoring Group on Somalia and Eritrea, 'Report of the Monitoring Group on Somalia and Eritrea Pursuant to Security Council Resolution 1916 (2010)', S/2011/433, New York: United Nations Security Council, 2011; UN Monitoring Group on Somalia and Eritrea, 'Report of the Monitoring Group on Somalia and Eritrea Pursuant to Security Council resolution 2002 (2011)', New York: United Nations Security Council, 2012; UN Monitoring Group on Somalia and Eritrea, 'Report of the Monitoring Group on Somalia and Eritrea Pursuant to Security Council Resolution 2060 (2012)', New York: United Nations Security Council, 2013.
204. SAHAN and IGAD, 'Human Trafficking and Smuggling on the Horn of Africa–Central Mediterranean Route', 2016, available at: http://www.igad.int/attachments/1284_ISSP%20Sahan%20HST%20Report%20%2018ii2016%20FINAL%20FINAL.pdf; UN Monitoring Group on Somalia and Eritrea, 'Report of the Monitoring Group on Somalia and Eritrea Pursuant to Security Council Resolution 1916 (2010)', S/2011/433, 2011.
205. Plaut, *Understanding Eritrea*.
206. Tinti and Reitano, *Migrant Refugee, Smuggler Saviour*.
207. Ibid.
208. Interview, Kassala, November 2017.
209. Tinti and Reitano, *Migrant Refugee, Smuggler Saviour*.
210. Interview, Khartoum, November 2017; interview, Kassala, November 2017.
211. Tinti and Reitano, *Migrant Refugee, Smuggler Saviour*.
212. Van Reisen, Estefanos, and Rijken, *Human Trafficking Cycle*.

213. Tinti and Reitano, *Migrant Refugee, Smuggler Saviour*.

214. Interview, Kassala, November 2017.

8. PEOPLE SMUGGLING VERSUS HUMAN TRAFFICKING

1.   David Gadd and Rose Broad, 'Troubling Recognitions in British Responses to Modern Slavery', *British Journal of Criminology* (2017); doi: 10.1093/bjc/azx082

2.   Kiril Sharapov, '"Traffickers and Their Victims": Anti-trafficking Policy in the UK', *Critical Sociology*, 43, 1 (2015), pp. 91–111.

3.   Interview, UK law enforcement, July 2017.

4.   Interview, UK law enforcement, July 2017.

5.   Interview, UK law enforcement, July 2017.

6.   Interview, UK law enforcement, July 2017.

7.   Sharapov, '"Traffickers and Their Victims"'.

8.   Interview, Belgium, February 2018.

9.   Nicola Mai, 'Migrant Workers in the UK Sex Industry: First Findings', Swindon: ESRC, 2009, available at: https://www.researchcatalogue. esrc.ac.uk/grants/RES-062-23-0137/outputs/read/be2a081c-47df-41fa-b995-8b14df29c558

10. Christiana Gregoriou and Ilse A. Ras, 'Representations of Transnational Human Trafficking: A Critical Review', in Christiana Gregoriou (ed.), *Representations of Transnational Human Trafficking: Present-Day News Media, True Crime, and Fiction*, London: Palgrave Pivot, 2018.

11. UN General Assembly, 'Protocol against the Smuggling of Migrants by Land, Sea and Air, Supplementing the United Nations Convention against Transnational Organized Crime', 12 December 2000.

12. UN General Assembly, 'Protocol to Prevent, Suppress and Punish Trafficking in Persons, Especially Women and Children, Supplementing the United Nations Convention against Transnational Organized Crime', 15 November 2000.

13. Albert Kraler and Dita Vogel, 'Undocumented Migration: Counting the Uncountable; Data and Trends across Europe', Report Prepared as Part of the CLANDESTINO Research Project, 2008, p. 7.

14. Interview, international law enforcement, Lagos, September 2017.

15. Interview, law enforcement, Benin City, September 2017.

16. 'Stories from the Field: Inside Kassala Safe House', Khartoum: IFRC, 2016.

17. Interview, international NGO, Khartoum, October 2017.

18. Interview, international NGO, Khartoum, October 2017.

19. Interview, Khartoum, November 2017.

20. Daniel Silverstone and Stephen Savage, 'Farmers, Factories and Funds: Organised Crime and Illicit Drugs Cultivation within the British Vietnamese Community', *Global Crime*, 11, 1 (2010), pp. 16–33.

21. Independent Anti-Slavery Commissioner, 'Combatting Modern Slavery Experienced by Vietnamese Nationals En Route to and within the UK', 2017; interview, Hanoi, October 2017.

22. Interview, Hanoi, October 2017.

23. Interview, Hanoi, October 2017.

24. Interview, Hanoi, October 2017.

25. Interview, Tirana, Albania, September 2017.

26. Samantha Punch. 'Moving for a Better Life: To Stay or to Go?', in Derek Kassem, Lisa Murphy and Elizabeth Taylor (eds), *Growing Up in Europe: Contemporary Horizons in Childhood and Youth Studies*, Berlin: De Gruyter, 1995. p. 202.

27. Ibid., p. 204.

28. Julia O'Connell Davidson, 'The Right to Locomotion?', in Prabha Kotiswaran (ed.), *Revisiting the Law and Governance of Trafficking, Forced Labour and Modern Slavery*, Cambridge: Cambridge University Press, 2017, p. 159.

29. Julia O'Connell Davidson 'Rights Talk, Wrong Comparison: Trafficking and Transatlantic Slavery', OpenDemocracy, 2015, pp. 72–5, available at: https://www.opendemocracy.net/en/beyond-trafficking-and-slavery/rights-talk-wrong-comparison-trafficking-and-transatlantic-sl/

30. Tuesday Reitano, 'Human Trafficking in Africa: Do We Need a New Definition?', Global Initiative against Organized Crime, 29 August 2017, available at: http://globalinitiative.net/does-human-trafficking-need-a-new-definition/

9. A CRIMINAL PYRAMID SCHEME

1. Stephen Ellis, *This Present Darkness: A History of Nigerian Organised Crime*, London: Hurst, 2016.

2. Marc Goodman, 'What Can Business Learn from Organised Crime?', *Harvard Business Review* (2011), available at: https://hbr.org/2011/11/what-business-can-learn-from-organised-crime

3. Highway 10 refers to the route along the 10th parallel, which separates West Africa and South America by 2,575 kilometres. Between the fifteenth and nineteenth centuries, it was used to move slaves east. During the Second World War, it became an aerial bridge to transport troops and equipment to the Mediterranean. It has now reopened as a transit route for cocaine. Antonio Mazzitelli, 'The New Transatlantic

Bonanza: Cocaine on Highway 10', Western Hemisphere Security Analysis Centre, 2011.

4. Charlie Edwards and Calum Jeffray, 'On Tap: Organised Crime and the Illicit Trade in Tobacco, Alcohol and Pharmaceuticals in the UK', London: RUSI, 2011.

5. Ibid.

6. Leo Sisti, 'The Montenegro Connection: Love, Tobacco and the Media', Reporting Project, n.d., available at: https://www.reportingproject.net/underground/index.php?option=com_content&view=article&id=7&Itemid=20

7. Interview, Lagos, Nigeria, August 2014.

8. 'Blue Sky M: Hundreds Rescued from Abandoned Cargo Ship', BBC News, 31 December 2014, available at: http://www.bbc.co.uk/news/world-asia-30646778

9. Lizzie Dearden, 'Abandoned Migrant "Ghost Ship" Arrives in Italy Carrying Hundreds of Syrian Refugees', The Independent, 3 January 2015, available at: http://www.independent.co.uk/news/world/abandoned-ghost-ship-carrying-hundreds-of-syrian-refugees-arrives-safely-in-italy-9955399.html

10. 'Italy Steps Up Migrant Boat Patrols after Tragedies', BBC News, 14 October 2013, available at: http://www.bbc.co.uk/news/world-europe-24515906

11. 'Frontex Joint Operation "Triton": Concerted Efforts to Manage Migration in the Central Mediterranean', European Commission Press Release, 7 October 2014, available at: http://europa.eu/rapid/press-release_MEMO-14-566_en.htm

12. Centre for Social Justice, 'A Modern Response to Modern Slavery', London: CSJ, 2015.

13. Phil Williams, 'Trafficking in Women: The Role of Transnational Organised Crime', in Sally Cameron and Edward Newman (eds), Trafficking in Humans: Social, Cultural and Political Dimensions, New York: United Nations University Press, 2007.

14. 'The Victims & Traffickers', Polaris Project, n.d., available at: https://polarisproject.org/victims-traffickers

15. Misha Glenny, McMafia: Crime without Frontiers, London: Bodley Head, 2008.

16. Elizabeth Hopper and José Hidalgo, 'Invisible Chains: Psychological Coercion of Human Trafficking Victims', Intercultural Human Rights Law Review, 1, 18 (2006), pp. 185–209.

17. Kevin Bales, Laurel Fletcher, and Eric Stover, Hidden Slaves: Forced Labour in the United States, Berkeley: University of California Press, 2005.

18. Donna Hughes, 'The "Natasha" Trade: The Transnational Shadow Market of Trafficking in Woman', *Journal of International Affairs*, 53, 2 (2000), pp. 1–18.

19. Elizabeth Kelly, 'Journeys of Jeopardy: A Review of Research on Trafficking in Woman and Children in Europe', Geneva: International Organization of Migration, 2002.

20. Maria Ioannou and Miriam S. D. Oostinga, 'An Empirical Framework of Control Methods of Victims of Human Trafficking for Sexual Exploitation', *Global Crime*, 16, 1 (2015), pp. 34–49.

21. Judith Herman, *Trauma and Recovery: The Aftermath of Violence; From Domestic Abuse to Political Terror*, New York: Basic Books, 1992.

22. Dee L. R. Graham, with Edna I. Rawlings and Roberta K. Rigsby, *Loving to Survive: Sexual Terror, Men's Violence, and Women's Lives*, New York: New York University Press, 1994.

23. See, e.g. Natalie Kitroeff, 'Stockholm Syndrome in the Pimp–Victim Relationship', NYTimes Blog, 3 May 2012, available at: https://kristof.blogs.nytimes.com/2012/05/03/stockholm-syndrome-in-the-pimp-victim-relationship/

24. Centre for Social Justice, 'Modern Response to Modern Slavery'.

25. Sharapov, '"Traffickers and Their Victims"'.

26. Ann De Shalit, Robert Heynen, and Emily van der Meulen, 'Human Trafficking and Media Myths: Federal Funding, Communication Strategies, and Canadian Antitrafficking Programs', *Canadian Journal of Communication*, 39, 3 (2014), pp. 385–412; Alexandra S. Moore and Elizabeth S. Goldberg, 'Victims, Perpetrators, and the Limits of Human Rights Discourse in Post-Palermo Fiction about Sex Trafficking', *The International Journal of Human Rights*, 19, 1 (2015), pp. 16–31; Anna Szörényi and Penelope Eate, 'Saving Virgins, Saving the USA: Heteronormative Masculinities and the Securitisation of Trafficking Discourse in Mainstream Narrative Film', *Social Semiotics*, 24, 5 (2014), pp. 608–22.

27. Interview, UK, July 2017.

28. Interview, Lagos, September 2017.

29. Simon Ebegbulem, '"Our Gods Will Destroy You": Oba of Benin Curse Human Traffickers', Vanguard Nigeria, 10 March 2018, available at: https://www.vanguardngr.com/2018/03/gods-will-destroy-oba-benin-curse-human-traffickers/

30. Interview, Lagos, September 2017.

31. Interview, Lagos, September 2017.

32. Interview, Kassala, November 2017.

33. Centre for Social Justice, 'Modern Response to Modern Slavery'.

10. CONCLUSION

1.   Home Office, 'Draft Modern Slavery Bill', Norwich: H.M. Stationery Office, 2013.
2.   Christiana Gregoriou and Ilse A. Ras, 'Representations of Transnational Human Trafficking: A Critical Review', in Christiana Gregoriou (ed.), *Representations of Transnational Human Trafficking: Present-Day News Media, True Crime, and Fiction*, London: Palgrave Pivot, 2018.
3.   Gillian Wylie, *The International Politics of Human Trafficking*, London: Palgrave, 2016.
4.   'Nigerian Crime and Corruption: No Fantasy; Why It Became so Ubiquitous', *The Economist*, 12 May 2016, available at: http://www.economist.com/news/books-and-arts/21698631-why-it-became-so-ubiquitous-no-fantasy
5.   'The World of Nigeria's Sex-Trafficking "Air Lords"', BBC News, 27 January 2016, available at: https://www.bbc.com/news/magazine-35244148
6.   Home Office, 'Country Policy and Information Note Vietnam: Victims of Trafficking', London: Independent Advisory Group on Country Information, 2018.
7.   Liz Kelly, '"You Can Find Anything You Want": A Critical Reflection on Research on Trafficking in Persons within and into Europe', *International Migration*, 43, 1–2 (2005), pp. 235–65.

INDEX

smuggling into, 142–146

exploitation of migrants, 138–141

FACT *see* Front pour l'alternance et la concorde au Tchad (Front for change and concord; FACT)

family, role in migration, 74–78

February Revolution (2011), 119

Felbab-Brown, Vanda, 9

Financial Crisis of 2008, 118

France, 20, 41, 66, 68, 73, 80, 91, 93

Frontex, 153

Front pour l'alternance et la concorde au Tchad (Front for change and concord; FACT), 52–53

Gaddafi, Muammar, 118, 119

Gadd, David, 134

Gangmasters Licensing Authority (GLA), 5–6

genocide, 11

Germany, 25, 41, 68, 71, 72, 79, 91, 92

Ghana, 110

GLA *see* Gangmasters Licensing Authority (GLA)

Glenny, Misha, 12, 154

Goodman, Marc, 150

Government of National Accord, 52

Grand Emir for Sahara, 42

Greece, 71, 78, 79

Greenacres Caravan Park, Bedfordshire, 10, 12

Gulag archipelago, 114

Haftar, Khalifa, 52, 53

hawala system, 37

Hemeti, Mohamed Hamdan Dagolo, 112

Henriksen, Rune, 19, 41, 51, 161

Hidalgo, José, 154

Hilal, Musa, 124

Hopper, Elizabeth, 154

Hughes, Donna, 154–155

human commodity, controlling, 153–155

Human Rights Council, UN, 11

Human Rights Watch, 121

report (2014), 100

human trafficking

definition of, 137

implications of, 168

industry, 1–17

versus people smuggling, 13–14, 133–148, 165–166

see also individual entries

human trafficking organised crime groups

changing tactics of, 68–70

structure of, 72–74

IGAD *see* Intergovernmental Authority on Development (IGAD)

Ikeora, May, 19

incomes to armed groups, 53–54

Institute for International Research on Criminal Policy, 4

Intergovernmental Authority on Development (IGAD), 130

Security Sector Programme, 102

International Labour Organization, 4

International Organization for Migration (IOM), 23, 43, 47

International Reproductive Rights Action Group, 30

Invisible Children campaign, 10

Ioannou, Maria, 155

IOM *see* International Organization for Migration (IOM)